POETIC OPERATIONS   ✕

ASTERISK: Gender, Trans-, and All That Comes After
a book series edited by Susan Stryker, Eliza Steinbock, and Jian Neo Chen

POETIC
OPERATIONS

TRANS OF COLOR ART
IN DIGITAL MEDIA

micha cárdenas

DUKE UNIVERSITY PRESS Durham and London 2022

Designed by Aimee C. Harrison
Typeset in Portrait Text Regular, IBM Plex Sans, and
Movement Direct by Copperline Book Services

Library of Congress Cataloging-in-Publication Data
Names: cárdenas, micha, [date] author.
Title: Poetic operations: trans of color art in digital media /
micha cárdenas.
Other titles: Asterisk (Duke University Press)
Description: Durham: Duke University Press, 2022. | Series:
Asterisk | Includes bibliographical references and index.
Identifiers: LCCN 2021014441 (print) | LCCN 2021014442 (ebook)
ISBN 9781478015031 (hardcover)
ISBN 9781478017653 (paperback)
ISBN 9781478022275 (ebook)
Subjects: LCSH: Transgender artists. | Transgender people's writings. |
Gender identity in art. | Minority artists. | Minority authors. | Digital
media. | BISAC: SOCIAL SCIENCE / LGBTQ Studies / Transgender
Studies | ART / Digital
Classification: LCC NX652. T73 C373 2022 (print) | LCC NX652. T73 (ebook) |
DDC 306.76/8—dc23
LC record available at https: //lccn.loc.gov/2021014441
LC ebook record available at https: //lccn.loc.gov/2021014442

Cover art: Cover art: "We Already Know and We Don't Yet Know,"
Autonets, by micha cárdenas, performed at the Hemispheric Institute of
Performance and Politics, Eighth Encuentro, São Paulo, 2013.
Photograph by Frances Pollitt.

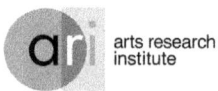

This project was supported in part by a
grant from the Arts Research Institute at
the University of California, Santa Cruz.

Duke University Press gratefully acknowledges the Critical Race and
Ethnic Studies Program at UC Santa Cruz, which provided funds
toward the publication of this book.

Portions of chapter 3 were published in the *Ada Journal of Gender, New
Media and Technology* as "Shifting Futures: Digital Trans of Color
Praxis," http://adanewmedia.org/2015/01/issue6-cardenas. Portions
of chapter 5 were published in *Scholar and Feminist Online* as "Trans of
Color Poetics," http://sfonline.barnard.edu/traversing-technologies
/micha-cardenas-trans-of-color-poetics-stitching-bodies-concepts
-and-algorithms.

For May, Judy, and chosen families everywhere

CONTENTS

ACKNOWLEDGMENTS

I must begin by acknowledging that most of the writing of this book took place on "the unceded territory of the Awaswas-speaking Uypi Tribe. The Amah Mutsun Tribal Band, comprising the descendants of indigenous people taken to missions Santa Cruz and San Juan Bautista during Spanish colonization of the Central Coast, is today working hard to restore traditional stewardship practices on these lands and to heal from historical trauma," to quote the UCSC land acknowledgment developed with the Amah Mutsun people. Additional writing took place on the lands of the Duwamish, Sammamish, Tongva, Mississauga, and New Credit peoples. The attempted genocide of native peoples in the Americas is the ground on which the contemporary digital economy is built, and my work tries to account for this fact.

As the work described in this book is deeply community-based, the number of people to thank is potentially expansive. Here, in the Art and Design: Games and Playable Media, Digital Arts and New Media, and Critical Race and Ethnic Studies programs at the University of California, Santa Cruz (UCSC), I have found such a wonderful community of scholars, who have provided a rich intellectual engagement that contributed to this book in innumerable ways. I am particularly grateful to Michael Chemers, A. M. Darke, Amy Mihyang Ginther, Jennifer Gonzalez, Camilla Hawthorne, Christine Hong, Jenny Kelly, Susana Ruiz, Warren Sack, Beth Stephens, Elizabeth Swensen, and Marianne Weems for your friendship and intellectual engagement. I am deeply grateful to Robin Hunicke for bringing me into the Games and Playable Media program. I am grateful to Ted Warburton, dean of the Arts Division; Assistant Dean Stephanie Moore; Bennett Williamson; and Dave McLaughlin for all their hard work to support my research and creative practice. I have been inspired by UCSC scholars, including Gloria Anzaldúa, Angela Davis, Donna Haraway, and Sandy Stone, for so long that I feel huge gratitude to be able to think and move in this place where they wrote so many of the texts that shaped me. The brilliant graduate students here, including Chris Kerich, Anne Napatalung, Clara Qin, Kiki Rosales, Dorothy Santos, and Kara Stone, gave me very important feedback on the later drafts of the book. I also want to thank my dear friends Lori Matsumoto and Farhana Basha for helping me get through this pandemic while finishing this book. Marcia Ochoa, I could never thank you enough for the ways you've showed up for me when I most needed it.

The community I was welcomed into at the University of Washington's Bothell and Seattle campuses provided a supportive environment that helped make this book possible. I am incredibly grateful to my friend Lauren Berliner, who gave me such important feedback at our Whiteley Center writing retreat, as well as to Ron Krabill and S. Charusheela, who mentored me through the process of turning my research into a book. The amazing students in my graduate cultural studies seminars "Trans of Color Poetics" and "Race, Gender and Sexuality in Science Fiction," including Emily Fuller, Daniel Kissinger, Frances Lee, Namita Paul, Ruth Sawyer, and Noir Soulkin provided valuable feedback on parts of this book and the ideas in it. Nejat Kedir and Kim Sharp both provided crucial, thoughtful, kind attention to this project. I will always be grateful to Bruce Burgett; his leadership and warm welcome brought me to Bothell. The interdisciplinary community of thinkers I met there is too large to list everyone, but I am grateful to all of you for the community based in our shared commitment to social justice, especially Anida Yoeu Ali, Dan Berger, Carrie Bodle, Amaranth Borsuk, Naomi Bragin, Sarah Dowling, Jose Fusté, Susan Harewood, Mark Kochanski, Minda Martin, Ariana Ochoa Camacho, Jason Pace, Julie Shayne, Jade Sotomayor, and Thea Tagle. The staff of the School of Interdisciplinary Arts and Sciences, including Miriam Bartha, Bill Humphreys, Lauresa Smith, Carmen Staab, and Simone Willynck have done essential work that facilitated parts of this research, for which I am deeply grateful.

My warm thanks go out to Kara Keeling and Tara McPherson, who both guided me through the conception and development of the concepts written here when I was at the University of Southern California (USC). I am profoundly indebted to both McPherson and Keeling for supporting me in developing a conceptual framework through the complex and at times messy work of balancing commitments to theory, activism, and art. Holly Willis, the chair of USC's Media Arts and Practice (iMAP) Department, offered important guidance on the questions of what constitutes practice-based research. In addition, Karen Tongson's leadership in the Center for Feminist Research seminar on race in popular culture was foundational to my theorization of the shift, which laid the theoretical groundwork for the rest of the book.

My intellectual community at USC, both in iMAP and throughout the entire school, inspired and influenced the ideas in this book so much. I am so profoundly grateful for the ongoing intellectual engagement of the brilliant scholars I met there: Treva Carrie, Samantha Gorman, Kai Green, Laila Shereen Sakr, Susana Ruiz, Adam Sulzdorf-Liszkiewicz, and all of the iMAP students. In addition, the staff of iMAP has put in many hours to facilitate the workshops and performances that were part of the research for this book, so my sincere thanks go to Jena Carter, Stacy Patterson, Elizabeth Ramsey, and Sonia Seetharaman for their continuing work to support the scholarship and art that is made in iMAP. Many USC faculty members have helped shape the trajectory of my work, including Steve Anderson, François Bar, Macarena Gomez-Barris, Jack Halberstam, Perry Hoberman, Richard Lemarchand, and Jen Stein.

The organizations I have worked with on these projects have also been fundamental to sustaining and invigorating these concepts, including Gender Justice L.A., ILL NANA/DiverseCity Dance Company, the Allied Media Projects, Detroit Represent, Strong and Beautiful, the Ruth Ellis Center, and Maggie's Sex Worker Action Project. The organizations that have hosted the workshops and performances have allowed these projects to develop far beyond my initial imagining, including the Zero1 Biennial; the HTMlles Festival; Temple University; Transmediale; the Gender, Bodies, and Technology Conference at Virginia Tech; the SCA Gallery at USC, hosted through iMAP; the Living as Form Nomadic Edition at Antioch College; and the Dark Side of the Digital Conference. All of the participants in my workshops and performances for both *Autonets* and *Redshift and Portalmetal* have also contributed to the ideas herein, for which I am grateful.

The Allied Media Conference and the family of brilliant artists and organizers that make up its murmuration have been a huge influence on the ideas here. I particularly have to thank adrienne marie brown, Alexis Pauline Gumbs, Jenny Lee, Mike Meddow, Diana Nucera, Anna Martine Whitehead, and Mo Willis for their continuing mind and heart expanding inspiration. In addition, my co-organizers of the International Trans Woman of Color Network Gathering at the 2014 Allied Media Conference—Lexi Adsit, Nina Malaya, and Luna Merbruja—made a huge contribution to the international movement to end violence against trans women of color, which, of course, had a great impact on the concepts in this book.

My thanks also go to Patrick Kielty, whom I worked with as a visiting scholar at the University of Toronto. In addition, the entire Toronto QTPOC arts community inspired me profoundly, including Ravyn Wngz, Sze-Yang Ade-Lam, Nisha Ahuja, Mel Campbell, Matthew Chin, Audrey Dwyer, Kumari Giles, Catherine Hernandez, Una Lee, Leroi Newbold, Juliette November, Eshan Rafi, Jes Sasche, Shaunga Tagore, Syrus Marcus Ware, Tobaron Waxman, and Dames Making Games Toronto. This entire project was shaped by their brilliant insights and constant magic of creation.

At Duke University Press, Elizabeth Ault has provided tireless guidance and support for this book. I thank her for her generous attention, for truly understanding my project, and for helping guide it to fruition. My thanks go to Susan Albury, Benjamin Kossak, Susan Deeks, and everyone at Duke University Press who helped make this book a reality. My thanks also goes to Cathy Hannabach and Megan Milks for their feedback on my manuscript. My deep, heartfelt thanks go to Susan Stryker for years of friendship and support and her decades of work to create the space that made this book possible, and especially for her work on the Asterisk series. Thanks also to Eliza Steinbock for her work to make this series possible. I am so honored to have this book be the first in the series, thank you.

The broader intellectual community of scholars working in queer new media studies has been a continual source of strength and inspiration while I worked on this book. I specifically thank Fiona Barnett, Jacob Gaboury, Jessica Marie Johnson, Alexis Lothian, Amanda Phillips, and Bo Ruberg.

I thank the people in my personal life who provided so much support throughout the writing of this book. Rox Samer, you are my *sestra*, and I am so grateful for your continued inspiration, friendship, and intellectual exchange. Ryan Li Dhalstrom and Saba Waheed provided essential support as I finished writing the first draft of this project, for which I am profoundly grateful. My friends Zach Blas, Nasrin Himada, Angela Eunsong Kim, Sam Nasstrom, Jasmina Tumbas, and Invincible Ill Weaver gave me ongoing support and theoretical and artistic inspiration throughout this writing. My father, Gabriel Cárdenas, pushed me to get my bachelor's degree and inspired me to be an artist from a very young age. My mother, Judith Louise Cárdenas, passed away just as this book was going into production. I mourn her and love her dearly and am so grateful to her. She instilled in me an early love of reading and cared for me through difficult times, which brought me here. To my daughter, I will always love you.

The list of people who have made this book possible is vast. I wish I could name all the trans people of color whose lives were stolen too soon, but that list does not have an end, yet. I am sure I am egregiously leaving out many people. Any errors in the book are entirely the fault of the author. I am so, so grateful to everyone who supported me through this time and for their contributions to the development of these ideas. Thank you to all those I have named and all those I should have named.

ALGORITHMIC ANALYSIS
INTRODUCTION

TURN YOUR HEAD and her gender changes. Her exquisitely unruly face, scarlet hair framing her gracefully arched eyebrows, is pictured in a shifting hologram on a neon pink ID card (figure I.1). Depending on the angle at which you look at the Peruvian artist Giuseppe Campuzano's artwork *DNI (De Natura Incertus)*, a manufactured national ID card, the sex marker shifts from "M" to "T," for *travesti*, and the image of his face changes.[1] The work performs the gesture of shifting optics by using a lenticular printing technique. Lenticular prints are used for holograms because they rely on a shifting of the viewer that corresponds to a change of image and can be used to present the illusion of a three-dimensional image. *DNI* is Campuzano's national identity card, a requirement for every Peruvian citizen older than eighteen, digitally modified to display an image of him in drag with a "T" gender marker. The gesture of a forged *DNI* is additionally subversive in that many travestis do not have access to a *DNI* card.[2] Campuzano's project was presented at the 2014 São Paulo Biennial (MAL).[3] The title of the artwork uses the initials of Peru's Documento Nacional de Identidad (National Identity Document) and reimagines it with the Latin phrase "De Natura Incertus" (Of Uncertain Nature). Campuzano's *DNI* uses the algorithmic media of identification

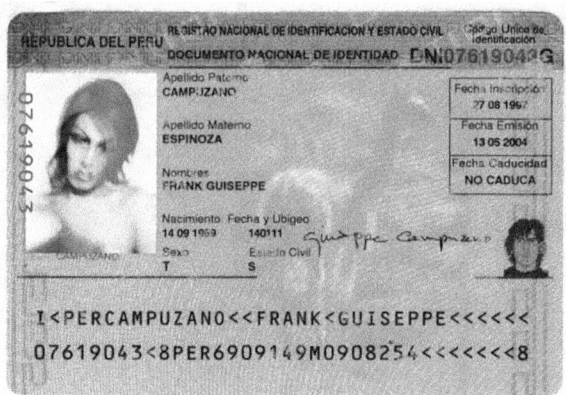

I.1 *DNI (De Natura Incertus)*, by Giuseppe Campuzano.

cards to simultaneously call into question ideologies of binary gender, national identity, and immigration.

In Campuzano's work, a trans of color survival strategy is made tangible through a poetic subversion of the algorithms of immigration control technologies. The rest of the card is intact, from the background image of a vicuña as a national symbol of Peru to the seemingly random numbers and "<" signs common to passports today that make their data more easily readable by electronic scanners (figure I.2). I alternate gender pronouns throughout the text to linguistically represent Campuzano's gender fluidity, following the method used by Malú Machuca Rose, whom I cite later in the chapter. By digitally cutting and stitching the image of her national identity card with this performative image of her female gender presentation and the letter "T," Campuzano uses art and performance to gesture to speculative possibilities of subversions of gender regulation.[4]

Campuzano's shifting and layered approach to visibility is a powerful introduction to the technologies of representation used by trans people of color. Identification cards such as the DNI are digital technological assemblages, often using bidimensional bar codes and radio frequency identification (RFID) transmitters. Campuzano's intervention into them requires studying these technologies, and forgery techniques, to simulate future possibilities for gender markers and photos on ID cards. The holographic watermark of the word *IDENTIDAD* is also present in Campuzano's *DNI*. The Peruvian DNI cards are designed to be read by algorithmic devices; thus, they can be understood as a physical embodiment of the algorithms that read them. Campuzano's *DNI* creates a fictional example of countersurveillance strategies that go beyond the visual, intervening in the sensor networks that would read the data on

I.2 *DNI (De Natura Incertus)*, by Giuseppe Campuzano.

a DNI card to confirm its validity. Algorithmic analysis invites us to look for algorithms—to identify the components and operations that make up the process we are analyzing—to understand them better, where a process can be an artwork, an identity, or a moment of violence. Campuzano creatively hacks identification and migration control algorithms, subverting them through what I call trans of color operations of cutting, shifting, and stitching. These operations are evident from the cutting out of the photos of her face to the shifting of lenticular images, the digitally stitching together of images, and the elaborate costumes she creates for those images. Cutting is an operation that helps identify the parts of an algorithm, but one should imagine cuts not so much as absolute separation as definitions for spaces of intra-action. The parts, or variables, shift over time. Stitching is the operation of attaching various parts together, which is essential to both intersectionality and assemblage, as I expand on in this chapter. The identification and elaboration of these poetic operations—cutting, stitching, and shifting—is central to my analysis and continues later in the chapter and throughout the book. Campuzano is reaching here not for simple visibility or invisibility but for a holographic body that can shift and change with the movement of the viewer. The emphasis on movement is decolonial, as Western modes of knowing emphasize the primacy of the visual over embodied movement. The Cameroonian theorist Achille Mbembe has described the optics of our necropolitical moment in terms of "hologrammization" to allow for "invisible killings."[5] While Mbembe is speaking of three-dimensional maps of occupied Palestine, the forms of visibility he describes have far-reaching relevance for communities targeted by racial and gender violence worldwide. Trans of color poetics go beyond binaries of visible and invisible, using methods, such as holograms, that rely on movement more than visuality.

In this book, I argue that by using algorithmic analysis to consider artworks that contribute to safety for trans people of color, survival strategies can be perceived, and from these strategies emerges a trans of color poetics: a repertoire of poetic operations. Poetics, whether of language, media, or movement, are the observable meeting points of matter and agency. While for Aristotle poetics described the essential qualities of a good poem, for the Caribbean theorist Édouard Glissant poetics are an expressive material force that flows, with political impact, between people and cultures.[6] Glissant's poetic imaginary begins with the cry of the enslaved African person thrown from a slave ship into the abyss. I build on his poetics and return to them throughout the book. The main focus of this book is the poetics of artwork made by trans people of color working in digital media, a body of work that has been undertheorized. The artworks I discuss all contribute—most explicitly and a few implicitly—to reducing violence against trans people of color by interrupting colonial control of embodiment, modulating perceptibility, fostering transformation, and building solidarity. Trans of color poetics can also be seen in the work of artists who do not identify as people of color or as trans or gender nonconforming whose poetics still increase safety for trans of color communities. An understanding of these poetics can aid work for gender and racial justice more broadly, especially in considerations of race and gender in technology. In this introduction, I describe algorithmic analysis further, while chapter 1 uses algorithmic analysis to describe trans of color poetics in greater detail.

One of the intentions of this book is to expand transgender studies by articulating an alternative genealogy for the field, adding a root to the rhizome. Understanding trans of color experience as far older than the word *transgender*, the book stitches a thread through decolonial theory, women of color feminism, and queer of color critique. Much of the beginning of transgender studies, as a field that has been developing in the US academy for the past thirty years, emerged out of a consideration of the visibility of white transgender people in Western contexts.[7] Sandy Stone's essay "The Empire Strikes Back: A Posttranssexual Manifesto," often cited as the origin of contemporary transgender studies, focuses on trans women in England

and California.[8] Still, Stone cites Gloria Anzaldúa's concept of mestiza consciousness as an inspiration for her idea of post-transsexual. Susan Stryker's book *Transgender History*, while very important to the foundation of the academic field, focuses largely on social movements in the United States. It does chronicle many important moments in the history of US trans of color art and activism, including Marsha P. Johnson and Sylvia Rivera's organization Street Transvestite Action Revolutionaries (STAR), a direct-action organization founded in New York in 1970 that provided food, housing, and support for trans people who had recently been released from jail.[9] *Transgender History* discusses intersectionality and mestizaje as foundational concepts for understanding transgender phenomena.[10] With the publication of the *Transgender Studies Reader 2* in 2013; the later formation of TSQ: *Transgender Studies Quarterly*; and the publication of *Queen for a Day* by Marcia Ochoa, *Black on Both Sides* by C. Riley Snorton, and *Trans Exploits* by Jian Neo Chen, significant effort has been made to expand trans of color scholarship.[11] *Poetic Operations* continues this trajectory, working toward decolonizing transgender studies by focusing on nonwhite trans people, trans people with ancestry outside Europe, people who have histories of colonial violence, and places outside the United States and Europe where one can see gender variance beyond rigid gender binaries. Doing so changes a discussion of the possible uses of digital media for trans justice, in that global South countries continue to have less access to the internet.[12] In addition, doing so troubles any simple definition of trans, because non-Western practices that are similar to transgender, such as two-spirit and travesti, rely on ontologies that defy Western conceptions of a single, unitary, separate self.[13] Destabilizing the persistent hegemony of global North countries over people in the global South by destabilizing the terminology through which those people's gendered, racialized bodies are understood is a method of decolonization. Trans of color poetics attempt to do this by destabilizing the concepts of trans and transgender by including gender-non-conforming people such as travestis, stitching together a new poetic formation based in global solidarity.

Campuzano's trans Latinx futures are imagined through his own travesti practices of shifting his appearance, showing different images of his face on the two alternate images on his speculative national ID card. Campuzano's usage of the lenticular is a reclaiming of the ability of the travesti to inhabit multiple genders, which he reads in Incan mythology. In an interview with the performance studies scholar Lawrence La Fountain-Stokes, Campuzano describes the travesti as "a transformative postidentity that replaces clean racial and racist lines with superimposed ethnicities, from the perspective of feminist and postcolonial studies."[14] In place of a rigid concept of racialized gender identity, Campuzano offers superimposition and multiplicity activated by movement:

> We can trace a transvestite genealogy between the androgynous ritual Moche and the Inca "men disguised as women." . . . The connection between the ritual androgyne and transvestite dancers as cultural mediators; in the hair, from sacred indigenous and colonial offerings to the mode of subsistence for the modern transvestite hairdresser; in the feathers shared by the Inka Manco Capac of the man-woman caste, the colonial androgynous archangel and the contemporary transvestite showgirl. Fragmentary thought and supposition as a challenge to a supposedly lineal, continuous and progressive knowledge. The transvestite as a revolution of the pretenses of originality and unity determined by dominant history and ethics.[15]

Campuzano's usage of "travesti" imagines a deep precolonial history of beings with the power to change their genders at will. The travesti's ability to shift between genders challenges the Western conception of identity, where one must have a single, static body and gender. It also challenges US-centric conceptions of transgender that would exclude transvestites or even see the term as derogatory.

While the word *travesti* is often translated as *transvestite*, as it is in this interview, that translation has been disputed by scholars who claim that the word is untranslatable.[16] Writing about Campuzano's usage of the word in her artwork, Malú Machuca Rose describes travesti as a methodology and an epistemology in their essay "Giuseppe Campuzano's Afterlife."[17] Rose claims travesti as their own identity and describes travestis as *curanderas* (healers) and *brujas* (witches). Campuzano, describing his *Museo Travesti del Perú* (TMP) project, says that it "travestida de museo, para travestir al museo" (it *transforms* into a museum in order to *travesti* the museum). La Fountain-Stokes translates this as "it cross-dresses as a museum in order to cross-dress the museum."[18]

Campuzano is using "travesti" the way that "trans" and "queer" are used as verbs. Here the grammar is important. "Travesti" becomes a verb; it is used as an *operation*, akin to saying "to queer" or "to trans." This specifically trans of color methodology of travesti could be read as describing the act of cross-dressing the museum, or of transforming the museum through healing rituals of performance. In the oft-cited introduction to the "Trans-" issue of *Women's Studies Quarterly*, Susan Stryker, Paisley Currah, and Lisa Jean Moore ask, "What kinds of intellectual labor can we begin to perform through the critical deployment of 'trans-' operations and movements?"[19] They argue for a usage of "trans" as a conceptual operation similar to the way that "queer" has been used as a conceptual operation when writers say they are "queering." Campuzano's "travesti" is an example of trans of color poetics that contain the operations of cutting, shifting, and stitching while still having their own specificity, including a larger repertoire of gestures. I propose that this process of identifying operations is part of a method I call algorithmic analysis.

Algorithms do not require digital technology and were invented far earlier than digital computers. They are similar in form to both recipes and rituals. Algorithms are not new. The word *algorithm* is a derivation of the name of the scholar Muhammad ibn Musa al-Khwarizmi, who lived from 780 to 850 AD and is credited with inventing algebra in his book *Dixit algorismus*.[20] His name was translated from Al-Khwarizmi in Persian to Algorithmi in Latin, which later became "algorithm" in English.[21] He proposed methods, algorithms, for solving calculations with uncertain quantities.

By starting with a list of parts and adding a list of operations, instructions for how those parts interact, one can create an algorithm. When I speak of algorithms, I am talking about code. I started writing algorithms in the fourth grade, then later studied computer science for my bachelor's degree and worked as a software engineer for five years. But to understand algorithms, you do not need to be a programmer. You can also understand an algorithm as a recipe. A recipe has ingredients and steps, just as an algorithm has variables and instructions. Think of the algorithm for cooking chicken: get the chicken, oil, spices, and a pan. Preheat the oven. Oil the pan. Put the chicken in the pan. Spice the chicken. Put the pan in the oven. The ingredients in the recipe correspond to the variables, and the steps correspond to the instructions, lines of code that describe how the variables are related. Throughout this book, I demonstrate three methods of algorithmic analysis: the identification of operations and operators, a method of breaking down a problem into its basic elements and instructions; the analysis of existing algorithms in media and technology, including reverse engineering; and the creation of new algorithms, in functional computer programming languages, pseudocode, or code poetry. I propose that algorithms can be useful for the study of arts and humanities, deepening our ability to theorize social formations, including race and gender. Algorithmic analysis examines algorithms, uses algorithmic methods such as identifying components and actions, and uses algorithms as tools for analysis and creative practice. The goal of algorithmic analysis is not to attempt to describe artworks with totalizing precision, but to see how algorithms can help to better understand art and poetry, as well as the social dynamics embodied in artworks. Adding a consideration of algorithms present in a work does not displace other ways of analyzing that work but adds to the many methods of analysis available to those engaging in critical analysis.

In his study "Symbols in African Ritual," Victor Turner defines ritual as "a stereotyped *sequence of activities* involving gestures, words, and objects, performed in a sequestered place, and designed to influence preternatural forces on behalf of the actors' goals and interests."[22] Similarly, algorithms include a set of instructions that are repeated in order to function. Algorithms may seem to influence preternatural forces when they accomplish tasks beyond human capacities, such as rapid data processing or recalling data from the internet far beyond the reach of a single human memory. Often rituals include specific ingredients, such as a wedding ring and wedding dress in the Western ritual of marriage. Similarly, algorithms often require specific input data to run properly. These rituals are culturally specific algorithms. Consider how a Jewish wedding might include the ingredient of a glass to be broken and a *chuppah* (wedding canopy). Wedding rituals also include a series of steps to be performed in order, such as a procession of the bride, the saying of vows, and an appeal to a supernatural power to bless the union. Performance studies scholars have considered ritual extensively to understand performance as acts that gain meaning through repetition. Computer scientists regularly describe what algorithms do with the verb *perform*.[23] In this book, I extend the precise ways that algorithms are used in computer science to a more indeterminate, poetic application. My aim is to challenge the way that algorithms have been limited by some fields, such as software engineering, which often ignore nonbinary genders and intersectionality, and largely ignored by other fields, such as trans studies and many humanities fields.

Poetic Operations learns from women of color feminism to articulate an algorithmic method of analysis and propose new operators of thought and action to work for the survival of trans people of color. Algorithmic analysis learns from and extends intersectional and assemblage models of thinking from the women of color and queer of color thinkers Kimberlé Williams Crenshaw and Jasbir Puar, respectively. The algorithmic model is intended not to replace intersectional or assemblage models, but to enhance and add to them. One of the largest contributions of women of color feminism is Crenshaw's concept of intersectionality, which states that by looking at the intersections of axes of oppression, formerly unseen forms of violence are revealed.[24] One can understand intersectionality as an algorithm, originally imagined with two elements—race and gender—and the operation of simultaneous coexistence in the same space of a body. It is important to note that the trans studies scholar Simon D. Elin Fisher has written about how Crenshaw's formulation of intersectionality was informed by Pauli Murray's concept of *Jane Crow*, showing that trans of color scholarship is not a recent development, but a constitutive part of the history of women of color feminist thought.[25] Murray was a gender-non-conforming Black journalist and activist who wrote in 1944 about the interactions of white supremacy and male supremacy.[26]

Puar has proposed assemblage as an extension of intersectionality to account for "forces that merge and dissipate time, space and body against linearity, coherency and permanency."[27] While Crenshaw used a mental image of an intersection of lines to understand the violence black women face, Puar applies Gilles Deleuze and Félix Guattari's concept of assemblage as a model for theorizing South Asian queer subjects.[28] Puar points to the original meaning of the word *assemblage*: "The original term in Deleuze and Guattari's work is not the French word *assemblage*, but *agencement*, a term that means design, layout, organization, arrangement, and relations."[29] An assemblage can be envisioned as a mental figure of a collage, an arrangement of parts and their relations. I am proposing that algorithms can be, as intersectionality and assemblage have been, a powerful way of figuring complex processes of identity and oppression. Just as intersectionality and assemblage provide important mental models for theorizing oppression, violence, and resistance, algorithms provide another model, one with infinitely more operations and elements. If one understands intersectionality as a list of axes of identity, and their relation as one of coexistence in a single location, or person, that is one model that can be described as an algorithm with an operation of simultaneity. Assemblage addresses the ways that conceptions of identity can be thought of as rigidly divided, instead offering a model of a system or machine with many parts in movement and many kinds of relation among the parts. This can also be expressed in algorithmic analysis, as the elements of algorithms can be variables that can have many relations expressed by different operators.

The category of trans people of color is complex and in motion, like the digital poetics I write about in this book. I use the concept *trans of color* here to refer to a grouping of experiences that is itself in a constant process of shifting. While there are many people who identify under the acronym QTPOC (queer and trans people of color), each of these categories is still contentious and rife with its own political contradictions. My motivations to focus on the formation "trans of color" are multiple. One motivation is to continue the theoretical trajectories laid out by queer of color scholars, such as José Muñoz and Roderick Ferguson, while exploring areas of trans of color experience for which their work laid the groundwork. Another motivation is to continue the ongoing work of women of color feminism and challenge feminism to create justice for trans people previously excluded by feminists. In her deeply important essay "The Transfeminist Manifesto" (2016), Emi Koyama describes how many feminist spaces violently refused entry to trans women.[30] While there has been important scholarship on the ways that trans and cisgender women worked together in the 1970s, my focus here is on establishing a longer genealogy of trans activism and embodiment by establishing a through line from centuries-old practices of travesti and two-spirit people to gender-non-conformity in people of color today.[31]

Another reason I am using the concept of trans of color, while including modes of being such as two-spirit or travesti (which may be considered other than trans), is to trouble the category of trans by showing its internal contradictions and violence. In *The Ruptures of American Capital*, Grace Hong writes "the category 'women of color' completely disorganizes the very idea of a stable and knowable identity," which also resonates with the categories that make up trans people of color.[32] In this book, I focus on self-identified Latinx, Black, Asian, and Indigenous artists who identify as trans, nonbinary, travesti, or two-spirit. This is not an attempt to be representative of all trans of color artists.

I understand the term *people of color*, like *women of color*, to be a political identification, not a biologically or geographically determined assignment. The term originated from a group of Black women at the National Women's Conference in 1977 who proposed the Black Women's Agenda and were willing to expand their proposal to build solidarity with other women present, including Asian, Indigenous, and Latinx women.[33] There are many people who might visually appear as a person of color who do not identify as a person of color or act in solidarity with the project of women of color feminism. Many Indigenous and Latinx people have skin tones that appear to be white and European, due to histories of colonization. I understand people of color to be defined by having histories of experiencing colonial violence that continue to this day in the forms of racialized, gendered violence.[34] Nevertheless, it is still helpful to identify distinctions in color and hair and body types because people who are more easily visibly identified as part of an oppressed ethnic group face more violence than those who do not. Among trans people, Black trans women are repeatedly the group that is the most targeted for murder. People who often pass as white, such as myself, experience the privileges associated with whiteness, including safety and economic gain, when they are perceived as white. There is much to say on these distinctions, and some activists have adopted the acronym QTBIPOC to acknowledge that Black and Indigenous peoples in the United States experience different levels of violence and may not want to be grouped together with the broader term *people of color*. As an action, rather than an inherent category, we could understand the terms *people of color* and QTBIPOC as algorithms in themselves or as shifting placeholders to be mobilized in larger algorithms.

Latinx is a category within the category of people of color, which is vast, incorporating a multitude of body types and cultures. The word *Latinx* is in flux, a recent adoption that moves beyond the gendered binary of the Spanish language. Spanish words ending in *a* or *o* are gendered feminine and masculine, respectively. To avoid this, activists have taken up the word *Latinx*, which replaces the *a/o* with an *x*. This formulation also uses an algorithmic syntax in which *x* can be understood to mean anything, like a variable in algebra or in computer code. As an assemblage, one might imagine Latinx to refer to South American and Central American peoples, their diasporas, and the relations among them, or to Latina, Latino, and nonbinary Latinx people. Yet if we understand Latinx as an algorithm that can be expanded into permutations of Latin-, with anything after it, we might imagine Latinx to include Latina, Latino, Latin@ (an earlier formation attempting to subvert the binary limitations of the Spanish language), Latine (a recent suggestion to follow Latinx as it is more easily pronounceable by Spanish speakers), and other words yet to be imagined.[35] The openness of variables as placeholders allows for future possibilities, as well as the future ways that algorithms may be performed.

The term *transgender* originates in Western medical definitions of transsexuality and can be a colonial imposition on non-Western trans subjects and people of color in Western countries.[36] While the word *transgender* was originally used in a medical context, it was soon taken up by activists in resistance to the term *transsexual*, which was seen as medicalizing.[37] Many people have adopted other terms, such as *trans* and *trans**, to refer to a broader coalition of identities grouped around experiences that might be described as transgender. Trans* (trans with an asterisk) uses a digital command line syntax to indicate trans-anything: transgender, transsexual, nonbinary, and more. In this term we can see how the logics expressed by algorithms describe the multiplicity of embodiment expressed in forms of movement that trans people of color have been living for centuries. When an asterisk is used in a command line—such as *"ls trans*"* in MacOS, iOS, or Android os—it means "list any files whose names begin with 'trans' and are followed with anything else." Here the asterisk operation is one of expansion and a way of indicating uncertainty. In this I see a reflection of the multiplicity of embodiments that have come together in coalition in the contemporary trans movement. Further, I understand the openness indicated by the asterisk to indicate a possible futurity in which other forms of embodiment are also referenced by trans*. The asterisk can also indicate a footnote, as Christina Sharpe describes "the asterisked" human as the human left behind, yet she also sees *trans** as an expansive term. She states, "The asterisk speaks to a range of configurations of Black being that take the form of translation, transatlantic, transgression, transgender, transformation, transmogrification, transcontinental, transfixed, trans-Mediterranean, transubstantiation (by which process we might understand the making of bodies into flesh and then into fungible commodities while retaining the appearance of flesh and blood), transmigration, and more."[38] Her description of the asterisk signifying transformation resonates with the operation I have called shifting, and I return to discussions of fungibility in relation to shifting in chapter 3. The "more" she references points to the unknown potential referenced by the command line asterisk. Sharpe uses the asterisk to link the excess that is Blackness to trans forms of embodiment, linking racialization and gender non-normativity in ways I explore through trans of color poetics. Beyond that, the openness of the asterisk points to the ways that trans studies has expanded beyond a concern with only transgender or transsexual experiences, out to the many vectors that require consideration in the ongoing construction of those categories, such as species boundaries, colonization, slavery, and racial capitalism. In this book I most often use the word *trans*, without the asterisk, to refer to people who feel that the gender they were assigned at birth does not always correspond to their lived gender, or their desired gender. This understanding draws on Strkyer's statement that the term *transgender* names "any and all kinds of variation from gender norms and expectations," a capacious definition that reflects her commitment to expanding transgender studies beyond its US-centricity.[39] I understand this expanded definition to resonate with the concept of trans* without having to indicate the asterisk in every usage. Still, the asterisk in *trans** can refer to trans of color, calling attention to the fact that we cannot theorize the multitude of trans* phenomena without taking into account how race is a technology that reifies and disrupts gender along colonial lines.

The asterisk in *trans** denotes a process, an action that must take place for the word to be given meaning. Throughout this book, my focus is on movement, gesture, operation, rather than on fixed categories. Writing in TSQ, Eva Hayward and Jami Weinstein write that trans* is "the movement that produces beingness"; it is "not a thing or being, it is rather the processes through which thingness and beingness are constituted."[40] With this process-oriented ontology in mind, *Poetic Operations* focuses on the movements, the operations at work, in trans of color poetics rather than on rigid categorizations. Algorithms are processes made up of operations, with elements in relation, and they are the focus of this study. Hayward and Weinstein describe the operation of the asterisk in *trans** as "the expressive force *between, with,* and *of* that enables the asterisk to stick to particular materializations."[41] The expressive force is the poetics that move with powerful effect in the expanded space opened up by the asterisk operator in trans*.

The profoundly interdisciplinary work of Gloria Anzaldúa is another important precursor for trans of color poetics, although she is often left out of narratives of the history of transgender studies. The original title of Anzaldúa's first book—"Borderlands: The New Mestiza = La Frontera"—reads like a simple algorithm, poetically conjuring relations among the English-speaking spaces of the border, the Spanish-speaking spaces, and the mestiza woman as the medium between them.[42] In the preface to *This Bridge We Call Home*, a follow-up to the important women of color feminist anthology *This Bridge Called My Back*, Anzaldúa writes, "For positive social change to occur we must imagine a reality that differs from what already exists."[43] Her *consciencia de la mestiza* (mixed-race consciousness), "a consciousness of the Borderlands," is linked to her description of being "half and half, mita' y mita' . . . both male and female . . . having an entry into both worlds."[44] Her work mixes English, Spanish, Nahuatl, poetry, history, theory, and personal narrative, using language as a technology to stitch together many passions. She describes shifting between states as an important part of her writing method. Similarly, this book includes theory, poetry, first-person accounts, source code, video, and interactive elements. I shift among writing modes throughout the book as a way to write theory poetically and challenge the assumptions of academic writing. In my earlier book *The Transreal*, I propose that transgender experiences of shifting can inform how viewers understand media art that spans multiple realities, including augmented reality, alternate reality, and mixed reality artworks.[45] Anzaldúa's description of creating new realities resonates with my formulation of transreal aesthetics as political aesthetics that cross multiple realities. I return to the transreal in later chapters. Interdisciplinary, performative, cross-genre writing, a mode heavily used by Anzaldúa, is an important part of my method, because the subject of this book is deeply personal to me.[46]

While algorithms are not new, what is new is the massive scale at which they have been deployed and adopted into the everyday lives of so many people around the globe. The ways that algorithms shape our lives today have come to widespread attention due to media coverage of Russian hacking of the 2016 election. To date, it has come to light not only that Democratic National Committee servers were hacked, but social media also was widely exploited to influence the campaign.[47] The Cambridge Analytica case allowed the public to see how a single firm, working with former Trump advisor Steve Bannon, was able to use Facebook's application programming interface (API) to access the data of millions of Americans.[48] The project sought to influence emotions and voter outcomes and effectively turned Facebook into Bannon's psychological warfare tool.[49] Still, the damage that algorithms have done to democracy are only part of the harm that has been caused by their misuse, which includes everyday acts of discrimination literally coded into objects and software used by millions.

Researchers including Kate Crawford and Joy Buolamwini have published articles in the *New York Times* about how racism is encoded into facial recognition systems and artificial intelligence (AI) image processing systems that have been widely deployed in many countries.[50] These scholars, along with scholars such as Safiya Umoja Noble and Virginia Eubanks, have articulated the violence of algorithms.[51] My intention is not to eschew or ignore that violence. Describing her method as Black feminist technology studies, Noble shows how search results benefit corporations and harm women of color.[52] She describes in great detail how top search results can be changed by paid advertising and search engine optimization methods that exploit Google's algorithms, leading to a lowest common denominator effect for sorting results by popularity and sensationalism. One of the images in her book shows a screen shot of a Google search the day after the election of Donald Trump with a top result pointing to a fabricated news site claiming that he won the popular vote, which is false.[53] The work of these scholars applies important intersectional critiques to the algorithms that infiltrate our daily lives. Still, I refuse to cede the power of algorithms to oppressive forces. It is precisely because of the violence that algorithms inflict on our lives that it is urgent to understand them, and to be able to use them for analysis and expression. Critique is not enough.

My usage of algorithms in this book is not intended to be positivist or re-ductive of unquantifiable phenomena into calculable numbers and formulae. Many of the arguments in this book will be unacceptable to computer scientists who understand algorithms as being defined by their predictable outcomes and lack of ambiguity. Instead, my offering here is to say that algorithms can be a useful model for thinking through issues relevant to artists and humanists, as well as for instructing computer scientists about how trans people of color are, and have been, using algorithms for their survival for centuries.

After the visibility of trans people of color increased in the United States in 2014, the violence seemed to worsen dramatically. The number of murders of trans people grew in 2015 by 50 percent. While fourteen transgender people were murdered in the United States in 2014, twenty-one were murdered in 2015, and these numbers reflect only the documented cases.[54] By the time Trump was elected in 2016, the number of murders of trans people was higher than it ever had been, up to twenty-seven.[55] The National Coalition of Anti-Violence Programs (NCAVP) reported, "As of August 23, 2017, NCAVP has recorded reports of 36 hate violence related homicides of LGBTQ and HIV affected people, the highest number ever recorded by NCAVP," with transgender women and people of color experiencing the highest rate of violence.[56] Transgender Europe reports that, globally, more than two thousand trans people were murdered from 2008 to 2016.[57] The continued increase in murders of trans women of color underscores the deep need for political strategies other than simple visibility or invisibility, which the anthology *Trap Door*, referring to the trap of visibility, addresses.[58] While the global situation is dire for trans people of color, their continued survival is a demonstration of powerful survival strategies.

Poetic Operations holds that the survival strategies of trans and gender-non-conforming people of color can serve as a powerful basis for both theory and artistic practice. This book offers alternative proposals for responding to a situation of violence that seems to be getting worse daily but that is, in fact, a continuation of centuries of colonial violence, as the editors of *Trap Door*—Tourmaline, Eric Stanley, and Johanna Burton—argue.[59] One can see a parallel between a perceived increase in violence against trans people and the increase in attention to their murders. In contrast to Katy Steinmetz's narrative of increasing acceptance for transgender people in her *Time* magazine cover story "The Transgender Tipping Point," the actress Laverne Cox has described the present moment as a "state of emergency for trans people."[60] Cox's description of the situation for trans people of color resonates with Mbembe's concept of necropolitics. Mbembe describes how governments work today as necropolitical because they no longer promise to ensure life for citizens; they also guarantee death for those deemed "Other" based on the ways that contemporary colonial capitalism is a continuation of slave plantations and colonies. Cox's statements express how the lived experiences of trans people of color demonstrate Mbembe's formulation.

The frequency of murders of trans women and the fact that the murders are often ignored indicate the importance of Mbembe's model of necropolitics for understanding trans lives. Under necropolitics, the state decides who will die, and nonstate actors often carry out the killing.[61] In "Trans Necropolitics," Jin Haritaworn and C. Riley Snorton argue that "visibility, legibility and intelligibility structure a grid of imposed value on the lives and deaths of black and brown trans women" and that, in certain instances of antiviolence activism, "trans women of color act as resources—both literally and metaphorically—for the articulation of visibility of a more privileged transgender subject."[62] Their claim underscores the need for more in-depth analyses of race within transgender studies, as well as the importance of contributing to the agency of trans women of color to control their own visibility and other material conditions, such as their economic position. *Poetic Operations* focuses on contemporary trans of color artists using digital technologies, in sharp contrast to the frequent occurrence of studies that refer only to trans people who have died. In this book, I focus on these artists' brilliant engagements with technology, language, movement, and embodiment.

Poetic Operations works to decolonize the digital by understanding the communicative capacities of digital technologies as an outcome of the settler colonial socioeconomic support structure of the United States. My project *Local Autonomy Networks* (*Autonets*), which I describe in chapters 2 and 5, attempts to make those capacities available through other means that do not rely on the same violent foundations. *Autonets* was a project I created to build abolitionist networks for safety for queer and trans people of color, starting with wearable electronics such as bracelets and hoodies, and using those prototypes in workshops and performances. Another decolonial method at work here is to reveal the communication methods of the body that predate digital technologies and show how they are embodied in current computing and communication metaphors.

This book learns from Chela Sandoval's methodology of the oppressed and the *particle group*'s science of the oppressed, both of which center oppressed subjects as agents of knowledge production in a process of anticolonial struggle. In *Methodology of the Oppressed*, Sandoval links her concept of differential consciousness, the ability to shift between "oppositional forms of consciousness," to both trans people and the digital when she says, "The differential maneuvering required here is a sleight of consciousness that activates a new space: a cyberspace, where the transcultural, transgendered, transsexual, transnational leaps necessary to the play of effective stratagems of oppositional praxis can begin."[63] Her grouping of trans and the digital together, in a Chicana feminist theory of decolonial social change, opens the way for a trans of color poetics that can use digital poetic gestures for the survival of trans people, in resistance to colonial drives to eradicate those who can move between genders. The *particle group*, a new media artist collective I have collaborated with, articulated science of the oppressed by reimagining science in the interests of oppressed people.[64]

Scholars writing about digital media art have often left the social dimensions of the work undertheorized, but this project is aligned with theorists engaging directly with issues of race, gender, and sexuality. New media criticism by Wendy Chun and Lisa Nakamura brilliantly engages intersectional analyses of race and gender, even though these concerns are often still marginalized in a larger field of digital studies. Queer new media critique is emerging in essays published by Zach Blas and Kara Keeling, who names this new configuration in her essay "Queer OS," citing a historical lack of such scholarship.[65] These feminist and queer approaches are addressing areas of concern that have been left unaccounted for by well-known digital scholars who eschew discussions of embodied difference in digital media, such as Lev Manovich. Part of my intent in using algorithmic analysis to describe trans of color poetics is to engage with media studies from the perspective of a trans person of color and to shape that intervention around the concerns of trans people of color, including, but not limited to, safety, violence, hypervisibility, surveillance, migration, incarceration, and access to health care.

Practice-Based Research

Poetic Operations engages in a materialist approach to understanding social change that begins with trans people in movement and uses their experiences to imagine more just futures. My approach is a hybrid of theory and practice, motivated by art and activism as much as by theory. Discussing my own practice-based research projects developed from 2011 to 2015, including *Autonets* (2011–14), *Pregnancy* (2015) and *Redshift and Portalmetal* (2015), as well as media made by other artists and authors, I consider the strategies for social change prototyped by media art, speculative design, and science fiction. Black female androids, communicator bracelets, and alien landscapes provide visions of possibility beyond the violence of the present moment. I discuss Janelle Monáe's androids in chapter 3 and communication bracelets and alien landscapes in my own work in chapters 4 and 5. Walidah Imarisha writes in *Octavia's Brood*, "Whenever we try to envision a world without war, without violence, without prisons, without capitalism, we are engaging in an exercise of speculative fiction."[66] Imarisha's joining of political and cultural work continues the path of women of color feminism. *Poetic Operations* also takes inspiration from the media justice movement made visible at the annual Allied Media Conference (AMC), whose politics aim to be visionary, as opposed to grievance-based, and who avow, "We presume our power, not our powerlessness."[67] I see this mode of working toward building alternatives instead of only focusing on critique as central to my methodology.[68]

The deep concern with safety and survival in these artworks is a kind of materialism, a move away from pure abstraction in art. To say this is materialism may seem at odds with how materialism has been used by media theorists such as Sarah Kember and Joanna Zylinska, whose book *Life after New Media* includes very few mentions of race or racial categories. Kember and Zylinska look to Karen Barad's materialism as a way to move beyond identity categories that have been tied to demands for representation. Yet Barad's move toward considering the agency of matter does not make concerns about race and gender less important. On the contrary, Barad states that their concern is with developing a theory of matter that reflects the social and political reality to create change. Discussing gender performativity as a process of materialization, Barad states, "What is at stake in this dynamic conception of matter is an unsettling of nature's presumed fixity and hence an opening up of the possibilities for change."[69] Barad has proposed a relation between identities based on these principles that she refers to as "intra-action," describing agency as co-constitutive between people and objects.[70] Their concept of intra-action describes a world where matter is not fixed but is changing over time in relation to the matter around it. As Barad states, the matter in our bodies is in a constant state of change. While trans people of color in digital media make shifting visible as a survival strategy, it is also an existential condition for everyone. Like the variables in an algorithm, we are in flux within a set of parameters. With this in mind, my concern is to understand the material factors facilitating the murder of trans women of color and to work toward preventing those murders by analyzing how digital media is used for violence and for survival.

While trans women of color have been a primary target of violence among LGBTQ communities, they are still left out of a great deal of scholarship. Yet simply writing about trans people of color is not enough to improve their situation. Action is also necessary. This book questions the division between theory and practice, between high theory and activism, and between the academy and the community by working directly with affected communities and understanding activism as always already engaged in theorizing. My aim as an interdisciplinary scholar is not to provide authoritative answers based on reading all the works in a given discipline so much as it is to ask questions, make connections, and create concepts.

Practice-based research is a form of research driven by creating art, media, performance, networks, or community engagement instead of relying only on close study of archives of text or media. For example, in his essay "Gaming the Humanities," Patrick Jagoda describes how the creation of digital games can be a rich site of experimentation for practice-based research in digital humanities.[71] *Poetic Operations* engages modes of practice-based research that include community-based design, community-based art, and performance-led research, which are well suited to the needs of trans politics and strive to go beyond representation. Community-based design has been described powerfully by Una Lee as a process in which community members, not just designers, have input into the design of technologies that impact them, a process I used in both *Autonets* and the *Transborder Immigrant Tool* (*TBT*). Lee is a co-organizer of the AMC and creative director of the And Also Too design studio in Toronto.[72] Community-based art practices involve dialogical processes of conversation, as described by Grant Kester, which are very present in my work on *Autonets*.[73] The artist collective Blast Theory has described a method of "performance-led research in the wild," in which artistic questions drive technological research, which resonates with my research practice.[74] Theorists such as Angela Davis, Dean Spade, and Colectivo Situaciones write from their experience of engaging in activism.[75] Learning from their work, this book emerges from a sustained practice of social engagement. My own art projects described in this book have addressed many different audiences during the practice-based research that led to this writing. The workshops I facilitated were intended for members of affected communities. The performances I cocreated were intended for numerous audiences, including art audiences and public audiences on streets. This book is intended to engage academic audiences by drawing on histories of women of color feminism to theorize trans of color poetics, while also hoping to inspire activists, artists, and anyone interested in trans of color lives to take action.

Poetic Operations resists the linear form of a book. The reader will note the frequent shifts in register in this book from first person to third person.

Because it is based in practice-based research, I often write from my experience of movement, performance, writing code, and creating electronic objects. Rather than separate these out, they are woven through each chapter, an integral part of my thinking. Chapter 4, "The Experience of Shifting," addresses how I see experience as a basis for creating art and theory. In chapter 4, I write about the digital games *Mainichi*, by Mattie Brice, and *Redshift*, which are both based on personal experiences of shifting one's appearance or location to avoid transphobic violence. Betsy Wing, the translator of *Poetics of Relation*, writes of Glissant, "The structure of *Poetics of Relation* is based more on associative principles than on any steady progress toward irrefutable proof; it is an enactment of its own poetics."[76] Similarly, this book contains cuts to media, frequent shifts, and the stitching together of concepts into a network of relations.

Algorithms also are not always linear; they can contain flow control statements that include event handlers, function calls, and break statements. In programming languages based on the C language, such as C++, a function is a named group of instructions. Functions can be activated by referring to their names. Events, such as a mouse click, can be linked to specific functions called event handlers, creating nonlinear flows through a particular piece of code.[77] A loop is a set of instructions that repeats until a certain condition is met, but by using the keyword *break*, code can force an exit from a loop.[78] I encourage readers to interrupt their reading when URLs for the online companion are mentioned, as the supporting media for this project are extensive and consisted of years of research creation. This book's digital components are available at http://scalar.usc.edu/works/poetic-operations.

The use of the Scalar digital authoring platform allows performance documentation to be featured alongside this text. As the project includes technological artifacts, performances, and workshops, the materials presented in the book include text, source code, photos, video, sound, and technical diagrams. In this way, the form of the project embodies the interdisciplinary approach that *Poetic Operations* takes to understanding trans of color art in digital media while also revealing the social and cultural implications of trans of color lives. The creation of this book's digital companion involved writing Cascading Style Sheets (CSS), HyperText Markup Language (HTML), and JavaScript code and working with database systems and digital video, image, and sound editing software. Encompassing both the print book and the online companion, this book is in itself an act of trans of color poetics, in both the language and the form it takes. Readers should understand that the media in the companion are as important as the text for experiencing the fullness of the arguments in this book.

The projects I describe here emerged through a process of exchange, overlap, and feedback among reading, performances, workshops, writing, presentations, and technological creations in hardware, software, and wearable electronics. My research questions were formed in—and continue to evolve through—the mixing of these practices. While my work explores intersections of theory and activism, performance and media art are also important to my methodology as parameters that provide direction, as archives for inspiration, and as sites for presentation.[79]

Operations: The Cut, the Stitch, the Shift

Poetic Operations is organized in a way that strives to enact the poetics it describes. Each chapter uses trans of color poetics to stitch together theory and practice while shifting between first-person and third-person registers when discussing artworks. The introduction begins by proposing the method of algorithmic analysis, which is used throughout the rest of the book. Using algorithmic analysis, chapter 1 proposes trans of color poetics as seen in the poetry of trans women of color, as well as the conceptual installation artwork of Giuseppe Campuzano. Chapter 2 goes more deeply into trans of color poetics by using the method of algorithmic analysis of identifying specific operations. The cut is the first operation introduced because it is the operation that allows one to break a problem into smaller components and operations. Once the operation of the cut is demonstrated, the operation of the shift is introduced in chapter 3 and elaborated in chapter 4. This operation provides a fundamental building block for writing algorithms, the variable. From there, chapter 5 introduces the stitch, which allows one to combine variables into algorithms, extending out beyond individual bodies. In the conclusion, I consider the contemporary relevance of algorithms in light of recent studies of algorithmic bias, digital redlining, and the emerging forms of visionary trans of color activism. The overall structure of the book, then, enacts algorithmic analysis in the way that it is organized by following the logic of writing an algorithm.

Trans of color poetics are perceptible in the gestures of the cut, the shift, and the stitch. Chapter 1 establishes the theoretical foundation for trans of color poetics, arguing that poetics can be part of the struggle for decolonization in that they can contribute to the survival of people harmed by colonial processes by transmitting survival strategies and building affective networks of care. The chapter begins and ends with the trans women of color poets Esdras Parra and Kai Cheng Thom grounding trans of color poetics in linguistic poetry to extend it to media and movement in later chapters. The chapter also considers Campuzano's *El Museo Travesti del Perú* in more depth to reveal a poetics of survival used by travestis. The differentiation between trans and trans of color is deepened in this consideration of travestis and two-spirit people via Campuzano's and Qwo-Li Driskill's descriptions of decolonial poetics with which trans of color poetics is in dialogue.

Chapter 2 applies the cut to describe methods for decolonizing digital technologies through collaboratively developed performances in public space that create embodied networks. The cut corresponds to the first method of algorithmic analysis: that of taking a problem and breaking it down into its components and operations. The chapter discusses *Autonets*, a project to create wearable communication networks for trans of color safety, inspired by the prison abolition movement, that do not rely on prisons, police, or corporations. In *Autonets* I created working prototypes of mesh network clothes and accessories that used signal strength to detect the proximity of other *Autonets* garments and display it to the wearer (figure I.3). I use the operation of the cut to analyze a performance of *Autonets* in São Paulo, Brazil.

Chapter 3 proposes a new operator of trans of color poetics, the shift, a form of movement in which one transforms one's shape, color, or location. The shift provides elements such as variables, which are not rigidly defined as static entities, that can be combined in algorithms. A body in the process of shifting can be understood to parallel a variable in an algorithm that can take on different values. The chapter argues that shifting is a form of movement particularly relevant to necropolitics, where simple visibility is replaced with modulation, sensors, AI computer vision algorithms, invisibility, and holograms. The chapter demonstrates shifting through the performance of the Black gender-non-conforming artist Janelle Monáe and the music videos for her science fiction concept album *Metropolis*. Considering examples that make shifting perceptible, including Monáe's music videos, as well as examples of my code poetry (poetry that uses the syntax of computer code as part of its poetics), I show how the shift can be used in algorithmic analysis. Shifting demonstrates how trans people of color were using algorithmic methods long before digital algorithms codified them.

Chapter 4 argues for the value of personal experience in trans of color theory through the example of games that use a first-person form of storytelling to portray the daily lives of trans people of color. Digital games are the paradigmatic example of algorithmic media. Direct experience can be a powerful

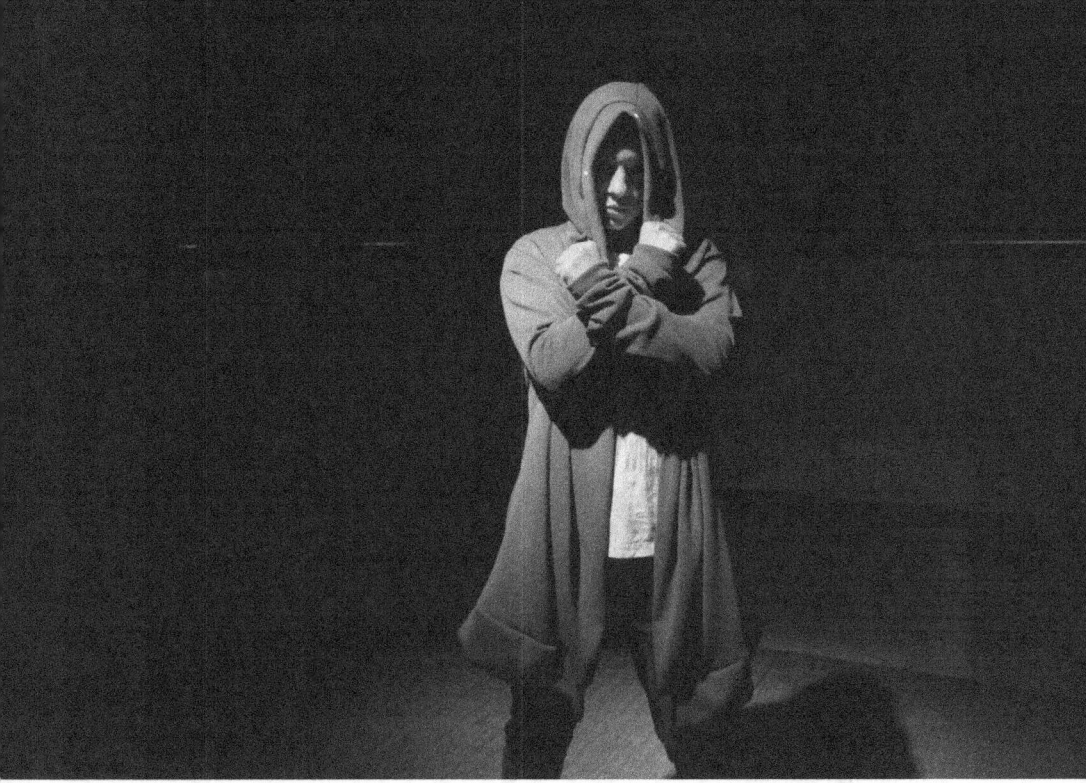

I.3 Jovan Wolfe of Gender Justice LA wearing *Autonets* mesh networked hoodie designed by micha cárdenas and Ben Klunker. Photograph by micha cárdenas.

basis for creating digital games about the survival of trans people of color. Personal games can bring audiences into those experiences—not to build empathy, but to work toward solidarity. Brice's *Mainichi* is analyzed in the chapter, a game about the daily life of a Black trans woman. Seeing the problem with audiences' attempts to gain empathy by playing the game, sidelining her ideas and focusing only on her suffering, Brice used *Mainichi* in an embodied performance to make players more directly implicated in their interactions with her.[80] Chapter 4 also considers the value of embodied experience from the point of view of a light-skinned, mixed-race Latinx trans woman of color, my own point of view, in my online game *Redshift* (figure I.4). I describe the poetic choices I made in the game to share my experiences in a way that blends with science fiction elements to allow audiences to consider choices I have to make while still protecting my own boundaries. In addition, I discuss the live performance of *Redshift* I created in collaboration with the two-spirit Black Cherokee performance artist Rayvn Wngz and how the performance brought algorithmic poetics to life through a collaborative gesture of decolonial solidarity.

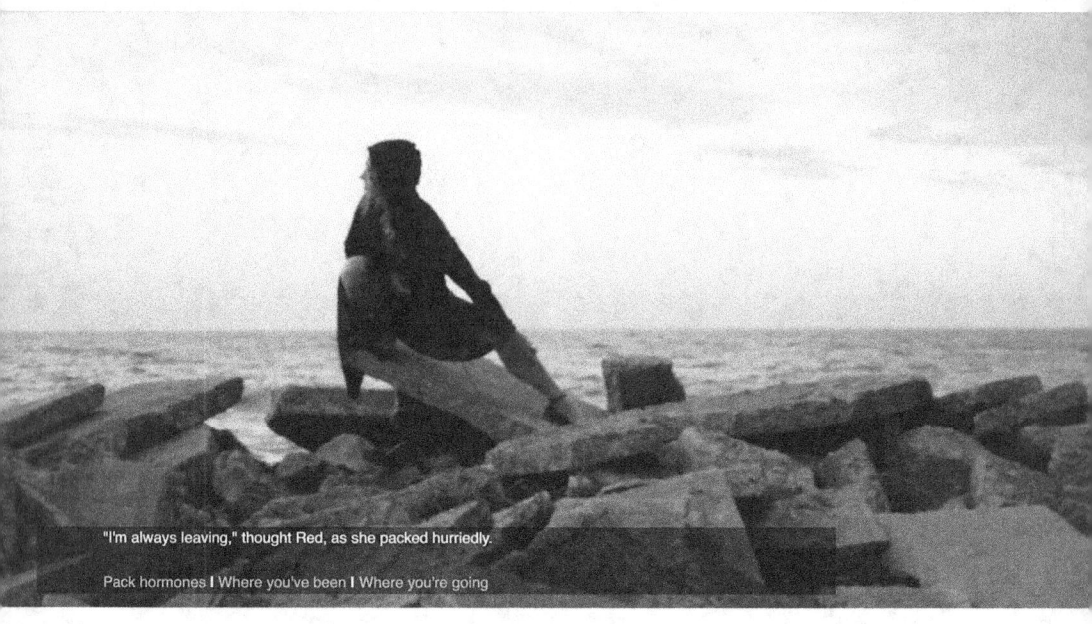

I'm always leaving," thought Red, as she packed hurriedly.

Pack hormones I Where you've been I Where you're going

I.4 Screen shot of the online game interface from *Redshift and Portalmetal*,
by micha cárdenas.

The stitch is a method of connecting elements by sewing, which I elaborate in chapter 5. Stitching is another operation of trans of color poetics that
allows the poetics to extend beyond the individual experience to bring about
both opacity and relation. Returning to Campuzano's *Museo Travesti del Perú*,
the stitch is shown to emerge from ancient embodied practices of gender
transgression and continue into media art practices today. Stitching reveals
intra-action, undoing the illusion of separateness that Western ontologies
have enforced. Chapter 5 considers applications of opacity, escaping surveillance through wireless mesh networks, wearable electronics, and mobile
phone applications. Contemporary artists use algorithmic media to create
speculative design and contestational design projects, including *The Transborder Immigrant Tool (TBT)*, by the Electronic Disturbance Theater; *Stealth
Wear*, by Adam Harvey; *Facial Weaponization Suite*, by Zach Blas; and *Autonets*.
The TBT used cheap recycled cell phones to help people find water on the
US-Mexico border through a custom global positioning system (GPS) application. *Stealth Wear* is part of a larger set of works created by Harvey, including *CV Dazzle*, in which the artist designs clothing, hairstyles, and makeup
that can defeat AI-based computer vision (CV) algorithms. Blas's *Facial Weap-*

onization Suite is rooted in a philosophical consideration of Glissant's concept of opacity, using algorithmically generated masks to move queer politics beyond demands for representation. The chapter also demonstrates how trans of color poetics can be performed by people who do not identify as trans people of color, as Blas and Harvey do not identify as part of that group. The artists discussed in the chapter use technologies of stitching to avoid surveillance at the algorithmic level. Trans of color poetics demonstrate how contemporary AI systems for CV, which are based on colonial assumptions such as the idea that gender is only binary, are fundamentally wrong. Computer vision algorithms do not see travestis, shifting between bodies. While this can be exploited, it also reveals the violence of exclusion at the epistemological level that is being encoded into these technologies. In contrast, the stitch can be used to create relation, decolonize digital communications, and build solidarity among people.

In the conclusion, I return to the words of Sylvia Rivera, a visionary activist working for trans Latinx futures, to consider the importance of developing poetics as a means of stopping the murders of trans women of color. I consider the emerging popular awareness of algorithms and more recent scholarship on the violence of algorithms. I follow the line from Rivera's vision for a trans movement to an expanded abolitionist vision described by Ravyn Wngz at a Black Lives Matter press conference in 2020.

In this book, I reflect on the process of continuing to face the deaths of my community members every day. To do so, I engage with the theory of necropolitics, which brings considerations of racism and colonialism into dialogue with highly technological contemporary forms of war and neocolonialism. To this theory I add trans of color experience and a visionary model of politics demonstrated in contemporary art, speculative media, and science fiction. I look to women of color feminism and queer of color critique to find modes of thought that can express the many dynamics of processes of identity in algorithmic analysis. By proposing trans of color poetics, I hope to open a space for many operations to be articulated, which can bring our experiences to life through poetry and performance. By proposing that the lives of trans people of color are an important basis for theory and art, I hope to create space for many more unimagined configurations of gender, sexuality, and other forms of difference, as well as the forms that have been said not to exist for so long.

TRANS OF COLOR POETICS

ONE

Si la voluntad te elige como potro
su figura de viento
hay que colocar la muela
en el ojo de la aguja
hay que ser potro primero
y luego buscar la perfección del hígado
los rostros del frío y del asombro
para ser de nuevo hombre.

If the will finds you as a yearling
its wind-like figure
you must place the molar
in the eye of the needle
you must be a yearling first
and then seek the liver's perfection
the faces of the cold and the wonder
to be human once more.

—ESDRAS PARRA (translation by Jamie Berrout)

IN A POEM ABOUT SHAPE-SHIFTING, the Venezuelan trans woman poet Esdras Parra (1937–2004) offers an algorithm for becoming human. "To be human once more," she writes, follow these steps. Parra's writing articulates the experiences of isolation that so many trans women of color experience, but it does so in a way that embodies solitude through rituals of healing in collaboration with an environment filled with agency. If you find yourself a "yearling," no longer human but a one-year old foal with lanky, unmanageable legs and sudden dependence, you will have to complete an impossible act of stitching with your teeth to become human again.

Parra's affective description of feeling the sudden newness and foreignness of one's body, even feeling inhuman or less than human, resonates deeply with me. Here the poetic gesture of stitching that is an act of liberation in Giuseppe Campuzano's work becomes an impossible act of forcing a body that does not fit through the eye of a needle, yet it is still a necessary act to regain a relationship to your body. For Parra, the steps needed to become human again draw on her upbringing in the Andes outside Caracas, Venezuela. In the "Autoretrato" (self-portrait essay) from her book *Antiguidad del frio*, Parra writes about how the mountain climates shaped her: "I am, somehow, those climates. Isolation and solitude pleases me. . . . (My mother was a small and vigorous *india* [Indigenous woman] born in those desolate mountains.)" In the essay, she describes how her poetics, concerned almost entirely with nonhuman phenomena and a solitary human experience of natural phenomena, is linked to her Indigenous ancestry and early experiences living outside urban areas. In Parra's work, trans of color poetics are actively in collaboration and messy coconstitution with nonhuman worlds and bodies. Shifting here goes beyond color or form to cross lines of species, as it also does in the writing of Gloria Anzaldúa. Stitching is not only to create clothing for a human body, but to suture the broken parts of oneself that make you feel like an animal, outside the onto-epistemologically delineated space of the human that provides coherence, reason, and protection.

Parra's work, with its attention to care and healing, is a powerful example of trans of color poetics. Poetics, in this book, refer to the choices involved in turning thought into action. That action can be directed toward the creation of an object, the creation of media, the ordering of words, or an expression of movement. Poetics are how the expressions of trans of color artists become poetry, become more than everyday speech, movement, or media. While this book takes inspiration from theorists in the field of queer of color critique, such as José Muñoz and Roderick Ferguson, I choose to focus on poetics as a generative mode of thinking that can also incorporate critique. *Poetic Operations* examines and develops trans of color poetics that can open possibilities of life for trans people of color in movement. I consider movement expansively to include elements of transnational migration, performance, and mobility. Trans of color poetics are a creation, an offering, not a prescription or a definition. I describe what I perceive in these works and how they contribute to a decolonial politics that aims to end the violence enacted to enforce gender binaries, racial hierarchies, and settler colonial rule. The algorithm of trans of color poetics can be understood as more of a ritual offering than a formula that seeks to render a totalizing depiction.

This chapter develops the theory of trans of color poetics, using algorithmic analysis to identify the poetic gestures of the cut, the shift, and the stitch. Here I use these tools to analyze linguistic poetry by trans of color poets, as well as contemporary art, to develop the repertoire of trans of color poetics as a basis for the turn to digital media in the following chapters, which go into more detail about each operation. Through thinking about care as acts taken toward collective survival, I show how trans of color poetics reflect Latinx, mestizx, and two-spirit ways of being in the world. In the introduction, I discussed Campuzano's *DNI (De Natura Incertus)*. In this chapter, I discuss Campuzano's conceptual project *El Museo Travesti de Perú* (TMP), and then my artwork *Pregnancy*, to show how they are informed by decolonial theory and women of color feminism. Finally, I turn to Kai Cheng Thom's work to consider how trans of color poetics gesture beyond the present realities of violence toward futures of community care through algorithms encoded as rituals. While these authors' and artists' conceptions of gender and identity exceed the Western definition of transgender, their poetics unite them.

Trans of color poetics begin with a history of expression older than US-centric notions of transgender and connect those gestures to how trans bodies of color move in contemporary digital media art. Campuzano states, "Articulated through a genealogy of Peruvian dance . . . the Museo Travesti served as a political artifact that preserved a mestizo memory translated into social inclusion for the transvestite: from carnivalesque mimesis to daily *poésis*."[1] Campuzano describes a shifting across both racial and gender lines, uniting the mestizo and the travesti, and performs those crossings through the stitching together of digital and nondigital artifacts into artworks, which he describes as poésis.[2] He differentiates between mimesis, or duplication, and poésis, or original creation. Poetics, then, can be understood as the choices involved in creating something new. In creating digital media, many choices are made about what elements to include, how to combine those elements, what relationships the elements will create together, what relationship the work will have with the audience, and what networks will be created or activated. Algorithmic poetics use the performativity of digital code to bring multiple layers of meaning to life in networks of signification.

Poetics should be understood here as the meeting of intention and expression; all the ways that matter is used to communicate, where matter includes concepts expressed as words, sound, or gesture. As I describe in the introduction, trans of color poetics, inspired largely by Édouard Glissant's poetics of relation, are also a network of elements in relation, yet here the elements are operators, and the relation is an algorithm. I learn from the operation of the cut described by Jacques Derrida and Gilles Deleuze to articulate the operations of the shift and the stitch. The shift describes how bodies can transform or move in space. The stitch indicates how elements such as fabric, concepts, people, code, and movements can be connected together.

Esdras Parra's Decolonial Poetics

Parra's longing to be human again is crucial here in opening the space of trans of color poetics to be not merely instrumental, even when the artists may be vitally struggling to live. Despite the desperate need to end the murderous violence we face—the small, mundane violence of misgendering and the unspeakable violence of the "aporia of isolation" that Trace Peterson describes—what Parra's writing shows us is the need we also have "to be human once more."[3] Is this not the goal of struggle: to be able to feel our tender humanity and share it with another?

As Parra's work shows, trans of color poetics speak to the ways that the bodies and lives of trans people of color can feel unimaginable in societies whose common sense imagines that we do not exist. Her example of the impossibility of finding that one's self is a baby horse recalls another trans of color poet, Trish Salah, and her unruly statement on poetics as a way of "writing recovery, writing graven, writing manifesting the body and its impossibility."[4] Impossibility is a condition that activates poetic imagination by exceeding the bounds of logic, which also finds resonance in the trans experience of exceeding the bounds of gender that are said to be inviolable.

> No amo lo predecible
> nada de extender los brazos para sentir el corazón
> ese tiempo que se pierde de vista

despierto respirando el aire de ayer
atravieso el arroyo negro
te señalo lo que no veo
no han existido otras manos que éstas
que recogen las piedras
un desierto a oscuras
un vuelo a ciegas en invierno
una caricia huraña
yo sólo escucho la luz de los árboles
el mundo es suyo
mío el deseo de porvenir.

I have no love for the predictable
no reaching out of the arms to feel the heart
the time that escapes from view
I wake up breathing yesterday's air
cross the black ravine
point out to you that which I do not see
no hands have ever existed save these
that gather the rocks
a desert in the darkness
a sightless flight in winter
a distant touch
all I listen to is the light of the trees
the world is theirs
longing for the future is mine.[5]

Parra's poetry moves in the deep quiet of solitude, finding healing outside of the world of people, sharing rituals of recovery. While the dislike she has of the predictable would seem to distance her from algorithmic considerations, Parra describes a ritual outside of the time of cisgender heteronormative life rhythms. Her hands have always existed, gathering rocks, walking in the desert, flying in the winter. In lines that speak to the depth of pain she feels, I feel I have shared these pains with her: "The world is theirs / longing for the future is mine." So much of trans experience is composed of that *longing* for a future body, future community, future child, and, in the case of trans women of color, a future world in which we can survive.

Translation is an act of care, which in this case is an act of trans women caring for one another. In her commentary on her translation process, Jamie Berrout writes in her Tumblr blog about how Parra's use of poetics emerges from her survival strategies and consciously challenges the obtrusive gaze of audiences that demand transparency, a demand Glissant has tied to the colonial encounter.[6] Writing about the political import of her own translation and publishing work, Berrout says in the introduction to her translation of *Este suelo secreto*,

> In our world, the lives of trans women of color mean little and our work, destined to fade into obscurity, has even less value. It is our bodies that have worth, but only when our selves are separated from them—a living trans woman equals nothing, a book by a trans woman equals nothing, but a list of names of dead trans women equals a platform and careers for our allies, but an institution that trans women's bodies are shepherded toward in the name of care, where they must suffer negligence and abuse, equals lucrative grants. In our world, trans women of color must do the work of caring after and valuing and lifting up each other.[7]

Berrout's critiques of the lack of care and attention given to trans women of color, and to their writing when they are alive, reflects Parra's own pain: "the world is theirs / longing for the future is mine." The cut is used throughout Parra's poems in breath cuts and line breaks. Here the cut of the line break emphasizes the separation between theirs and mine, *suyo* and *mio*, present and future, to resonate with a deep, shining pain. In Berrout's English translation the word order is different, creating more time between "theirs" and "mine." The cut of isolation, of existing in nature, far from anyone else, is both a transphobic circumstance and a profound poetic choice in Parra's poetry. In Parra's world, a decolonial possibility exists far outside of the cities of humans, defying linear time with hands that have always existed. She stitches together the lines of her poem in a way that weaves the pain of the present with an image of future possibility, creating a fabric of space outside of linear time.

A Decolonial Poetics, Shifting outside of Categories

Trans of color poetics are a gesture of solidarity animated by a poetic ambiguity that make them more capacious. The formation "trans of color" reveals the limitations of the Western medical definition of transgender and calls for solidarity beyond its bounds. I include Campuzano, who identifies as travesti, here in my description of trans of color poetics in an effort to make the term more expansive and to decolonize transgender studies. Yet in so doing, the term *trans of color* needs to be understood as not indexical, not an authoritative description of a rigid category. Thinking of trans of color poetics as an algorithm allows one to imagine the category of trans of color as a shifting variable, as part of a process that exists only when it is performed, with an appearance that can change rapidly based on the needs and desires of the moment.

In *TMP*, shifting can be seen in Campuzano's ability to inhabit a multiplicity of genders, undermining the border between them. The *TMP*'s critical intervention into questioning the modernist foundations of the museum, and the racial and gender normativity that museums reproduce, put her work in dialogue with contemporary art in venues from the São Paulo Biennial to contemporary art museums, including the Museum of Contemporary Art in Krakow.[8] In *TMP*, Campuzano creates a conceptual museum, with no physical home, to refigure the nation of Peru as a travesti.[9] Campuzano states, "The Museo Travesti is a political project that starts by challenging knowledge in order achieve a dislocation of power, transferring the androgynes and transvestites from the margins to the center of Peruvian history as a transformative strategy for moving from memory to social recognition . . . [and] situating transvestites not as subjects that belong to society, but as subjects that transform our societies."[10] Much like the shifting of the mestiza in Anzaldúa's *Borderlands/La Frontera* or the movement among several resistant strategies of Chela Sandoval's differential consciousness, Campuzano applies the mutability of the transvestite to the nation, saying, "If there were such a thing as a Peruvian essence, it would be constant metamorphosis. A Peru, an America, immersed in the transvestite processes of imposition and agency that are constitutive of its subjects."[11] His claim resonates with Marcia Ochoa's linking of trans and transnational in her analysis of the spectacular femininity of *transformistas*, trans women, and beauty queens in Venezuela.[12] Campuzano's centering of the figure of the transvestite as a figure of power destabilizes Western teleologies that would present transgender as a more advanced, or more radical, choice of gender.

Using imagery from Incan culture, Campuzano gestures toward a long history of nonbinary gender formations. She uses the figure of the travesti to subvert binaries of colonizer and colonized and savage and civilized, in resistance to an official history of Peru that would see those binaries as fixed and real.[13] She uses this multiplicity of identity to challenge the laws that govern identification necessary for migration through a speculative digital simulation of alternative possibilities of identification. Her reference to a precolonial history that challenges gender binaries echoes Anzaldúa's claim, "I know things older than Freud, older than gender," when she claims that she can "enter into the Serpent," further challenging gendered binaries of embodiment through a practice of shifting she calls the Coatlicue state, from the Aztec goddess.[14] Anzaldúa's writing, like Campuzano's, uses her embodied acts of gender transgression to challenge a spectrum of borders, including the border between genders and the border between the secular and the sacred. Malú Machuca Rose brings these layers of trans of color performance, queer kinship, and spirituality together in their essay on Campuzano "to claim a legacy of *travesti* as *curandera*," or spiritual healer.[15]

Rose describes Campuzano's poetics as a gesture of impurity, considering the artist's HIV-positive status as important to her work. Rose states, "The central aim of Campuzano's travesti project is not to find the travestis in Peruvian history but, rather, to make out of her travesti body a map, a museum, an epistemology, to create on her body a way of coming to know the world and weave oneself into it."[16] Rose adds that many people engaged in trans movement activism in Peru reject the word *travesti*, using "transgender" to gain access to resources from the global North, which makes Campuzano's usage of the word an intentional gesture to inhabit the margins as a site of power.[17] In this beautifully written first-person account of working with Campuzano and her collaborator Germain Machuca, and mourning Campuzano's passing, Rose describes how Campuzano's performance of travesti refuses a national history of Peru that would envision Indigenous people as separate from the state and instead embraces the impurity of lost connections to Indigenous ancestors, a trans of color form of kinship. In this sense, trans of color poetics can be understood as a performed imaginary of connections that blur the firm lines of reality and call into question the Western category of "trans," exceeding the umbrella for a group of categories with an ever-growing woven fabric of kinship. I return to the expansive project TMP in more detail in chapter 5.

By acknowledging the multiple ways that gender is imagined, and the ways those different conceptions are contoured by racialized and colonial acts, trans of color poetics call into question the dominance of any single way of conceptualizing gender. The global distribution of the US concept of transgender reproduces colonial systems of knowledge, imposing Western conceptions of the self and the body onto non-Western subjects such as travestis and two-spirit people.[18] Trans of color poetics perform a decolonial challenge to the idea of transgender by questioning Western notions of the self as unified, unchanging, and separate. The concept of transgender relies on Western systems of knowledge that imagine an individual subject with a discrete gender, who crosses a line to another discrete gender. This figuration has been widely critiqued, as in Sandy Stone's *The War of Desire and Technology*, which sees the multiplicity of identity evidenced in the common experience of internet chat room users and their ability to choose and change their identities frequently, a clear example of algorithmically enabled shifting identity.[19]

By thinking algorithmically about identities as variables, groups in processes of shifting, trans of color poetics allow us to see opportunities for solidarity and collective action while also upholding the unique identities of groups who may not identify as trans. For example, I include Indigenous two-spirit identities, imagined as "inclusive of Indigenous people who identify as GLBTQ or through nationally specific terms from Indigenous languages," in the idea of trans of color poetics as an effort to challenge the colonial limitations of transgender studies.[20] Still, doing so risks imposing Western labels on experiences to which they do not apply. Qwo-Li Driskill has further developed two-spirit identity into two-spirit critique, an important relation for trans of color poetics that sees the acknowledgment of Indigenous peoples and knowledge as essential for breaking down gender, racial, and sexual systems of oppression rooted in settler colonialism. The concept of two-spirit is also a grouping that describes many names that different tribes use to describe themselves, such as the Cherokee term *asegi udanto*, which "refers . . . specifically to people who either fall outside of men's and women's roles or who mix men's and women's roles," as Driskill describes.[21]

I understand critique as a form of love. Critique means that I care about you enough to read your work and come back to you and tell you what I did not agree with. Critique can be a kind of intimacy, when I care enough to tell you how your writing hurt me. Cherríe Moraga's book *A Xicana Codex of Changing Consciousness* (2011) contains a chapter in which she equates trans masculine identity with the genocidal act of making a culture disappear, which is a deeply problematic misunderstanding on her part.[22] I read the lack of trans women as a tension in the founding of women of color feminism.[23] In 2005, M. Jacqui Alexander's reflections on *This Bridge Called My Back*, and its profoundly transformational effect, does mention transgender people, while it does not address their earlier absence.[24] Alexander's decolonial argument is that connection across difference is profoundly important, decolonial, spiritual, personal work. I see the project of creating a trans of color poetics as part of a larger project of building a trans of color feminism, which includes scholarship and art, to account for the historical lack of trans women in feminist theory and art.

To account for this historical lack of care for the lives of trans women, I am using an algorithmic method to describe the elements of a trans of color poetics that are imbricated with trans of color survival. Trans people exist across multiple identities and survive in community. Ending violence against trans people of color is part of a project of ending the racialized, gendered violence of colonization. Édouard Glissant has argued that poetics can work to undo the effects of colonization. In *Caribbean Discourse*, Glissant states, "The most violent challenge to an established order can emerge from a natural poetics, when there is a continuity between the challenged order and the disorder that negates it."[25] In *Poetics of Relation*, he elaborates this, saying,

> I began wondering if we did not still need such founding works today, ones that would use a similar dialectics of rerouting, asserting, for example, political strength but, simultaneously, the rhizome of a multiple relationship with the Other and basing every community's reasons for existence on a modern form of the sacred, which would be, all in all, a Poetics of Relation.... Whereas the Western nation is first of all an "opposite," for colonized peoples identity will be primarily "opposed to"—that is, a limitation from the beginning. Decolonization will have done its real work when it goes beyond this limit.[26]

Here Glissant's description of decolonization overcoming the opposition of separate identities through the poetics of relation resonates with trans of color poetics that are both decolonial and rhizomatic. He describes the real work of decolonization, in a Caribbean context, as the work of overcoming identity as necessarily oppositional. His description resonates with women of color feminism's formulation of identity in difference, in which the identity woman of color is formed in solidarity with women of different ethnicities. Similarly, trans of color poetics offer a set of practices that bridge multiple ethnicities and genders. In describing trans of color poetics, I am seeking to stitch together the kind of community Glissant describes, which relies on multiple relationships with those who may be considered other. In the place of further and further division into separate categories of identity, I am advocating for a coalitional strategy of solidarity, like women of color feminism, for gender-variant people from across the globe to work for safety and joy together. Similarly, like women of color feminism, trans of color poetics are a formulation that challenges their own definitions, bringing together forms of gender nonconformity that do not neatly fall into the category of transgender. Glissant uses the concept of poetics in solidarity with decolonial struggle, describing a "Poetics of Relation, in which each and every identity is extended through a relationship with the Other."[27] In a poetics of relation, Glissant states, "Creolization . . . approximates the idea of Relation for us as nearly as possible. . . . If we posit métissage as, generally speaking, the meeting and synthesis of two differences, creolization seems to be a limitless métissage, its elements diffracted and its consequences unforeseeable."[28] One can understand creolization as a poetic resistance to colonialism, an insurgent challenge to the purity of an imposed colonial language, which also changes the original language in the process.[29] This mixing process can be seen as a link between women of color feminism and trans of color poetics, which goes beyond language to engage in activism through art.

There is a conflict between the totalizing logic of colonialism and the multiplicity of elements that poetics arise from, whether those elements are words, lines, gestures, or images. Algorithmic processes can be used to enact a totalizing logic, or they can be mobilized to challenge totalitarianism. In *Poetic Intention*, Glissant states, "If it does indeed sanction and embody a poetic thought, is not every poetics today just and heavy with the conception and total activation of the diverse poetics of the world?"[30] Here Glissant, having seen numerous anticolonial revolutions, understands all poetics that allow the embodiment of poetic thought to be in relation with all of the other diverse poetics operating in the world. He mentions wildly different poetics, including Baudelaire's French poetics of depth, poetics of duration, poetics of the Occident, and poetics of the nation.[31] These different conceptions of poetics show the way that he imagines poetics as a material force that either can flow into the abyss within a person, such as poetics of depth, or can ripple across a country's struggle for independence. Inspired by Glissant, I am committed to developing forms of poetics that can nurture rich vibrant relations among diverse peoples struggling to overcome the violence of ideologies that seek to impose any single standard of gendered, racialized, or other forms of being. Trans of color poetics can nurture these relations among gender-variant people who may be widely separated geographically or culturally.

My choice to focus on poetics in this book, more than aesthetics, is a decolonial gesture. In *Borderlands/La Frontera*, Anzaldúa states that "ethnocentrism is the tyranny of Western aesthetics," strongly linking practices of the separation of art objects from performance rituals, for the purpose of aesthetic consideration, to the disempowerment of Indigenous peoples.[32] In his analysis of aesthetics, Clyde Taylor, filmmaker in the L.A. Rebellion and professor emeritus at New York University, describes how the concept of aesthetics is inextricable from histories of white supremacy. In *The Mask of Art: Breaking the Aesthetic Contract—Film and Literature*, he writes: "The aesthetic played a major role in the narration of transcendent Whiteness and an indispensable role in the development of modern, pseudo-scientific racism. . . . [R]acism was elevated during the European Enlightenment to an institutionalized corpus of scholarly knowledge."[33] The L.A. Rebellion was a group of Black filmmakers working in Los Angeles in the late 1960s, in the aftermath of the Watts uprising, toward a vision of a society with gender and racial justice.[34] In describing the foundations of Black Aesthetics, Taylor shows how Western aesthetic thinking is linked to the logics of colonialism. As such, my effort here looks to poetics as an alternative. I am not claiming that poetics are inherently always decolonial, or that aesthetic theory should be discarded, but my goal in this book, as a poet and artist who works with media and performance, is to articulate a poetics, a set of gestures that can be used in support of decolonial politics and ethics. Poetics describe movement, resonance, affect, and connection across and between bodies. Thus, I am more interested in the creative possibilities of poetics, learning from the decolonial poetics of relation that Glissant articulates as being outside of the self-other separation enacted by Western Enlightenment ontologies, instead seeing all things as connected in relation. Instead of being concerned with what sensory qualities artists can use in creating objects, what one might describe as aesthetics, I am concerned with the ways that artists can use movement and tempo, what shifts in register or affect they can perform, and what networks of relations they can create to stitch together to bring about specific forms of relation such as solidarity and safety. These movements and networks are central to what I conceive of as poetics, and they are present in Parra's and Campuzano's work, and in mine.

Trans of Color Poetics in *Pregnancy*

Like Parra, I long for a future. My own longing for a future of having a child is captured in my series of poems titled *Pregnancy*. I first encountered Parra's poems when *Pregnancy* was curated into the *Museum of Transgender History and Art* (MOTHA) at the Henry Art Gallery in Seattle. A conceptual museum like Campuzano's *Museo Travesti del Perú*, MOTHA finds a temporary home in whatever museum the project gets curated into. In this case, the artist who created MOTHA, Chris Vargas, collaborated with the curator at the Henry, Nina Bozicnik, to identify trans artists local to the Coast Salish Pacific Northwest region. As part of that exhibition, the curators invited me to perform some of Parra's poems, and Berrout's translations, as well as my own poems from *Pregnancy*.[35]

Pregnancy refuses to separate the linguistic from the material, combining poetry and bioart into a visual format in which my biological material is always seen in motion, under a microscope, alongside my poems. The poems describe a time when I stopped taking my prescribed estrogen to bank reproductive tissue for a future child before receiving gender confirmation surgery. I understand the poems as a conceptual experiment, in the tradition of Hélène Cixous's urge to write the body in all of its various states, including chemical states. In one poem I respond to Paul Preciado's experiments with testosterone, saying that this process is not merely an experiment but also a process in which I need to engage in order to survive. Another poem describes the possibility of fighting back against the genocidal drives of both colonization and transphobia by having children and building a family. The poems conclude with reflections on Anzaldúa's descriptions of her own body as alien and in transformation, asking, "How many people are inside me?" next to an image swirling with gametes. A primary goal of the project was to share with other trans women the knowledge that doctors had lied to me and told me that I would be nonreproductive from the moment I began taking estrogen. I learned from other trans women that one can follow certain steps and have the possibility of producing gametes after just a few months. With a kid's microscope at home, I was able to see the changes in my biology happening, document them, and share them with others. *Pregnancy* translates and encodes the knowledge I learned about how trans women can have reproductive capacities into poetry, images, and video (figure 1.1).

Theorists of new media have described digital poetics through the lenses of theater, historical layering, and game mechanics. While Brenda Laurel's pioneering book *Computers as Theater* applied Aristotelian poetics to human computer interaction, using Aristotle's four causes and six elements, this book takes a similar approach using the decolonial poetics of Glissant and Anzaldúa.[36] Laurel defines poetics as "a body of theory that treats a poetic or aesthetic domain" and uses that to analyze digital games and software interfaces.[37] In her analysis of the poetics of the digital game *Assassin's Creed III: Liberation*, the cultural studies scholar Soraya Murray builds on Lisbeth Klastrup's poetics of virtual worlds to define poetics of digital games as "the perceptible game elements, and how they converge and bring into being particular aesthetic and expressive effects for the player."[38] Murray's description of poetics focuses largely on game mechanics as poetics, in that they are gestures of play that are not just visual. Both of these definitions include aes-

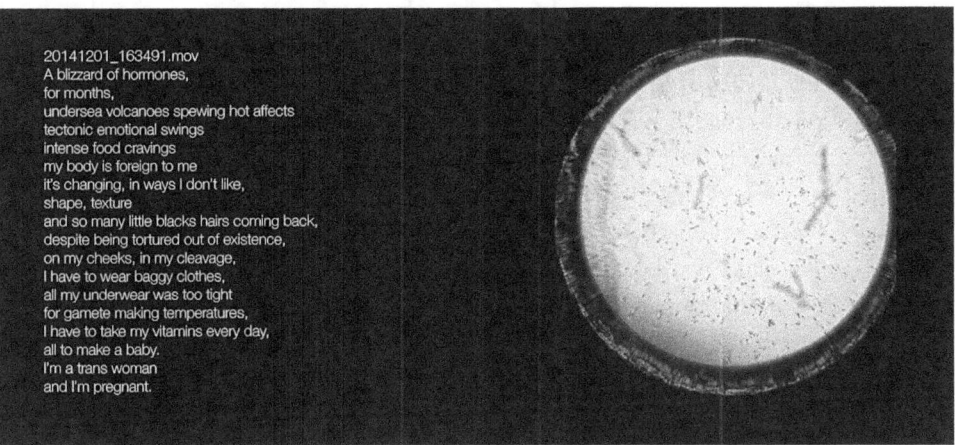

20141201_163491.mov
A blizzard of hormones,
for months,
undersea volcanoes spewing hot affects
tectonic emotional swings
intense food cravings
my body is foreign to me
it's changing, in ways I don't like,
shape, texture
and so many little blacks hairs coming back,
despite being tortured out of existence,
on my cheeks, in my cleavage,
I have to wear baggy clothes,
all my underwear was too tight
for gamete making temperatures,
I have to take my vitamins every day,
all to make a baby.
I'm a trans woman
and I'm pregnant.

1.1 Still image from *Pregnancy*, by micha cárdenas.

thetics, but my own usage of "poetics" is part of a turn toward developing a decolonial poetics. My discussion focuses mostly on operations, nonvisual elements, embodied gesture, and ways of using time that divert from Western aesthetics' focus on the visual, the linguistic, and linear time.

Operators enact operations, a word that has its own resonances with transgender desires for transformation. In *Intensive Science and Virtual Philosophy*, the artist, philosopher, and Princeton University lecturer Manuel DeLanda describes the ontology of Deleuze's writing. As a materialist philosopher, Deleuze seeks to describe the world not in terms of objects and categories, but as processes, movements, and operations. DeLanda describes one of Deleuze's forms of movement, the line of flight, as an operator.[39] A line of flight can be imagined as an escape route, a path of transformation, or a path taken by a person or object as they move from one realm to another. In logic, an operator is a conjunction that describes a logical operation, such as "and," "or," or "but," whereas in mathematics, an operator describes a function. Similarly, in programming languages operators define the fundamental operations possible in a language, such as in the C language: assignment ($=$), comparison ($==$), or multiplication ($*$). The description of conceptual operators is a fundamental part of developing a language. Poetics are a way to use particular operators of language toward a given conceptual goal. Glissant focuses on the creolization of language as a central part of his poetics of relation. As Glissant does, I combine Deleuze's process ontology with decolonial thought to articulate trans of color poetics. Decolonization is a process. It requires one to see people, places, and things not as they are in the present but as they were and are in the past, present, and future simultaneously.[40] Instead of categorizing bodies by asking what a body is, Deleuze asks the reader instead to ask, "What can a body do?"[41] Actions are described by operators. Deleuze focuses on action, describing bodies and objects in a world in process. This shift in focus from "what is" to "what can be done" is a central inspiration for this book's focus and method.

In *Pregnancy*, trans of color poetics are used to create a narrative of an imagined trans woman scientist documenting her own body for herself, not for a voyeuristic viewer. The time stamps at the top of each poem follow an algorithmic format of file name conventions, intended to show progression in time, but also to gesture toward a kind of scientific mode of documentation. In parts of the video, one can see the lens of the microscope slide into place, revealing the technology that is cutting into space to create these round, planetary images lit from below. The microscope image shows biological tissue in constantly shifting and morphing forms. There are no images of the whole body, a choice that resists the voyeuristic way that cisgender audiences often interact with art by trans women, seeking to know the truth of our pain. In its place is a literal representation of my body's tissue under the microscope, reframing and highlighting how the cisgender gaze can feel intrusive, as well as the colonial violence of Western science that penetrates bodies in its demand for transparency, its demand to know. The moving images of body fluid are stitched into a narrative through lyric poetry that tells the viewer the story of the narrator's emotional journey to try to bank her sperm to have a baby. The poems and videos are stitched together into the superstructure of the digital video, arranging them in time, into a series of steps the narrator follows to become biologically reproductive again, even while she is poetically reproductive the entire time. In the final poem of the video, the narrator refers to Anzaldúa's writing on how her body contains many forms, so she is "never alone," to which the narrator responds by asking, *"How many people are inside me?"* The microscope image next to the poem is dense, full of small moving particles. In the final shot of the video, the image of the body fluid under the microscope fills the frame, slowly shifting upward, a geography of forms moving under the eye of the microscope. In subtle waves of blue, yellow, and purple one can clearly see a multitude of motile sperm, swimming through the frame, shifting their bodies to try to survive. These poetic statements and the closing shot challenge the Western unitary conception of identity, the idea that we only have one body and one identity.

Similarly, the diasporic poetry of Kai Cheng Thom uses gesture, language, and performative ritual to challenge simple conceptions of identity by describing a ritual that can be understood as an algorithm, a list of cardinal directions and a series of steps, words, and movements intended to be performed by the reader. While the title of the poem is "Prayer," it also uses gestures common to Wiccan spells, gesturing toward the cardinal directions:

Prayer

[To the East]
For the colonizers, and the shadow of their violence
For my ancestors, and the echo of their silence

[To the West]
You have known me, with your body's violence
Remember me, with touch and silence

[To the North]
God damn God and His Creation's violence
God damn God, who answers with silence

[To the South]
Forgive me, for my violence
Save me, with the gift of silence
M'goi, Megwetch, Ashe, Amen

—KAI CHENG THOM[42]

Thom's poetry is abundantly full of sweet fruits of wisdom gained from shifting across and among national, ethnic, and gender borders. In "Prayer," Thom describes a ritual, common to numerous spiritual practices, of praying to the four directions. Yet in her ritual, she links colonial violence to the personal violence inflicted on her body, to a God who would create people who commit violence, and, finally, to her own accountability for any acts of violence she has committed. The form of the poem includes bracketed movement instructions for one who would perform the prayer. The poem concludes with words of blessing that enact the cultures Thom is engaged with in her home of Montreal, Iroquois territory, including the Cantonese word *m goi*, the Cherokee word *Megwetch*, the Nigerian Yoruba word *ashe*, and the Hebrew word *amen*. Thom's decolonial poetic here is diasporic, committed to justice for Indigenous peoples while finding ways to survive and find pleasure in the place where she has been brought by her parents.

Thom writes in *A Place Called No Homeland*:

> some bodies can't be touched / some poems
> cannot be written / just felt
>
> diaspora haunted, we
> hunt for pregnant pauses / give birth
> from unwanted yellow wombs / bodies
> like invisible-ink poems / ghost children drawing maps in the margins /
> of a place called No Homeland.[43]

Thom's raucous, "femme femme fabulous" poetry addresses and seeks to undo the violence of settler colonialism in Canada while dancing the tenderness of her own trauma and desire in overlapping and mixing processes of movement, transformation, and opening.[44] Starting as "unwanted yellow wombs" birthing "ghost children," Thom's poems describe moments of intimate relationships and activist disappointments to find a place of healing deeply personal wounds:

> There is no need for silence
> there is no need for shame
> your body is a map of the divine.[45]

In Thom's words I hear the echo of Anzaldúa's wish that her writing will create actual maps for survival for other women of color. In her introduction to her translations of Parra's poems, Berrout writes, "Any trans woman of color who writes saves other trans women—by showing that her life is possible, that our lives collectively are possible, by claiming space for us, by giving white trans women another chance to stand with us, by fighting the deadly stereotypes and lies against us, by creating a history of us, by projecting her voice for future girls like us—and therefore saves herself."[46] In Thom's trans of color poetics, the assaults and displacements she experienced make of her body "a map of the divine," offering a way forward for other trans femmes of color toward healing. This is the hope of trans of color poetics: to be able to increase the life chances of trans people of color. Perhaps it is an overly ambitious hope, but it can be a horizon to reach for, and I see trans of color artists reaching for this horizon, caring for themselves and for one another.

THE DECOLONIAL CUT TWO

THE STREET IS LINED with bulbous trees and palm fronds. Wide green leaves drip rainwater onto the hot street and the bodies of the people who have gathered here to see the next performance in the Hemispheric Institute of Performance and Politics' Eighth Encuentro in São Paulo, Brazil. This performance of *Local Autonomy Networks* (*Autonets*), on January 18, 2013 (figure 2.1), has been announced by the Encuentro Program as codeveloped by workshop participants to respond to gendered racialized violence by building community-based safety strategies. The eight performers are all wearing black and gray—some in dresses, some in jeans, and all in hoodies or bracelets with microprocessors, sensors, and LED lights sewn into them. They move as a group from within the crowd. They step forward on the sidewalk. One performer places her hands on her face and tilts her head up to the sky. The other performers, who are Black, Latinx, and white, do the same. The woman who first put her hands to her face doubles over, a gesture of pain and grief. The other performers do the same, moving together solemnly. Their silence makes space for street noise: cars passing, brakes screaming, people calling out to one another in Portuguese. The gestures are not perfectly in sync; there is an element of improvisation. One performer steps away from the group. The remaining performers turn; now a different performer stands in front. He begins another gesture, spinning both arms in a circle, ending

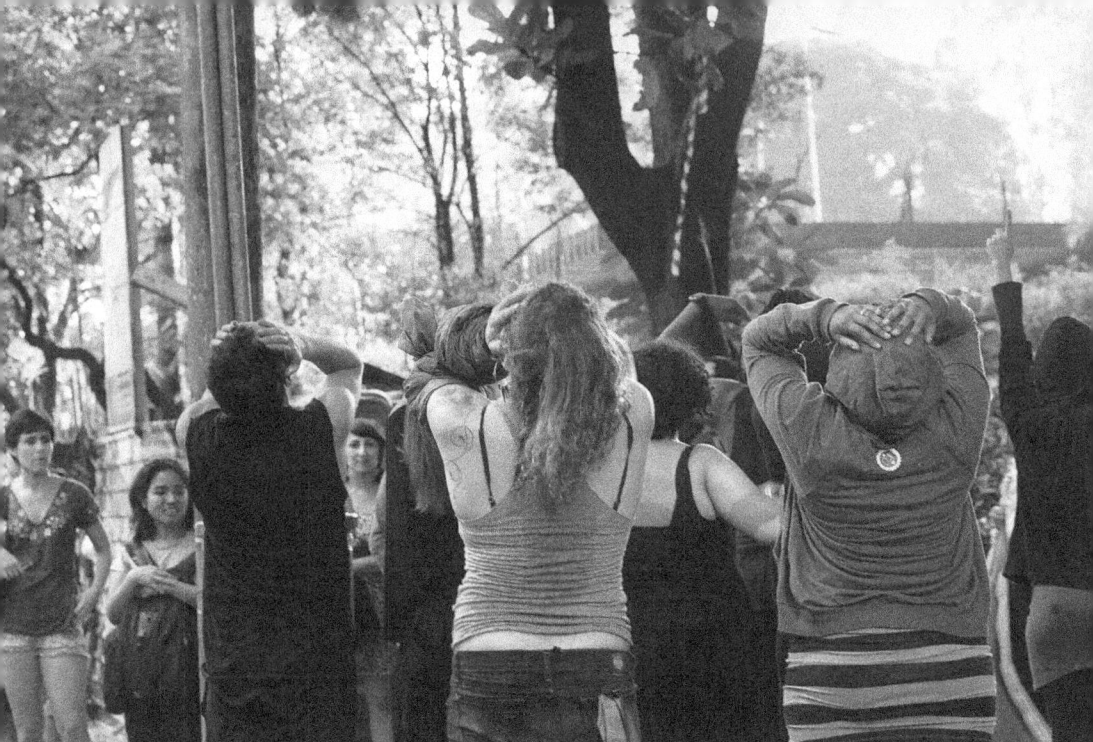

2.1 "We Already Know and We Don't Yet Know," *Autonets*, by micha cárdenas, performed at the Hemispheric Institute of Performance and Politics, Eighth Encuentro, São Paulo, 2013. Photograph by Frances Pollitt. The video is accessible at http://scalar.usc.edu/works/poetic-operations/we-already-know-and-we-dont-yet-know.

with both hands pointing: one at the floor, the other at the sky. Another performer stands behind him, mirroring the gesture. The group moves into the middle of the street. My gesture at this point is to lie still on a low wall, head down, arm dangling limply. Another female performer lies on the ground beneath me, reaching her arm up. A third steps up and begins gently touching my hair.

This chapter argues that cutting is an operation of trans of color poetics. I demonstrate one method of algorithmic analysis: that of breaking a problem down into underlying operations by analyzing performances using the operation of the cut. The chapter focuses on two performances from my collaborative project *Autonets*—one in São Paulo, and another in Los Angeles. Movement makes a cut by creating a relation between time and space and among bodies, rhythms, and architecture. Embodied physical movement, or gesture, which is part of dance but is a broader category than dance, enacts a cut into fields of mediation. The material act of cutting, of separating a single entity into two, can also be used as a mental operation to separate elements of an artwork being considered, or a gesture in an artwork, or a block of code. In this chapter, the cut is the operation being described, but it is also the operation being used. The operation of breaking a problem down into underlying operations, or cutting, is demonstrated here by describing the operation of the cut in examples of performance.

The cut is an operation that is so familiar that it resists definition. Everyone is familiar with cutting with scissors. Poststructuralist theorists have applied this gesture to thought and action. In *Molecular Revolution in Brazil*, Félix Guattari and Suely Rolnik define the cut by pointing to what is being cut, saying, "The term 'cut' is inseparable from the term 'flow,'" where material and semiotic flows are described as that which precedes subjects and objects.[1] The cut is central to their process ontology, where everything is understood as process, movement, and flow. Cutting is a necessary operation for the emergence of singularities, strata, assemblages, and machines. Their definition of the cut references *Anti-Oedipus*, saying, "'Desiring machines' are characterized as systems for cutting flows."[2] *Anti-Oedipus*, which Michel Foucault described as "an Introduction to the Non-Fascist Life," is Deleuze and Guattari's attempt to describe desire and the subject in a poststructuralist way that is not reliant on previous attempts to codify human psychology, such as psychoanalysis. In the place of the subject, Deleuze and Guattari use a materialist approach to describe drives as desiring machines that constitute the subject. They state, "Every machine, in the first place, is related to a continual material flow (hylé), that it cuts into."[3] They see these machines as running a kind of code, saying, "Every machine has a sort of code built into it, stored up inside it." They use this theory to break down and challenge binary conceptions of sex and gender, calling for "not one or even two sexes, but *n* sexes."[4] Cutting is an operation that is important to trans of color poetics because it is the gesture that allows autonomy, interrupts surveillance, and enables opacity. Édouard Glissant describes opacity as a right of all peoples: the right not to be known, the right to refuse the encounter with the colonizer.[5] Opacity is a way of making a decolonial cut. Artists and performers cut flows of mediation with their movement. The cut allows them to experience a moment of opacity to the prying eyes of art audiences and policing apparatuses. In this way, trans of color poetics become not just poetics of survival, but poetics that stretch toward liberation. I describe in this chapter how the cut facilitates opacity in a way that works toward decolonization, refusing the colonial drive to know the interiority of trans people of color.

"Tightrope/Cuerdo Floja," by 2boys.tv

The Eighth Encuentro of the Hemispheric Institute of Performance and Politics combined academic conference and performance art festival throughout the city of São Paulo. The Encuentros, held biennially, include hundreds of performers and academics and have perhaps thousands of attendees who see the performances. Each Encuentro that I attended was a transformative experience. Attending the Encuentro in São Paulo was my first time traveling to Brazil. The Hemispheric Institute says that the São Paulo Encuentro "sought to examine the broad intersections between urban space, performance and political/artistic action in the Americas. From the critical poetics of body art to the occupation of public space by social movements, the event invited participants to explore the borders, identities and practices through which subjectivities, hegemonies and counter-hegemonies are constructed in the spaces of the city and beyond."[6] *Autonets* brought these concerns to life, engaging queer and trans liberation through embodied poetics in public space.

One performance at the Encuentro was "Tightrope/Cuerdo Floja," by the Canadian artist group 2boys.tv in collaboration with Radwan Moumneh, Alexis O'Hara, and a group of local drag queens and genderqueer performers.[7] The description of the performance states, "A chorus of local drag queens and genderqueer performers function as profane shamans, witnesses and guides through our collective memorial."[8] The performance points to the long history of extreme violence in Brazil against queer and trans people, from the widespread anti-LGBT violence under the dictatorship that took power in 1965 to the murder of queer trans people by the police in the 1980s, documented in Rita Moreira's award-winning film *Hunting Season/Temporada de caça*.[9] Using a combination of cabaret and house ball performance, 2boys.tv—Stephen Lawson and Aaron Pollard—create a stylized collective ritual of mourning. Beginning with a procession in the street, the performance moved into a large performance hall, with a huge screen created out of newspaper pages spanning from the stage to the ceiling. One scene in the performance saw a ball announcer introducing various performers by name as they came onstage, modeled their intricate costumes, then took their place in a lineup of various poses behind the screen, their shadows projected larger than life-size from a light behind the screen. The costumes were presumably created for this performance, stitched by hand, highly fashionable versions of mourning clothes. One outfit included a bulbous skirt created out of garbage bags, which the queen performed with, swirling it from side to side and for a moment being enveloped by it. The multilingual performance continued with musical performances; spoken word; and monologues in English, Spanish, Portuguese, and French. The monologues dealt with themes of memory. For much of the show, the group of local queens were at the side of the stage, kneeling with their heads down, one of them wearing a wide-brimmed black hat and a translucent tube dress divided by wide black stripes.

The show demonstrated 2boys.tv's technique of combining performance and digital projection to create a powerful ritual, cutting space and time to change perception. At one point, a woman speaking in Spanish about how her memory is failing had a screen of digital code projected behind her. The scene behind her changed to various images, including a starscape, demonstrating editing of digital video as it corresponded to the cutting of film. Yet her words, combined with a screen full of obscure code, might have referred to the ephemerality of digital memory, where forgetting becomes data loss, an irrevocable cut (figure 2.2). At another point, what looked like a female shadow on the screen began to dance, and her impossible movement revealed that she was actually a projection. In a final scene, performers stood in a line singing a low, solemn song in chorus, with the faces of variously gendered people projected onto their bodies (figure 2.3). The cut was used powerfully in these effects. The manipulation of the edges of the visible and the sources of images cut the space, generating these hybrid digital and analog illusions.

Performance art is algorithmic. Performance artists often set out to create a ritual, with an intentional beginning and end and a set of steps to be repeated over a meaningful duration. Consider the Fluxus scores, artworks that can be understood as a precursor to performance art. They consist of written steps to take to bring the artwork to life. The following score was written by Yoko Ono:

VOICE PIECE FOR SOPRANO
    To Simone Morris

Scream.
1. against the wind
2. against the wall
3. against the sky

1961 Autumn[10]

From scores such as these, performance artists began to create their own simple rituals as artwork and enact them. For example, in *AAA AAA* (1978), by

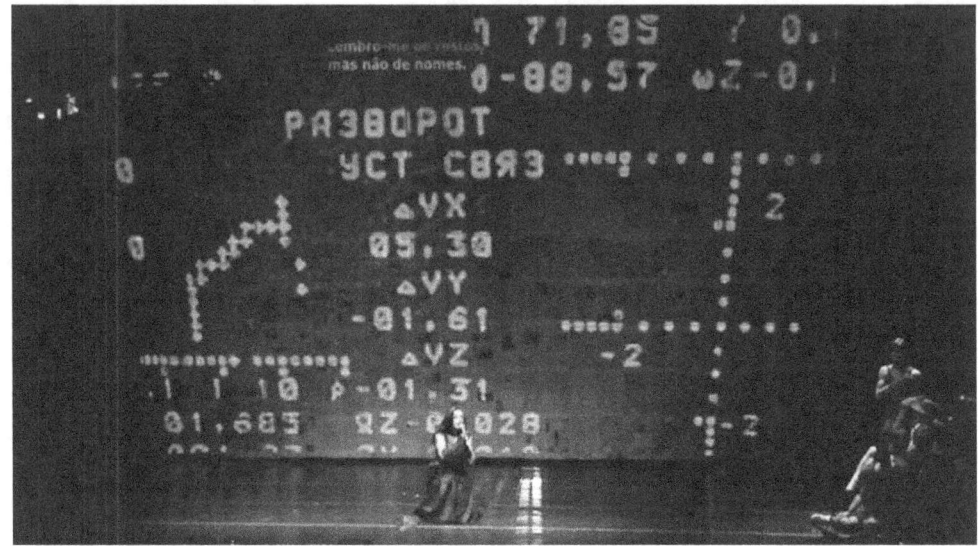

2.2 2boys.tv with Radwan Moumneh and Alexis O'Hara, "Tightrope/Cuerdo Floja," performed at the Hemispheric Institute of Performance and Politics, Eighth Encuentro, *São Paulo, 2013*.

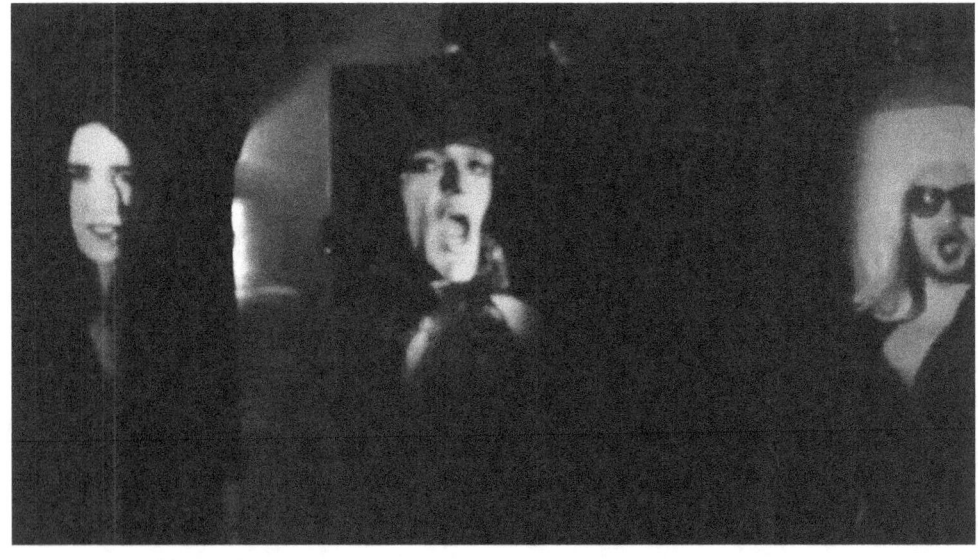

2.3 2boys.tv with Radwan Moumneh and Alexis O'Hara, "Tightrope/Cuerdo Floja," performed at the Hemispheric Institute of Performance and Politics, Eighth Encuentro, *São Paulo, 2013*.

Marina Abramović and Ulay, they followed these instructions: "We are facing each other both producing a continuous vocal sound. We slowly build up the tension, our faces coming closer together until we are screaming into each other's open mouths."[11] By understanding these instructions as an algorithm one can see how algorithms can describe performance. In this way, algorithms, performance, and rituals overlap and can deepen our understanding of each form.

"We Already Know and We Don't Yet Know"

The performance I cocreated at the Eighth Encuentro is titled "We Already Know and We Don't Yet Know"; it is part of my *Autonets* project. It was curated into the "Urban Interventions" series in the Encuentro, alongside groups such as Brazil's Erro Gruppo, whose work also explores violence and risk through public intervention. *Autonets* aimed to create networks of communication, inspired by the prison abolition movement, to be used for community-based responses to violence. The project began when I created a line of wearable electronic clothing and accessories that contained wireless transmitters. When activated, the garments would alert everyone else wearing an *Autonets* garment who was part of the local network that someone needed help. The São Paulo workshop used Theater of the Oppressed to invite participants to communicate the ways that violence and safety feel, affectively, via embodied gesture. The title referenced how participants in earlier workshops in the series had articulated to me that we already know violence in our bodies. We know what violence feels like on an affective level, but we don't yet know what a world without prisons looks like. We need to build abolitionist infrastructures for community-based safety. While circumstances of violence were so widely different across different contexts, there were still poignant points of similarity, which performance could illustrate.

I met members of Cero29 at the previous Encuentro, which was held in 2009 in Bogotá, where I was teaching a workshop on hacktivism at the Universidad Nacional de Colombia. After my workshop, we agreed to continue collaborating. Cero29 is a collective of artists in Bogotá who create artwork about the intersections of media technologies and politics. We began working on a proposal for the next Encuentro, which happen every two years; the next one would be in São Paulo. The goal had been to create wearable networked clothing that did not rely on corporate cellular networks. Months before "We Already Know" was performed, while looking into the pixelated image of a Skype video call, I listened as my collaborator in Bogotá told me

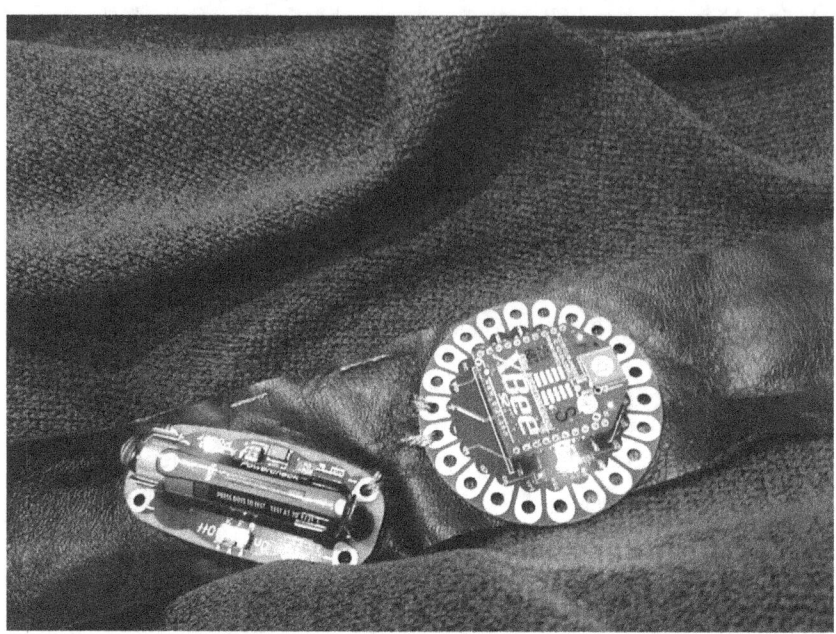

2.4 *Autonets* mesh networked bracelet.

that the wearable electronics I had been developing for a year were too expensive to be useful. I decided then to shift what I had been working on to address their concerns. It was a hot day in Los Angeles for me and a cool day in the cloudy mountain city of Bogotá for them. The resulting prototypes I had made cost about $100 each—close to the cost of some smartphones and out of reach for many students in Bogotá, the audience Cero29 had in mind.

When my collaborators told me that the technology I was building was too expensive for most people in Bogotá, or São Paulo, I suggested that we do something different. Through our discussions we came up with a workshop designed to improve participants' ability to communicate with their bodies to increase their safety. For example, how do you tell a friend you need to leave a bar when they are sitting next to the person making you feel unsafe? I worked with Cero29 to create a community-based design workshop for the São Paulo Encuentro, expanding *Autonets* to consider the possibilities of building communications networks that do not rely on digital technologies (figure 2.4).

Both design and software development use iterative methodologies in which one creates a particular iteration of an idea, often in the form of a prototype, and then tests that iteration for its possibilities and limitations before moving on to the next iteration. In reflecting on how the *Autonets* project shifted over time, I do not consider each step in this experimental process to be a failure. Discovering the limitations of wearable electronics could be considered a failure only insofar as failure is understood to be an essential part of any learning process. I understand each step as an iteration. Throughout this book I describe this process of creating prototypes with different design methodologies and then using those prototypes to start conversations in more detail. I regularly use exhibitions as opportunities for creating and testing new prototypes. In the development of larger projects, such as my augmented reality game *Sin Sol*, I have used exhibitions as development milestones, where each new exhibition presents a new prototype, instead of waiting for a "perfect" version of the artwork, which is not my goal.[12] With *Autonets*, I see the biggest success of the project in opening a space for conversations about how to create practical community agreements to prevent violence. Trans of color poetics are often more about improvising, modulating, and learning on the fly than about presenting a perfected product to a mass audience. The algorithms used are not perfected; they are provisional, to be tinkered with and improvised alongside of. My own work, an expression of trans of color poetics, frequently takes the form of a series of experiments, in dialogue with affected communities, that result in works of performance art.

Community-based design is a bottom-up, rather than top-down, approach to design. Instead of the ideas of a designer being imposed on a community problem, such as violence against trans people of color, community-based design in my work has meant meeting with and listening to trans people of color about violence they face and how they survive. To create a community-based design process inspired by artists and activists doing similar work, such as Una Lee, the Critical Art Ensemble, and Natalie Jeremijenko, I had conversations with people in thirteen cities and in the United States, Canada, Brazil, and Germany about the *Autonets* prototypes. I asked what forms of violence they were facing and how autonomous networks might help reduce it. After numerous discussions about *Autonets* prototypes with workshop participants and with the Cero29 collective, I began to come to the conclusion that wearable electronics were not the most viable option for creating safety networks at that time.

The next stage of the *Autonets* project emerged as I worked with Cero29. It focused on the research question, "Can digital communications be decolonized?" In other words, can the benefits of digital technologies be abstracted and replicated through other mediums, other material instantiations—namely, the human body? The performance studies scholar Diana Taylor writes in *The Archive and the Repertoire* about points of congruence between Indigenous worldviews and digital technologies and describes the colonial impositions that caused embodied communication to become devalued.[13] While this phase of the project had theoretical goals of applying decolonial theory to digital communications, it also had the practical research goal of teaching participants, especially low-income and marginalized participants, concrete methods for safety they could use in their daily lives. Trans of color poetics often stem from using survival strategies to inform how an artwork will be created, and those survival strategies are decolonial acts that resist the cis-heteronormative violence of colonialism.

The workshop sought to abstract and learn from digital technologies, moving beyond them to broader considerations of racialized and gendered movement, decolonizing the digital. Using embodied movement as a mode of communication is not necessarily a decolonial act, but it has been suppressed by colonizers in favor of the written word in order to institutionalize their power. Taylor differentiates between the archive, which is made up of physical objects such as documents that survive over long periods of time, and the repertoire, which is ephemeral, embodied, and performed.[14] She describes how the archive, by definition, is linked to government power and how the repertoire has been used to maintain cultural memory.[15] Taylor states, "It is only because Western culture is wedded to the word, whether written or spoken, that language claims such epistemic and explanatory power."[16] Because of the focus on the word in Western culture, one can see the practice of systems of embodied knowledge and communication as supporting a decolonial move away from Western culture. Taylor points out how the archive is meant to decouple knowledge from the body, whereas a repertoire of embodied movement relies on a specific body, in a specific place, to make meaning, as in the decolonial practices of Gloria Anzaldúa's *conciencia de la mestiza* and Walter Mignolo's geo-body-politics.[17] She uses the digital to trouble any simple binary between the archive and the repertoire, and she is cautious to state that "embodied performances have often contributed to the maintenance of a repressive social order" in the Americas.[18]

The *Autonets* performances described here demonstrate Sarah Kember and Joanna Zylinska's use of the cut as an act that creates relations and networks and reveals forms of mediation in *Life after New Media*.[19] They argue that new media studies should shift its focus from objects such as iPhones to processes of mediation. They advocate for cuts that are ethical interruptions of mediation, which they describe as "processes of temporarily stabilizing the world into media, agents, relations and networks."[20] Kember and Zylinska describe a cut as a "both a conceptual and [a] material intervention into the 'media flow' that has a cultural significance."[21] Both of the performances of *Autonets* discussed in this chapter make cuts into flows of the art circuits where their images are distributed, as well as into the surveillance networks of the state, to make desires and hopes for livable lives for trans people of color perceptible. They also consciously build relations and networks of trans people and their allies in an effort to expand the space and time in which livable trans lives can be possible.

Feminist engagements in media studies make negative comments about the cut of gender-related surgery. This continues a decades-long genealogy of feminist critiques of the surgeries deemed "cosmetic surgery" as not medically necessary or as the appropriation of cisgender women's bodies.[22] In a foundational text for transgender studies, "The Empire Strikes Back: A Posttranssexual Manifesto," Sandy Stone responded to Janice Raymond's claims for eradicating transgender surgeries, which were part of her larger argument that transgender people should not exist. Stone responded by saying, "We can seize upon the textual violence inscribed in the transsexual body and turn it into a reconstructive force."[23] Many scholars have described Stone's essay as the founding moment of transgender studies, arguing that transgender people did not need to hide themselves but, instead, could write scholarly works about their experience.[24] Stone was a student at the University of California, Santa Cruz, studying under Donna Haraway, whose ideas are cited numerous times in the essay. Haraway's writing also influenced numerous artists. In the early 1990s, feminist artists and theorists, including VNS Matrix and Sadie Plant, were inspired by Haraway to reimagine feminism with all of the creative potential they saw in the newly emerging cyberspace of the internet. The movement was described as cyberfeminism.[25] Cyberfeminist texts such as the essay "Stolen Rhetoric" by the art group subRosa in the book *Domain Errors!* speak with equivalence about women and uteruses, as if all women have a uterus, an assumption that excludes transgender women from cyberfeminism, even while other elements of cyberfeminism, such as reimagining the gendered embodiment through technological extensions, may open space in feminism for trans women. subRosa describe reproductive technologies such as in vitro fertilization, which cuts into an egg to fertilize it, as a form of colonization of women's bodies, despite the importance of these technologies to transgender people attempting to conceive children.[26] A more subtly problematic claim is made by Lisa Nakamura, who says in *Cybertypes*, "Identity online is . . . still mired in oppressive roles. . . . Chosen identities enabled by technology, such as online avatars, cosmetic and transgender surgery and body modifications, and other cyberprostheses are not breaking the mold of unitary identity but rather shifting identity into the realm of the 'virtual.'"[27] Here Nakamura groups transgender surgery with avatars that reproduce oppressive institutions online. She goes on, in the next paragraph, to state, "This kind of technology's greatest promise to us is to eradicate otherness" and "reinforce a 'postbody' ideology that reproduces the assumptions of the old one."[28] Nakamura's claim has no basis in the difficult experience of deciding to receive gender confirmation surgery, which can be an act of self-love, embracing one's difference. Nakamura's remarks are some of the rare considerations of trans people, who are mostly erased from considerations of digital media. Looking instead to transgender theorists can better illuminate how the cut of transgender surgery can be a poetic gesture.

Writing in *Transgender Migrations* about the cut as part of sexual reassignment surgery, Eva Hayward says, "*The cut is possibility*. . . . The cut is not just an action; the cut is part of the ongoing materialization by which a transsexual tentatively and mutably becomes."[29] Hayward sees the cut not as something imposed on transsexual women, but as part of their becoming. She goes on, saying, "The point of view of the looker (those who might 'read' her) is not the most important feature of trans-subjectivity—the trans-woman wishes to be of her body, to 'speak' from her body."[30] Sexual reassignment surgery is not always an attempt to leave the body behind in favor of the mind or to succumb to oppressive social dynamics, but, as described by Hayward, it is a process of expressivity. This is reflected in the recent turn to call the procedure Gender Confirmation Surgery.[31] Hayward likens the experience of transgender women across species lines to the home building methods of spiders, asking, "Might web building best articulate (with the word's multiple meanings) the act of extending bodily substance through sex transition; that is to ask, do webbing and the capacity to weave remind us that trans-sexuality is also an expression of the body as an address and habitat?"[32] Her formulation of transgender bodily transition as a form of expression takes the metaphor of weaving, an action close to stitching, but in the context of weaving a web there is no separation between the acting body and the elements being woven together. Following Hayward's thinking, one can understand the cut involved in transgender surgeries to be part of a poetics, a process of making decisions about the material world to give form to an idea.

The cut is an operation that resonates with transspecies considerations, establishing relations in the many directions indicated by trans*. Returning to the asterisk, Eva Hayward and Jami Weinstein write about the spider's web in relation to trans*. They write that "the asterisk makes many philosophical points, it is a sensuous node," describing how spiders use their web as a sensory extension. The form of the asterisk character * can be seen in the spider web itself, visually. Considering the phrase "trapped in the wrong body," which is often used to reductively describe trans* experiences, Hayward and Weinstein write about the spider web as trap, saying, "For the spider, its trap is its nearby-ness, its where-ness, its with-ness."[33] In this way we see again how the cut is a separation that facilitates relation. The spider cuts individual strands of web from its body to exist in a larger relation with the world. Similarly, poetics are gestures, words, and objects that are intentionally shaped in response to the world, multiplying one's relations and connections to the world. "We Already Know" uses cutting of space to make a network of relations perceptible between the performers and the many trans people who have experienced violence.

The performance "We Already Know" responds to the brutal fact of the murders of hundreds of transgender people. By the time the performance took place in São Paulo, at least 265 transgender people had been killed in the previous year, according to Transgender Europe's Trans Murder Monitoring project, with the most murders—126—occurring in Brazil.[34] After three days of conversation about community-based responses to violence as a way to work toward prison abolition by building alternatives to the prison-industrial complex, the prompts to create the gestures in the performance were simply the words *safety* and *protection*.

In "We Already Know," the bodies of the eight performers create cuts in fields of mediation by moving in a public space with a shared speed. The fields of mediation being engaged with in this context include digital video, photography, and networked media. As can be seen in figure 5.3, a photo of the performance, an audience member is engaged in photographing the event with a digital camera. The audience included international art festival attendees and residents of São Paulo. The photo documentation of the performance is also in digital photography. Kember and Zylinska describe photography as an art that creates a cut by temporarily stabilizing an image. In the case of digital photography, this is a digital cut. The video of the performance was taken by an audience member in the form of digital video shot with an iPhone and later uploaded to social media. The video demonstrates that the performers, by moving in this context with poetic intention, cut into multiple fields of mediation.

While the speed of the gestures can be seen more clearly in the video, a cut is created in the photograph by the position of the bodies. By having a shared position, and being oriented in space toward the audience, it is apparent that these movements are a performative gesture. In addition, by moving with a shared appearance and wearing similar kinds, and colors, of clothing, the performers in the photo differentiate themselves from the audience and call attention to their movement.

Dance allows one to see many links between movement and digital technology. Repetition is an arrangement of action in time that allows movement to create a cut in the rhythms of daily motion. Repeated movement allows one to see a relation to the procedurality of digital technology, which relies on repeating a series of steps in an algorithm. Choreography, or improvisation parameters, can also be seen as a series of instructions, like an algorithm.

Parallels between code and movement can be understood if code is understood poetically, as a mode of representation that can never fully represent that which is described. While algorithms are often understood only in terms of precision, they can be written at any level of abstraction and thus are similar to poetic writing. While it can be described in words, the richness of movement requires a great deal of linguistic work to be described accurately, in detail. Even then, language can never fully capture human movement. Still, some dance practitioners have experimented with algorithms in dance through digital code. Margo Apostolos, an associate professor of dance at the University of Southern California (USC), has created dance choreography scores for robots by writing software algorithms for their movement.[35] In addition, Merce Cunningham worked extensively with developing choreography in software for both virtual human models and human dancers.[36]

Representing dance requires a highly complex series of instructions, akin to semantic programming languages, which use human readable language to describe many machine-level assembly language commands. When incorporating language for specific movements—as in the case of dance traditions such as ballet, in which one may learn over time to do a *jeté* or a *relevé*—we begin to achieve a level of abstraction on the order of object-oriented programming languages. Considering that such moves can have multiple parameters, such as a *relevé* in *plie* at a particular speed, one can see echoes of parameters of function calls to objects in object-oriented languages. This is not to say that traditional Western forms of dance such as ballet are more advanced or more useful for decolonial politics. On the contrary, non-Western forms of dance are certainly more relevant to an effort to unseat Western hegemony.

Yet my own practice of dance has focused on contemporary ballet, which learns from traditional ballet to create new forms of movement.

There are many ways computer code and choreography differ profoundly. A line of code in a language such as C is translated by a compiler into assembly language instructions that create a precise movement of electrical charges within a microprocessor to be executed in order on a time scale of milliseconds. In contrast, a movement instruction, such as one to raise your hand, may spur a huge variety of possible movements, with the details to be filled in by the body and brain of the person moving. Was the hand raised with the wrist straight or bent? Were the fingers bent or straight? To what degree? At what speed was the hand raised? If this movement was programmed into a robot arm controlled by servos, the movement parameters would each have to be specified in exact detail. Even in that case, though, there is an interplay between the materiality of the body and the code that still determines the quality of movement.

The performers in "We Already Know" followed an algorithm that consisted of an ordered series of operations. The performance can be cut into a series of steps. We developed individual gestures in response to the prompt, informed by our discussions over the course of the workshop, and shared those gestures with the rest of the group. We learned from the wireless networks of the *Autonets* prototypes and reimagined how to create networks in our various local contexts. Through movement exercises, the "We Already Know" participants and I developed an affective connection to one another as performers. We learned one another's gestures and made a plan for moving through the public space of São Paulo. We went to the site and discussed how we could activate our gestures, a reflection of our affective responses to violence and imagination of possibilities for community-based responses to violence. To do so, we developed methods for communicating about movement based on a dance technique called flocking. We agreed to follow these steps in the performance:

1 Stand in a group. While moving with the group, performers would keep their *Autonets* garments turned on, which would enable the LED lights. Whoever was at the front of the group was the leader. The leader initiated their gesture.

2 When other performers saw the leader start their gesture, they also started the gesture, attempting to move in unison as best they could.

3 When the leader finished their gesture, they turned their body to pass leadership. When the leader turned, all performers turned our bod-

ies until the leader stopped and a new person was at the front of the group, signaling that person to be the leader.

4 In addition, performers could split off and do individual improvised gestures at any time, then rejoin the group. When stepping away from the group, the performer would turn off their *Autonets* hoodie or brace-let. The lights on the garments were only enabled when someone re-joined the performing group.[37]

The performers continued these steps, moving down the street toward Praça Roosevelt, until the duration of the performance ended. The audi-ence followed the performers down the street and onto the public square as the sun set between the skyscrapers. The effect of the performance is unknown—perhaps at best a momentary procession of mourning and an expression of the incomprehensibility of violence. The violence of murders of trans people of color cuts through logic, cuts off expression, and inter-rupts the poetics of the victim with a cold permanence. These are unethical cuts.

In "We Already Know," the rhythms and tempo of the movements in space created a shared circle with the audience. Performance and game stud-ies scholars refer to the way ritual creates space separate from everyday life as the magic circle of play.[38] Richard Schechner states, "Performances consist of twice-behaved, coded, transmittable behaviors. . . . [O]ne definition of perfor-mance is: ritualized behavior conditioned and/or permeated by play."[39] His definition uses the word *code* to define performance as that which is repeat-able, inviting comparison to algorithms. "We Already Know" created a circle of play in which performers improvised according to the agreed-on steps in the algorithm, as well as a magic circle with the audience watching the per-formance. Here we see trans of color poetics' ability to delineate space, to hold a space of emotional resonance that is delicately, subtly cut out of the rituals of everyday life being enacted in this public space.

The performance cuts into fields of mediation that structure everyday life. Gender, race, sexuality, and ability act as fields of mediation, mediat-ing the perception of bodies, and these fields can be cut in the way that dig-ital fields of mediation can. There is a danger of making the definition of a field of mediation too broad to have any meaning. Since Kember and Zylins-ka's definition of mediation includes "a thesis that mediation can be seen as another term for 'life,' for being-in and emerging-with the world," it seems within their scope to consider gender and race as fields of mediation.[40] Both of these fields of mediation, as well as sexuality and ability, can be seen as material fields, constituted by matter such as clothing, skin and hair, as well immaterial elements such as gesture.

In "We Already Know," the performers' gestures of cutting, from changing their relation to the audience using movement and gaze, to cutting into fields of mediation with a memory of trans murders, evokes the cut as a part of trans of color experience. Kember and Zylinska state "the practice of cutting is crucial not just to our being in and relating to the world, but also to our becoming-with-the-world, as well as becoming-different-from-the-world."[41] Becoming with and becoming different from the world are particularly relevant to trans of color poetics that consider people whose lives rely on becoming different from one's assigned gender at birth, even in a racialized context in which such a choice may be seen to add danger to an already precarious existence. The ability to separate oneself from the violent demands of a gender assigned at birth is an act of cutting—of severing ties and breaking expectations. To move into a trans becoming is to become different from the world, to place oneself outside the rhythms and demands of gender on one's body. Trans people of color do this in contexts such as Brazil and the United States, where racialized bodies are subject to death at the whim of police, thus increasing the danger they face exponentially.

Toward Trans of Color Poetics

By asking how the performers in "We Already Know" make cuts across the fields of mediation created by gender and sexuality, and how the cuts intersect with considerations of race, class, and nationality, one can see trans of color poetics extending queer of color critique. While queer of color critique added a more in-depth racial analysis to queer theory, a trans of color analysis of this performance adds a specific consideration of transgender bodies, in transition and movement, from which emerges a trans of color poetics. Writing by Teresa de Lauretis, who coined the phrase *queer theory*, included racial analysis as an important vector of analysis for queer theory, expanding beyond what she saw as gay and lesbian studies' focus on sexuality to the detriment of considerations of race.[42] Despite this initial impulse, as queer theory became more widely known, it became associated with studies of primarily white authors in the work of writers such as Eve Kosofsky Sedgwick and Judith Butler. Thus, when authors such as Jose Muñoz, Roderick Ferguson, and Juana María Rodríguez published their studies on queer of color subjects in performance, literature, and photography, queer of color critique became a recognizable field within queer theory. I am not proposing here that trans of color poetics operate only through bodies that can be categorized as trans of color, or that only trans of color theorists can write trans of color analysis. Instead, I claim that artworks that work to increase survival for trans people of color make certain poetic gestures perceptible and that algorithmic analysis can enable one to identify and use those gestures. In "We Already Know," most of the performers were non-trans-identified individuals who use gestures of cutting that are a part of trans of color poetics.

Rodríguez theorizes queer Latina gesture in performance and everyday life. She is "thinking about discourse as constituting a corporeal practice," pointing to the potentiality of gesture to be a form of communication that is imbricated with power, as well as with gender and sexuality.[43] José Muñoz's consideration of gesture in *Cruising Utopia* also sees the political potential of gesture. Describing a scene from the play *The Toilet*, in which a queer man holds his lover's head in his hands after a violent beating, Muñoz states, "The gesture interrupts the normative flow of time and movement. . . . [T]he politics of queer utopia are similarly not based on prescriptive ends, but, instead, on the significance of a critical function that resonates like the temporal interruption of the gesture."[44] Gesture can be an act of cutting that interrupts heteronormative time and space.

Studies of gesture allow us to consider the implications for this linking of algorithms, code, and movement. Rodríguez, citing comprehensive studies of gesture from *Gesture in Naples and Gesture in Classical Antiquity* in 1832 to *Sin Palabras: Gestiario Argentino/Speechless: A Dictionary of Argentine Gestures*, sees "the way in which gesture—like law, and indeed like gender and race—is regulatory, citational, and iterative, always dependent on previous codes of signification in order to generate and discipline meaning."[45] These are all characteristics of computer code: code regulates behavior; it cites code libraries, and it is iterative, relying on function definitions to build larger functionality. Rodríguez states that "gestures reveal the inscription of social and cultural laws, transforming our individual movements into an archive of received social behaviors and norms."[46] Here her description of the broad function of gesture allows one to see the larger implications of algorithms: both of them are methods of inscribing social and cultural laws, and both archive social norms.

The performers' individual gestures make up the content of "We Already Know," using movement to bring attention to their embodiment. One gesture is led by a Black woman and involves her hand, three fingers folded to reference the shape of a gun. This gesture proceeds into her placing her hands behind her head, a possible reference to being arrested. The gesture is performed by everyone in the group simultaneously and invites the watching audience into a consideration of two different forms of violence. Performed by the multiple bodies of these performers, it becomes a consideration of violence against, and violence perpetrated by, women of color, men of color, and transgender women of color. By enacting this moment in the public space of the street, the performance becomes a consideration of these forms of violence as they may occur in public spaces. The temporal and spatial coincidence of these particular movements on these bodies in this space creates a cut that establishes a relation between eight bodies on the street and previous and future moments of violence and incarceration.

One field of mediation that can be understood to be operating on this street in Brazil is the field defined by police surveillance technologies. Dora Silva Santana describes an experience of police violence in the Lapa neighborhood of Rio de Janeiro during the World Cup championship. She writes, "Mega events mobilize high surveillance of black bodies through racial profiling and, in this case, intersect with transphobia" and links those to the experiences of racially gendered practices of police violence against Black people in the African diaspora around the world.[47] One art collective, the Surveillance Camera Players, were dedicated to doing performances in front of CCTV surveillance cameras to call attention to the pervasive nature of surveillance in New York City.[48] In 2013, Geraldo Alckmin, the governor of São Paulo, announced that the city would be adopting the Domain Awareness System, a software system developed by Microsoft for the New York Police Department designed to leverage "big data" by connecting a citywide network of CCTV systems to databases using algorithms to detect "suspicious" behavior.[49] The system required localization, or modifications to translate the language and the metaphors of the software to a Brazilian context, which PRODESP, the state-owned software development firm, referred to as "tropicalization."[50] As bodies acting in public space and in networks of surveillance, these gestures can make a cut into the records of police databases by presenting forms of embodiment that exceed the ontological classification schemes of databases in the form of trans of color, gender-non-conforming, and poetic movement embodiments. One of the challenges of the São Paulo system, renamed Detecta, was to algorithmically detect suspicious forms of movement. By performing a public ritual of mourning of the lives of murdered Brazilian trans people, and protesting that violence, the performers create an interruption, a cut, in the logics of how movement can be categorized. Their movement, recorded into the system, demonstrates the way that the algorithm necessarily fails to categorize the range of human activity. Trans people of color in performance interact with police networks to reveal layers of safety, precarity, and performativity while cutting through the assumed ontologies of algorithmic policing systems.

In the performances discussed here, "We Already Know" and "Tightrope," one can see the operation of the cut operating as a gesture of trans of color poetics. These performances use separations, breaks, and interruptions to evoke mourning for trans of color lives lost and to imagine futures of care. This chapter has used the cut as a method of algorithmic analysis to break down the performances into their underlying components and instructions. I return to "We Already Know" in chapter 4, using the operation of the stitch to understand the operations happening among bodies in the performance. In another performance in this series, created in Los Angeles, I used similar techniques from Theater of the Oppressed to engage participants in the creation of a collaborative performance about safety for trans and gender-nonconforming people of color. The police violence against trans people that one can see in São Paulo is also very real in the United States, and while the contexts differ, they have many similarities.

"Local Autonomy Networks: Los Angeles with Gender Justice LA"

Performance can be a way to use ritual to move through feelings such as grief, mourning, and anger, feelings that participants in my workshops in São Paulo and Los Angeles expressed fiercely. The operation of cutting that I described in "We Already Know" can also be seen in the collaborative performance I created in Los Angeles. The performance, titled "Local Autonomy Networks: Los Angeles with Gender Justice LA" (figure 2.5), took place on a sidewalk just outside the USC campus in 2014. Gender Justice LA (GJLA) is a nonprofit organization based in Los Angeles that focuses on improving the lives of genderqueer and transgender people of color and low-income people. I used the School of Cinematic Arts gallery at USC to hold a Theater of the Oppressed workshop with GJLA, which was open to USC students to attend. The *Autonets* performance at USC was a response to the vulnerability created by the (purportedly neutral) new policy of asking for student IDs at the entrances to the campus. When I asked the participants in my workshop with GJLA what kinds of violence they faced on a daily basis, they said the university was inflicting violence on them. They stated that the newly instituted

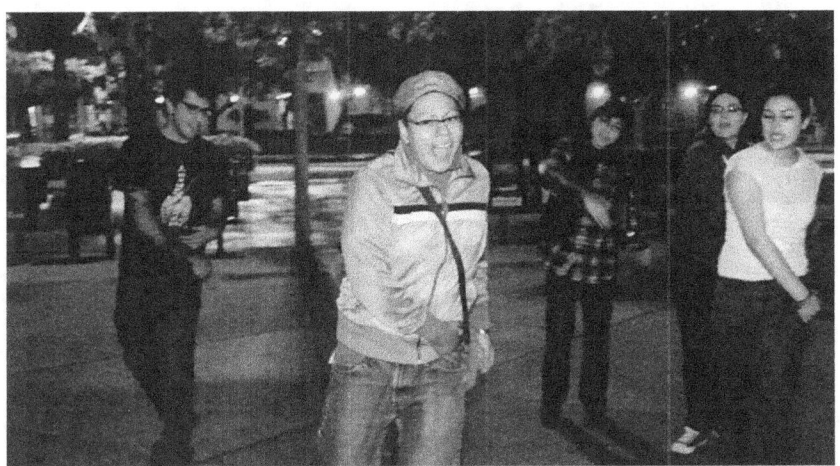

2.5 "Local Autonomy Networks: Los Angeles with Gender Justice LA," by micha cárdenas, performed at the University of Southern California, 2014.

practice at USC of setting up border fences at night and installing digitally enabled checkpoints for checking official ID cards (school ID or state ID), and reading their magnetic stripes' contents for storage in a database, had created an unsafe situation for the trans and gender-non-conforming participants of their group. As it is often difficult for transgender people and genderqueer people to change their official identifications to match their appearance, the policy, they stated, effectively excluded their group from campus. Further, they were concerned about the ramifications for members of their group, or anyone coming to campus, who might be undocumented and therefore also unable to show identification.

During the performance, a police officer approached the group, asked to speak to me, and asked for my government identification card. Interactions such as these can be recorded in a police report and entered into a digital database. The Los Angeles Police Department (LAPD) website describes how the department uses computer statistics (COMPSTAT) and predictive policing, which rely on algorithmically sorting massive amounts of information to identify patterns of activity, directing police where to go before crime has occurred.[51] Organizers with the Stop LAPD Spying Coalition in Los Angeles have repeatedly protested these methods, articulating how the algorithms encode racist police practices (figure 2.6).[52] The coalition points out that the data on which the COMPSTAT system relies is based on racist assump-

This is the expected rate of crimes in box n at time t, or the "hotness of the spot." The hotness of the spot is equal to the sum of the short and long term components of the model.

This is the short-term component of the model. It's short-term because it weights more recent crimes more heavily in predictions-this offsets the other part of the model by allowing the model to respond to more recent trends.

$$\lambda_n(t) = \mu_n + \sum_{t_n^i < t} \theta \omega e^{-\omega(t - t_n^i)}$$

This is the long-term component of the model. It's long-term because it's based on the historical average rates of crimes in the spot, and it weights all events that have happened equally regardless of when they happened.

2.6 Equation for the likelihood of future crime at a given location based on the frequency of historical crimes encoded in the algorithm of the Los Angeles Police Department's Predpol software for predictive policing. *Source:* Stop LAPD Spying Coalition, "Before the Bullet Hits the Body: Predictive Policing in Los Angeles," May 8, 2018, https://stoplapdspying.org/before-the-bullet-hits-the-body -dismantling-predictive-policing-in-los-angeles.

tions from the point of collection, such as categorizing people who commit crimes according to simple racial categories and binary genders. Further, it states, "The covert characteristics of predictive policing—algorithms that use historic crime data to generate predictions about location based crime or Chronic Offender Bulletins/heat lists that turn individuals into prime suspects before they have committed a crime, the inability of a person or community to know, much less challenge, their designation as a likely offender— all threaten due process and our human rights."[53] The coalition's work is an important example of activists engaging in algorithmic analysis of the logics that are part of how the LAPD disproportionately targets communities of color.

The work of the Stop LAPD Spying Coalition brings to light the ways that police surveillance causes harm, and the ways that artists and activists can respond. Their claims are an example of what Toby Beauchamp describes, saying, "Surveillance and security . . . produce the very categories and figures of gendered deviance that they purport to simply identify."[54] Similarly, the performers in the *Autonets* performance with GJLA sought to bring to light the harm caused by the surveillance practice of requesting state-issued identification documents from anyone entering the USC campus, and the ways that the practice ensnares anyone entering campus, from local community members to guest artists and students, in an algorithmic system of surveillance, categorization, and control.

The moment of police interaction with the performance demonstrates the need for what professor and attorney Dean Spade has termed a critical trans politics.[55] Not only do the movements of people in public space enter into a field of mediation by being recorded by police with the means described earlier, but some of these recordings are remediated into other databases. Spade writes about how IDs are used as a means of causing harm to transgender people and reducing their life chances by increasing their risk of violence. He says, "The declaration of the War on Terror ushered in a range of policy reforms and new government practices that have drastically increased surveillance. . . . [N]ew practices have emerged and various agencies now compare their entire data sets and seek out mismatched information."[56] The practice of recording people's movements in multiple databases and then comparing the data in those databases reveals the danger of living in multiple fields of mediation. While these dangers exist as a concern for everyone, they are acutely present for transgender people who may have mismatching identification, such as a driver's license with a female gender and a passport with a male gender, and the potential for the restriction of movement that this may cause—across national borders, into bathrooms, or into employment. Spade writes, "The use of gender as a category of data for sorting populations—something that is taken as neutral and obvious to most administrators—operates as a vector of vulnerability."[57] Spade's claim contradicts the common claim that algorithms, such as sorting algorithms, are neutral and shows how they are regularly used to reproduce harm against trans people of color. The operation Spade describes clearly demonstrates an operation of necropolitics, in which the deaths of marginalized populations are carried out through neglect. Supposedly neutral systems algorithmically distribute increased life chances for white cisgender people and decreased life chances for trans people of color through the operation of digital identity document tracking across multiple databases. These harms disproportionately affect trans people of color, including immigrants who have to produce documents more often and Black and Latinx trans people who are more often targeted by police for imprisonment.

In response to this situation, we created a performance around a question asked by one of the participants, Chella Coleman, a Black trans woman: "Does this look like safety to you?" The answer was that armed guards, police, and checkpoints are dangerous for many reasons. One reason is that they recall traumatic experiences for participants, students, and GJLA members who previously lived in Mexico and Palestine. In both of these places, checkpoints at border crossings are visceral embodiments of racist gender policing, where border agents have the ability to use one's racial or gender categories as cause to restrict one's movement or to inflict extreme violence, including murder. The memory of the fear of loss or violence experienced at a checkpoint lives on as trauma in the bodies of those who experience it, and checkpoints such as this one at USC may cause people to relive that fear.

As the performers move through public space, they activate their own bodies as archives of traumatic memory and transform those memories. In the Los Angeles *Autonets* performance, many of the roughly twenty participants were transgender or genderqueer people of color. In the discussions of the kinds of violence they faced resulting from identity-policing tactics, many described or depicted personal experiences. My gesture in this performance, in response to the prompt "safety," was based on my memory of traumatic experiences traveling in airports. With current security policies in airports around the world, I am frequently faced with the choice of having a full body search or entering into the field of mediation of a full-body millimeter wave scanner, which can create pictures of my naked body through my clothes.[58] The full body search involves having Transportation Security Administration (TSA) officers put their fingers inside the waistband of my clothes, their hands in-between and under my breasts, their hands up the inside of my legs until they touch my crotch, and the back of their hands dragged across my crotch area. This is a deeply disturbing experience that I have had repeatedly. I face having my gender judged to determine whether I need a male or female officer to search me, and I face having my race and religion appraised, although based on current prevailing Islamophobic fears on which US airport security practices are based, I experience less harassment due to my light skin and non-Muslim clothing.[59]

With these experiences in mind, I created a gesture for the other participants and myself to repeat throughout the performance. I assumed the pose required by the millimeter wave scanner, then enacted my utopian desire to escape the scanner and free my body from the position being imposed on it by spinning out of this position in an arc with my arms open. With this gesture, I created a cut in the flow of bodies moving on the sidewalk and through the campus entry checkpoint. This cut enacts a critique of the practices of corporeal control at security checkpoints. Whether or not the viewer of this act understands the gesture's full context is doubtful, but I hope that the gesture has some affective resonance for viewers.

One kind of ethical cut is a cut that opens possibilities for decolonization. Kember and Zylinska describe an ethical cut into a field of mediation as one that opens possibilities of life, saying, "Cutting well means cutting (film, tape, reality) in a way that does not lose sight of the horizon of duration or foreclose on the creative possibility of life enabled by this horizon."[60] In describing decolonization as an ethical and political project that opens possibilities for life, I am not using the term *decolonization* as a vague placeholder for liberation. Following Eve Tuck and K. Wayne Yang, I agree that decolonial struggle must work for both the repatriation of land to Indigenous peoples and a dismantling of the mechanisms by which this land has been held, including prisons.[61] Regarding "We Already Know," the original people of the land known as São Paulo are the Tupi people, including the Tupiniquim, Guaianas, and Guarani, who have been under attack in many ways since the election of Brazil's new extreme right-wing president Jair Bolsonaro. In Los Angeles, the Gabrieliño-Tongva people were present before Spanish colonization.[62] While my performances did not work for repatriation of land directly to these peoples, they did work to undo the ongoing violence of colonial institutions of police and gender binaries. Tuck and Yang state, "Ghetto colonialism, prisons, and under resourced compulsory schooling are specializations of settler colonialism in North America; they are produced by the collapsing of internal, external, and settler colonialisms, into new blended categories."[63] In differentiating decolonization as a specific struggle to return land to Indigenous peoples from a broader conception of social justice, Tuck and Yang make a crucial point about freedom, citing Audre Lorde, who writes, "Freedom is a possibility that is not just mentally generated; it is particular and felt."[64] One impulse driving this book is to differentiate what is "particular and felt" about trans of color experience that can then be felt in artworks using trans of color poetics.

Lorde's beautiful observation lends support to the idea that an embodied gesture can be a kind of cut that moves toward decolonization by offering a temporary stabilization of a feeling of freedom—freedom from colonial worldviews that become embodied through everyday gestures. Tuck and Yang point out that, "in North America and other settings, settler sovereignty imposes sexuality, legality, raciality, language, religion and property in specific ways."[65] I propose that a cut into a flow of mediation that supports colonialism, such as the binary gender system or the informational apparatus of policing systems, can be a decolonizing cut. These cuts can aid the project of removing settler sovereignty and returning Indigenous sovereignty, particularly when enacted by native people, such as two-spirit people. By considering the connections Tuck and Yang make, I see cuts that open creative possibilities for decolonization, prison abolition, and gender justice as ethical cuts, adding specificity to Kember and Zylinska's claim.

Demanding, or creating, opacity can be a decolonial act. In *Poetics of Relation*, Glissant writes, "If we examine the process of 'understanding' people and ideas from the perspective of Western thought, we discover that its basis is this requirement for transparency."[66] Glissant links the concept of transparency, a common element in discussions of internet freedom and communication rights, to the Western knowledge systems that enact colonialism. He calls on people to "agree not merely to the right to difference, but . . . agree also to the right to opacity," which can be seen as pointing to the need to go beyond an acknowledgment of difference to a right to reject the colonial demand to make one's self knowable, which is evident in the moment of colonial encounter.[67] Enacting opacity is one way of shifting, modulating the degree to which one allows one's fullness to be perceived. In both of the *Autonets* performances I describe in this chapter, one can see a movement toward becoming opaque. In "We Already Know," there is a gesture of the performers suddenly enacting repeated movements in public space—enacting a ritual without explanation. While some of the viewers were participants in the art event and may have gone as far as to read the title and description of the performance, even those informed viewers do not know the process and prompts behind the specific movements in this performance. Most viewers probably do not know the motivations for the performance. As a gesture toward opacity, this is significant in that it leaves viewers in the position of needing to look closely to try to interpret the moves for their meaning. A different choice, which one often sees in Theater of the Oppressed, would be for one performer to explain to the audience the context and motivations for the performance before it begins, then perform the movement. In contrast, we chose in this performance to leave the meaning open to allow the full poetic ambiguity of the gestures to convey more affect, instead of a specific logical communication.

Opacity allows for a protection of one's interiority from prying eyes, a serious concern for trans people of color who are routinely subjected to invasive forms of surveillance, and even invasive attempts by allies to know the truth of their lives. Opacity is not simply about visibility, or a rejection of visibility. Glissant states "the right to opacity . . . would be the real foundation of Relation, in freedoms."[68] Opacity allows for boundaries to be maintained, which in turn allow relation between distinct individuals to be negotiated. Describing opacity as part of a poetics of relation, Glissant states "the opaque is not the obscure, though it is possible for it to be so . . . it is that which cannot be reduced."[69] In this way, one can understand a demand for opacity from trans people of color to be a rejection of a colonial cisgender gaze that would attempt to render their identities and bodies into gender binaries and racial taxonomies. Instead, opacity maintains the irreducible fullness of their being. Trans of color poetics enacts opacity over transparency when artists choose to create works that are for other trans people of color, often focusing on sharing survival strategies and building community over attempts to render bare the truth of their lives to white cisgender audiences. The Los Angeles performance of *Autonets* uses opacity to eschew the kinds of legibility that are associated with protest for the kind of presence and emotion that is perceived to be performance.

In "Local Autonomy Networks: Los Angeles with Gender Justice LA," the performers are primarily genderqueer and transgender people of color who are performing at the checkpoint at the entrance to the USC campus. The performance is based in a demand for opacity, a demand to not have to produce the official identification that attempts to render one's gender transparent in exchange for allowing one to move across the borders of campus. The police officer at the checkpoint asked whether the performance was a protest, to which I replied that it was a performance of a utopian visioning of community-based safety. Unsatisfied, he asked again whether the performance was a protest. I told him that each performer had been invited to create their own, embodied expression of the concept of safety, and that many of them were wearing prototypes of a mesh networked safety device with LED lights and wireless transmitters. Choosing to rely on opacity, I refused to tell the officer that, yes, it was in fact a protest against this very checkpoint and that the organizers and I considered it both a performance and a protest. I was learning from a strategy that the art group Critical Art Ensemble has called "aesthetics of confusion."[70] While their use of aesthetics is more grounded in Aristotelian poetics, my focus on trans of color poetics grounds itself in the experience of relation in the Caribbean in the words of Glissant, where the confusion of the encounter is the place from which the openness of poetics unfolds.

In our organizing meeting for the performance/protest action, we discussed how the point was not to engage with the local security or police officers, because they are not the decision makers about this policy. Instead, we decided that our goals were both to propel our message about disagreeing with this policy widely through the announcements of the action and to build community, safety, and resilience through creating and enacting the performance. It became a mechanism by which we could build community-based responses to violence by developing methods to keep ourselves safe and then practice the skills necessary to enact them in the street, such as nonverbal communication, coming together as a group and separating, and using sound and light as cues for group movement in public space. These goals of the performance remained opaque to some onlookers, though, and to the police officer, to whom it appeared that we were "just dancing," despite the presence of drums and chants.

The police demanded that all performers show their IDs to reenter the campus after the performance was over. We refused. Again, we chose a strategy of opacity, refusing to allow the state to identify all of the members of our group and subject each member to a requirement for transparency in the form of a state ID that matched their appearance. I informed the officer that all of the performers were my guests, and I was a doctoral student holding a workshop, but the workshop participants were not registered as such and did not all have IDs to show. Without any explanation, the officer agreed to let us all back onto the campus. At this moment, the officer was perhaps choosing not to escalate the situation, or not to have to do the work of forcibly checking IDs, but was in effect also revealing the arbitrariness of the new ID checking policy. Our choice to remain opaque to the demands of the state ultimately had a positive outcome, revealing the unnecessary nature of the ID checking policy. Our opacity, along with our choice to move in a large group of more than twenty people and use some of the protection provided by our claim of creating art, allowed us to cut through the field of mediation of the campus border checkpoint.

Opacity is a mode of visibility beyond visible and invisible that can be enacted with the operation of the cut. Forms of movement that enable modulations of perceptibility are essential to trans of color poetics. I have considered how movement itself can act as a technology of communication and how this can be extended through wearable electronics. The two performances of *Autonets* described here are attempts at ethical cuts relying on the decolonial strategy of opacity described by Glissant. These performances, developed in an international performance art context and distributed through hemispheric networks of mediated communication, can be said to enact the concept of an ethical cut. The performances were attempts to dismantle structures that support colonialism by reducing violence against transgender people of color without relying on prisons and police. Present forms of digital communication are dependent on corporate and state structures that are incompatible with visionary trans of color politics. *Autonets* used algorithms, both as code and as rituals of performance, to create cuts in the fields of mediation of gender, race, sexuality, and police surveillance. The performances refuse expectations of transparent political and technical efficacy, instead using opacity to open a space of imagination for decolonial, abolitionist, trans politics. In the next chapter, I continue elaborating trans of color poetics by describing another operation that modulates perceptibility—the shift—in the science fiction imaginary of the gender-non-conforming artist Janelle Monáe.

THE SHIFT   THREE

THE ANDROID CINDI MAYWEATHER reaches her hand up to her ear, inputs
a code, and flickers from white to black. Her gesture could be described as
hacking the black and white binary, yet this is more than a binary transition.[1]
Her skin flickers from a white artificial skin of plastic or metal to the brown
skin of a human African American nonbinary person. The crossing is in multiple planes. By slowing the video down in digital video editing software, one
can see that it also includes a slight movement and a slight change of shape.
The shift is created by the algorithmically generated imagery of the morph.
The scene is quick, a second at the beginning of "Many Moons," a video in
Janelle Monáe's extensive seven-part concept series *Metropolis*. *Dazed* magazine describes the video as demonstrating a "signature Afrofuturistic aesthetic: an exploration of real world issues of race, class, gender, and politics
in a sci-fi setting."[2] Monáe describes the album, *Metropolis*, as a postapocalyp-
tic science fiction "emotion picture."[3] What I want to call attention to in this
short scene are not the states before or after the flicker, but the ability to shift
visibility that the android possesses. Shifting is a gesture of modulating one's
perceptibility by changing one's form, location, or appearance, which is part
of the repertoire of trans of color poetics.

   In this chapter, I propose a new operator, the shift, based on artwork by
trans and gender-non-conforming artists of color, Janelle Monáe and myself.

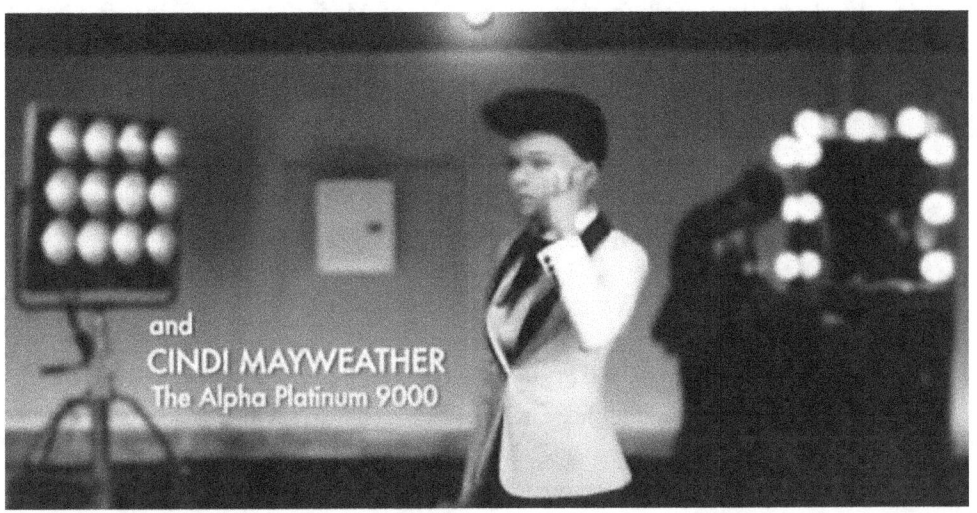

3.1 Still image from the video "Many Moons" showing the android Cindi Mayweather (Janelle Monáe) shifting from white to black. The video is available at https://scalar.usc.edu/works/poetic-operations/many-moons-hd-excerpt -slowed.

One method of algorithmic analysis is to break a problem down into its components and operations. In the previous chapter, I considered the operation of the cut in media art and performance as a gesture of trans of color poetics. Here I demonstrate how shifting can be observed and understood through algorithmic analysis. The shift, or the modulation perceptibility, can be seen enacted by oppressed peoples and by institutions of neoliberal power that define the contemporary moment. Shifting is one factor enabling transphobic violence to exist simultaneously with the discourse of an emerging transgender rights movement. A focus on a static state of visibility or invisibility is insufficient to account for what Kara Keeling has referred to as the "digital regime of the image," characterized by a mutable, flickering signifier.[4] Mutability is a skill practiced by many trans women of color who face multiple forms of violence each day, shifting their body and appearance as necessary for survival, at one moment passing invisibly as a cisgender woman and at another standing onstage speaking out against racist, transphobic violence. Shifting invites one to imagine gender beyond binaries, as an infinite field of expressive texture. In place of rigid categories, the ability to modulate gender at will points to a future in which gender can be a multidimensional, multispectral field of play.

In *Metropolis*, the album that features "Many Moons," the android, Cindi Mayweather, is being hunted. I read this fictional account as a reference to the frequent murders of Black and gender-non-con-forming people in the contemporary United States. Monáe has stated that Cindi Mayweather, the main character of her *Metropolis* multialbum concept series, could "absolutely" be a transgender woman.[5] Her claim places her work in dialogue with other examples of transgender women in popular culture, such as Laverne Cox's character Sophia Burset on *Orange Is the New Black*. While the character of Cindi Mayweather is performed by Monáe, who does not identify as a transgender woman, this is often the case for transgender characters. Further, by retroactively gesturing to the possibility of Cindi Mayweather's gender, Monáe's comment illustrates how trans characters do not necessarily need simple representational visibility to be present. Characters may shift at any moment in their past or future, so their trans or cisgender status cannot be determined simply by looking at them. Further, in a performance of the song "Americans" from the album *Dirty Computer* on *The Late Show with Stephen Colbert*, Monáe featured MJ Rodriguez, a Black Latinx trans actress who starts on the *Pose* television series, as the central performer.[6] In doing so, Monáe is doing more than representing the possibility of trans women characters in her story about androids in the United States.

The politics of shifting are not fixed; nor are they guaranteed, for they may still fall prey to the Western logics and neoliberal economics from which the digital emerged. Shifting also harbors possibility. It moves us beyond the regime of the visible. This chapter begins with the indeterminacy of trans of color visibility in the moment of passing and moves on to consider the political context of shifting and its importance to algorithmic analysis. Shifting is an operation of trans of color poetics, beyond a binary of visible or invisible, and artwork by many trans and gender-non-conforming artists of color make this operation perceptible. Using algorithmic analysis, I analyze artworks by Monáe, identify moments where algorithms are at work, and offer a code poem about Monáe's work. Shifting corresponds to the variables in an algorithm, whose value can change in an instant, and this shifting corresponds to trans of color as an identity, and category, in flux.

From Demands for Visibility to Performance of Modulation

Women of color feminist theorists have proposed powerful models for thinking through the complexity of identity in movement along multiple axes. The intersectional model proposed by Kimberlé Crenshaw can describe the everyday process that racialized trans women go through when they consider how these characteristics interact at specific points, such as being both trans and Latina. The assemblage model elaborated by Jasbir Puar helps us to understand many of these components of identity by accounting for time and transition, a model of many curved lines intersecting. An algorithmic model can add detail to how this calculation may work: in motion, in different locations, in different kinds of light, in different socioeconomic contexts, or based on any number of changing variables at a given time. Puar's assemblage model extends Crenshaw's by using the image of the assemblage from Gilles Deleuze and Félix Guattari. In *A Thousand Plateaus*, they write, "In a book, as in all things, there are lines of articulation or segmentarity, strata and territories; but also lines of flight, movements of deterritorialization and destratification. Comparative rates of flow on these lines produce phenomena of relative slowness and viscosity, or, on the contrary, of acceleration and rupture. All this, lines and measurable speeds constitutes an assemblage."[7]

Following this, one can understand an assemblage as a set of curved lines, and one can draw a set of curved lines with an algorithm.[8] By describing the steps in such an algorithm, one can begin to see how an algorithmic approach allows one to think through the details of multiple variables in an intersectional identity or an assemblage and to be able to consider them over time, not merely as a monolithic assemblage—just a set of curved lines—but as forms that have specific maxima and minima. This may lead to a detailed consideration of questions such as the passing status of Cindi Mayweather as depicted by the algorithms that render her transformation, or the ways in which a woman who escaped slavery might perform racialized genders. Algorithmic approaches may include creating a simulation of a scenario using algorithms or a close study of existing digital media.

As digital media is constituted through algorithms, much of the media through which audiences see trans women of color is enacted by algorithms, and these algorithms can be analyzed for their effects on the constitution of identities in movement. The algorithms that make digital media possible include algorithms for rendering images on-screen from a given media file, the compression algorithms that allow quick transmission of video and photos over the internet, and the algorithms of social media networks through which people find digital media.

Trans of color studies have wrestled with the challenges of visibility and invisibility, pointing to the need for more than simple demands for representation in necropolitical regimes. I agree with Keeling's claim that academic studies that seek to make queer and trans people visible are often problematic. Keeling states, "A 'looking' for M—that begins by asking where s/he is now inevitably operates by harnessing the capacity of those temporal structures and epistemological enterprises of policing and surveillance inherent in any framing of questions of representation and visibility."[9] Thus, other methods for scholarship are necessary that do not seek to locate people who need less visibility to stay safe. In the article "On Trans* Chican@s," Francisco Galarte points out the need for "exploring what is unannounced, listening for the iterations of silences," which resonates with my interest in understanding modes of invisibility and imperceptibility.[10] The trans studies scholar Aren Aizura claims that "invocations of invisibility and dehumanization don't quite tell the whole story."[11] Aizura also sees the importance of understanding the murder of trans people through the analytic of necropolitics, saying, "We cannot theorize a trans necropolitics without exploring the mobility of gender variant bodies and the circuits of capital they/we exploit and are exploited by."[12] Aizura describes the need to think beyond invisibility under necropolitics to also consider movement and economic context. The shift is one form of movement, such as movement across national borders, that allows trans people of color to escape violence daily. Transgender studies scholars have described the problems with using trans people's lives as a rhetorical figure without ever considering the lives of actual trans people, as has been done by numerous queer theorists. My intention here is not to imagine trans people of color as a metaphor, which Viviane Namaste has critiqued as one way of erasing the lives of actual trans people.[13] Instead, I look to the Monáe's poetics, and my own poetry, to better understand methods of modulating perceptibility that may be useful for reducing violence against trans people of color.

While shifting is not limited to transgender people's experience, it has a strong resonance with the trans gesture of passing, or choosing not to pass. Passing can offer a kind of invisibility. Contemporary science fiction is rich with scenes of shifting from visible to invisible, from William Gibson's book *Neuromancer*, with the Panther Moderns media terrorist organization who wear mimetic polycarbon suits, to Mamoru Oshii's animated film *Ghost in the Shell* (1995), with thermoptic camouflage (figure 3.2).[14] These scenes can be understood as speculative precursors to the nanotechnological efforts to create materials that can bend light to create invisibility for soldiers, which made significant progress in March 2014.[15] Li Gao, Debashis Chanda, and their collaborators at the University of Central Florida are working on fabrics for invisibility cloaks and stealth technologies by creating nanomaterials that are small enough to operate on quantum principles.[16] These material connec-

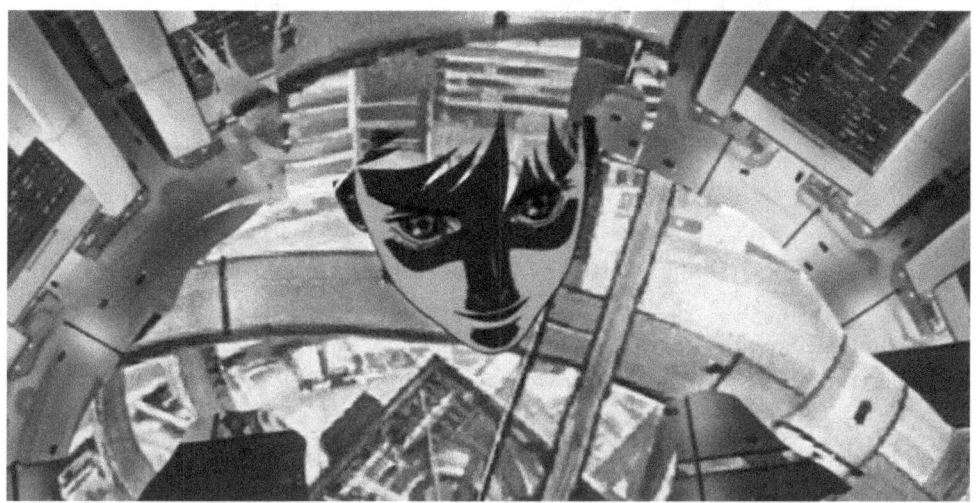

3.2 Excerpt from *Ghost in the Shell* showing thermoptic camouflage. The video is available at https://scalar.usc.edu/works/poetic-operations/ghost-in-the-shell -falling-fade.

tions between speculative fiction and contemporary reality demonstrate one of the ways media makes every day experiences visible. Yet shifting, as I describe here, deals more with the specific materiality of a shift from perceptibility to imperceptibility and considers the space between these two states.[17]

Passing is a technique of modulating visibility to be perceived as belonging to a particular category, such as a particular gender or race. There is an extensive body of literature on racial passing.[18] Passing is a gesture that brings the contemporary racialized trans subject into an analogous relationship with the flickering digital signifier. The performative utterance of making one's body read in a certain way reveals its mutability, reveals that one's body, like the digital image, can be a sign with more than one signifier. Yet in the case of passing as a particular racialized gender, unlike the neoliberal liquid ease of the digital, when trans people of color fail to pass seamlessly and reveal that they are in a process of shifting, when they are read as trans instead of cisgender, they are subjected to extreme, incomprehensible violence.

Around midnight on August 17, 2013, Islan Nettles was walking home with friends to her apartment in Harlem when she was violently murdered, according to news reports.[19] A group of men began flirting with her, and it is hard to know what happened next that led to such extreme violence. Did she walk under a brighter street light? Did the pitch of her voice out her? Did she get closer to the men as she walked past them on the street? The twenty-year-old Paris Wilson perceived something that caused his perception of Nettles to change, and he then attacked her, knocked her to the ground, and beat her until she stopped responding. She died in a hospital four days later. The beautiful mercury of her existence was halted by an act of absolute hate, meant to enforce absolute fixity, in a cruel series of rapid-fire gestures. Passing is not simply a question of being or becoming visible or invisible; instead, it is a question of attaining a particular kind of visibility. Often, for trans women of color, the question of passing can be determined by the amount of light and the color of light reflected from one's face and neck. Reflected light may determine one's ability to survive or not, as in the case of Nettles, a Black trans woman who was murdered in New York after a person catcalling her decided that she was a trans woman.[20] Instances of violence such as this one recall with great urgency the stakes of trans of color poetics and the churning magma of forces through which they are forged. While Monáe's depictions of shifting do not come from an experience of a trans woman of color attempting to pass, the experience of being a Black gender-non-conforming person in America resonates with many similar possibilities of violent response, and authors such as C. Riley Snorton refute the distinction between transness and Blackness that would separate out Monáe's experience. Passing is not simply a question of identity; it is a poetics of relation in which each element is shaped by its relations within larger networks, as Édouard Glissant has articulated. Passing involves both the modulation of visibility by the person who is passing and the reception of that image by the viewer, who makes a decision about whether or not a person fits into a particular category.

Passing requires an observer: it involves the modulation of light, but that light needs to reach a retina, and in this moment the quantum mechanics of light are necessary to consider. Karen Barad's concept of intra-action uses quantum mechanics to envision the matter that makes up bodies as lively material in processes of movement, becoming and passing, not passive material on which simple static categories of race and gender can be imposed.[21] As passing relies on the judgment of an observer, its usefulness for coalitional politics of race and gender must be questioned. If oppressed people's value to one another is defined by our passing status, we are leaving our political definitions in the hands of those who wish us harm. By focusing on the moment of shifting, I hope to highlight the uncertain boundaries of the categories of people of color, and trans of color, focusing on the agency of people to self-identify with those categories when they prove useful for building collective justice.

Shifting is a process of experimenting with the malleability of reality by moving in collaboration with the lively matter which bodies are composed of. Barad's intra-action is an operation that forms part of her concept of "agential realism," which attempts to move beyond the binaries of constructivism and realism in a way that exceeds simple representation. Agential realism attributes agency not only to subjects—for example, to theorists and physicists—but also to matter itself. She is aware of the politics of the work she does, seeing it as more than a mental exercise to understand quantum physics. Barad writes, "Reflection is insufficient; intervention is key."[22] She looks to the physicist Niels Bohr, who says, "Theorizing must be understood as an embodied practice, rather than a spectator sport of matching linguistic representations to existing things."[23] Barad concludes that "experimenting and theorizing are dynamic practices that play a constitutive role in the production of objects and subjects and matter and meaning."[24] These claims show how theory can be a way of engaging in practice, how the borders between the two are not always so clear but instead have their own intra-action. Informed by a study of quantum physics, Barad's analysis is useful to stitch together threads of theory and practice into practice-based research. There are multiple forms of materiality at play here, from the materiality of matter and light, to the materiality of digital media as a means for examining sociopolitical and economic processes, to the material realities of the lives and deaths of oppressed peoples.

Like Barad, who describes a multiplicity of possible states particles can be in, Keeling describes multiple possible futures in which trans Black youth may be able to live—without violence—holding open a space of potential. The multiplicity of matter and time can be seen in Keeling's analysis of violence against trans people of color who do not try to pass as people with normative binary genders. Keeling discusses Sakia Gunn's life to consider the temporality of Black queer lives.[25] The question of passing resonates with necropolitical gravity for masculine trans and gender-non-conforming people of color such as Gunn, a masculine Black person described by some as trans who was murdered in New Jersey at just fifteen years old.[26] Moments such as Gunn's murder reveal how the trans or gender-non-conforming person of color comes to be perceived by some as less than human, as disposable.

The moment in which Cindi Mayweather shifts demonstrates how the first necessary step for her to become visible is for her to shift from inhuman to human, from android skin to a skin that passes as a human Black woman. Keeling links passing, the digital, and black subjectivity together, saying, "Even the European has been simply passing for 'the human' all along and . . . black subjectivity and black culture, those very concepts created to serve as 'the human's' Other, provide the most fertile soil to till for ways to understand what it means to be 'human' in the digital age."[27] Here Keeling demonstrates that, because the category of human has been used flexibly to include people of European descent, focusing on Black culture can best help one see the contours of the changing nature of the human in digital environments. Snorton describes this malleability, which can be seen in the fact that slavery forced a shift from human to being deemed less than human, as the fungibility of Black flesh. Snorton describes how fungibility was transferred from objects of exchange, such as cattle, onto the bodies of Black people under slavery. He states, "Captive flesh figures a critical genealogy of gender as mutable and as an amendable form of being."[28] Snorton describes Monáe's song "Hell You Talmbout (Say Their Names)" as a digital repository of the names of Black people, including Black trans people, in whose honor the #BlackLivesMatter movement has mobilized. He goes on to describe the song, which uses a powerful, constant drum rhythm to call out names of black trans women murdered by police, including Mya Hall and Deonna Mason, followed by the exhortation to "say her name!"[29] Monáe has performed the song at #BlackLivesMatter protests, as well as in concerts.[30] Snorton calls the song's demand to say her name a practice of remembering that works to end the conditions that ensure Black and trans death in the present and as an investment in securing Black and trans existence in the present and into the future. The song is an important moment of solidarity between Black trans women and a Black artist whose gender is not limited to Western binary constructs, both because of Monáe's exclusion from those categories as a Black woman but also because of Monáe's stated identification. In simple, short, direct tweet on January 10, 2020, Monáe stated "#IAmNonbinary."[31] "Hell You Talmbout (Say Their Names)" mobilizes a trans of color poetics of shifting into hypervisibility to remember the lives of Black trans people whose lives are in the past while working for the safety of Black trans people in the future.

Monáe creates a brilliant moment of theory in action by performing a queer, gender-non-conforming Black android, a commodity, shifting their appearance to be perceived as human to escape captivity by inciting a revolution. Both Sylvia Wynter and Walter Mignolo have articulated how the Western conception of the human has been used historically to determine who is less than human and, therefore, who is expendable.[32] In her essay "Unsettling the Coloniality of Being/Power/Truth/Freedom," Wynter writes, "The struggle of our new millennium will be one between the ongoing imperative of securing the well-being of our present ethnoclass (i.e., Western bourgeois) conception of the human, Man, which overrepresents itself as if it were the human itself, and that of securing the well-being, and therefore the full cognitive and behavioral autonomy of the human species itself."[33] In "Many Moons," Monáe makes visible the need for oppressed groups of people to consciously take on the form of human and the need to shift into being perceived as human to survive. Monáe makes Wynter's claims perceptible through an imagination of the near-future, while Wynter's claims show the epistemological shifts necessary for a path toward liberatory futures. Monáe's creation of the scene of shifting is praxis, combining theory and practice. The shift performed uses digital algorithms of CGI effects to depict the algorithms of survival in an android, giving viewers a glimpse of the survival strategies Monáe has had to learn to survive, including passing as human in situations where her gender and race would cause her viewers to perceive her as less than human. Gender-non-conforming bodies are often seen as pathologically flawed, and therefore less than human, and therefore disposable. The moment of passing exists in a space of multiple possible futures, but, as Barad explains, numerous theories by physicists hold that until the moment of measurement, these multiple possibilities all exist with equal reality.[34] Digital renderings of in-between moments of shifting, with their uncertainty and multiplicity, may be the most accurate representation of reality.

The poetics of shifting along lines of race, gender, and species can also be seen in digital games. D. Fox Harrell is a professor of digital media and artificial intelligence (AI) at the Massachusetts Institute of Technology whose Imagination, Computation, and Expression Laboratory has created numerous projects exploring the dynamics of racial and cultural passing in digital media. One such project Harrell created is "Chameleonia: Shadow Play," based on W. E. B. Dubois's idea of double consciousness, in which players must transform their avatar and their avatar's shadow to pass through various locations, such as at work. In the game, Harrell says, "The player character represents the user's view of herself, while the shadow represents the socially constructed self."[35] In her analysis of the poetics of the digital game *Assassin's Creed III: Liberation*, Soraya Murray cites Harrell's concept of phantasmal media, which describes how cultural worldviews are encoded into algorithms and data structures. Murray describes *Liberation*'s Persona system, a game mechanic in which the main character, Aveline de Grandpré, must shift her appearance among being a charming lady in a dress, a slave, and a notorious assassin. Grandpré is a Black woman in colonial America in the 1760s. The game is remarkable as a rare example that depicts the racial violence of slavery in the United States. Still, Murray finds that the poetics of the game—in particular, its mechanics—still reinforce colonialist tropes about exoticized women. She states, "Power relationships between playable and non-playable characters are determined by the game mechanics, which (as Harrell theorizes) embody particular cultural meanings in the game's system of computational expression."[36] Murray cites the game critic Jagger Gravning's claims that the game depicts a transgender or gender-fluid narrative because at multiple points in the story Aveline must shift her gender to survive. Murray describes multiple scenes in which "combatants in pursuit sometimes refer to Aveline using a male pronoun, calling out: 'He's getting away!' or 'He's trying to shake us!'"[37] The game demonstrates ways that passing along racial and gender lines are linked, echoing Snorton's concept of the fungibility of black bodies in *Black on Both Sides*. Snorton states, "Gender indefiniteness would become a critical modality of political and cultural maneuvering within figurations of blackness, illustrated, for example, by the frequency with which narratives of fugitivity included cross-gendered modes of escape."[38] Snorton uses the word *fungible*, coined to describe cattle as something subject to monetary compensation, to describe both the conditions of oppression under slavery of being defined as less than human and the strategies used by slaves to shift how they were perceived in order to escape captivity. Both *Liberation* and "Chameleonia" point to the long histories of shifting present in Monáe's performance of Cindi Mayweather.

The meaning of racialized passing has been an issue of contention between transgender studies and queer theory, such as in the writing of Judith Butler and Jay Prosser. In *Bodies That Matter*, Butler discusses the film *Paris Is Burning*, which follows the lives of a number of trans women of color and drag performers in the New York ball scene in the mid- to late 1980s. After seeing an interview and performance by a trans woman named Venus Xtravaganza, the film's viewers learn that she was murdered. Butler's use of Xtravaganza's story is intended to display the limits of performativity. Instead of "liberation from hegemonic constraint," Butler says, Xtravaganza's denaturalization of sex ultimately results in her death, ultimately reinscribing heterosexuality.[39] Prosser's main contention is that Butler criticizes Xtravaganza as reproducing heteronormativity for desiring a life in which she would be safe. Prosser points to the ethical value of Butler's theory, which values transgression above a desire for normalcy, even at the expense of Xtravaganza's life. Butler sees Xtravaganza's death as "a tragic misreading of the social map of power" that "falsely constitutes black women as a site of privilege" by someone who "cannot overcome being a Latina."[40]

While Butler's argument is deeply rigorous, her discussion of Venus Xtravaganza is based on a lack of understanding of trans women of color's experiences, which include many more dimensions than Butler considers in her dismissal of Xtravaganza. Butler rightly points to how the violence of racism still affects cisgender Black women, despite their cisgender privilege. Yet when she states that Black trans women's "'identification' is composed of a denial, an envy, which is the envy of a phantasm of black women," she repeats a common trope in queer and feminist theory in which trans women are understood as deluded or suffering from false consciousness.[41] Butler applies this same charge of false consciousness to Xtravaganza. I propose, instead, that Xtravaganza's death was the result of a calculated risk that trans women understand they are taking; that her reading of the social map of power was accurate, but there is still a fundamental uncertainty in the act of passing. There are many variables one must calculate in the act of passing to avoid different forms of violence, such as whether or not one will be read as cisgender, Black, white, or Latina and how these readings interact.

One can never absolutely know whether one is passing or not. Say, for example, that a Black trans woman walks up to a coffee counter, as in a scene in *Mainichi*, a small art game by the designer Mattie Brice to which I return in chapter 4. If the person at the counter addresses the woman using the pronouns she prefers, is that because she is being perceived as a cisgender woman or is it simple politeness? To ask the barista would be to introduce uncertainty, tainting the value of the answer by introducing an observer, similar to the Heisenberg uncertainty principle that Barad discusses. Passing is thus, necessarily covert. To announce that one is passing is to no longer pass. To be perceived as a cisgender woman is different from being perceived as a trans woman who is passing as a cisgender woman. When passing occurs, it is imperceptible. Passing is both an aporia and a part of everyday life for many trans people. Cisgender Black and Latina women and trans women alike are subject to the unknowably complex relational logic of passing, every day: racial passing, gender passing, passing as members of economic classes. The uncertainty is a place of equivalence between trans of color experience and digital media, with pixels that change too rapidly to perceive. The uncertainty of passing is made visible and audible in the moment of the shift in Monáe's film, as well as in many other works of science fiction.

Visibility under Necropolitics

To understand the violence that is the penalty for failing to pass, and the larger sociopolitical structure in which shifting becomes a crucial act of survival, a deeper consideration of necropolitics is useful. Necropolitics, as described by Achille Mbembe, uses modes of visibility that go beyond a binary of being visible or not. Shifting is one proposal for how to understand visibility under necropolitics and how to operate within necropolitical forms of visibility. Contemporary scholars including M. Jacqui Alexander and Chandra Talpade Mohanty, who write about the legacy of women of color feminism, point to the ongoing project of colonialism as a means for understanding global inequity. Alexander states that Third World women now live all around the globe and that neocolonialism operates through the economic form of neoliberalism.[42] Thus, one can understand the constant threat of death that Mbembe describes in the colonies as existing today for people of color everywhere who have histories of colonization.

There are moments when shifting requires assuming a position of spectacular visibility, as in the case of gender-non-conforming artists such as Monáe, or in the case of social movements such as online protest movements. In Monáe's "Many Moons," Cindi Mayweather shifts from white to Black just before stepping onstage for a performance. Mayweather is performing for an android auction with clear reference to a slave auction, where each android is presented as a shifting, flickering hologram. Her position is one of hypervisibility, which she is using to covertly inspire the audience to revolt.

What matters most for trans of color poetics is not the moment of being opaque or invisible, or the moment of being visible and therefore represented, but the ability to shift between being visible and invisible at will. Thinking beyond demands for visibility in queer activism, the artist and theorist Zach Blas builds on Glissant's concept of opacity when discussing the relevance of the Anonymous online protest movement for queer politics. He calls techniques used by Anonymous "informatic opacity," the ability to be opaque to informatic surveillance, as seen in the US National Security Agency's PRISM program and biometric facial recognition systems.[43] I argue for a focus on movement over position not only to account for the fields of mediation that form the ground for contemporary Western identities, but also to account for the lives of trans people of color for whom shape-shifting is not only a desire, but a necessity for survival, and a daily practice. Movement from invisible to highly visible and back is a necessary skill in an environment that seeks to control one's visibility. The ability to be nonidentifiable is exercised daily by trans people who simply pass—for example, by trans femmes of color who can be unnoticed when passing through a dangerous situation.

The control of movement and visibility under necropolitics has important implications for trans people of color's ability to survive. Reading Frantz Fanon's accounts of colonial space, Mbembe states that the goal of the occupation of Palestine is to "render any movement impossible."[44] Yet the modulation of visibility is not only a form of resistance; it is also a form of oppression. Mbembe points out that the Israeli occupation of Palestine relies on techniques of visibility that include "hologrammatization," which allows killing to be precisely targeted, and invisibility, where "invisible killing is added to outright executions."[45] Mbembe is referring to a process of making three-dimensional maps of territories for use by armed forces, a scene that has been depicted in many science fiction films. The hologrammatization of trans people's identity can be seen in the everyday deployments of holograms on recent driver's licenses and passports, another form of media that relies on shifting light to particular angles to be seen. These holograms serve to further control trans people's access to identification that matches their identity. Holograms are media whose image changes depending on the viewer's perspective, which one can see happening in the moment of passing, in which a person's identity may seem to differ depending on the viewpoint of the observer. Yet holograms are also increasingly part of popular music, as is evidenced by Monáe's performance as a hologram in a duet with the rapper M.I.A. in 2014, using the same projection screens used to create the hologram of Tupac Shakur at the Coachella Music Festival in 2012.[46] Monáe joined M.I.A.'s performance of the song "Bad Girls" as a hologram, and M.I.A. joined Monáe's performance of her song "Q.U.E.E.N." Monáe's holographic performance makes Mbembe's claims of the increasing hologrammatization of colonized people literal, yet it subverts the technology to imagine Black gender-non-conforming futures of time-traveling rebels.

In an interview in *Rolling Stone* magazine in 2018, Monáe shifts again, describing her sexuality in terms of a process of opening and transformation. While the interviewer describes this as a moment of coming out and says that Monáe identified as bisexual first, she quotes Monáe as saying, "Later I read about pansexuality and was like, 'Oh, these are things that I identify with too.' I'm open to learning more about who I am."[47] In this moment of spectacular visibility, Monáe is using the multiplicity that holograms make perceptible, describing herself as having multiple sexual orientations and describing her future orientations as shifting over time through a process of learning. The article points to the queer storyline in the song "Q.U.E.E.N.," in which Cindi Mayweather is attracted to a female "dirty computer" named Mary Apple. Later, in the epic Afro-futuristic film for the album *Dirty Computer*, Mary is performed by Tessa Thompson. In the video, Monáe continues her gender shifting from earlier albums, such as in the video for "Make Me Feel." The viewer sees Monáe's character entering a queer bar with Mary, looking wide-eyed and new to the scene, with her hair down, red lipstick on, and wearing a jeweled bustier.[48] In *Dirty Computer*, Cindi Mayweather is referred to by her number, "Jane 57821." This is a continuity with Monáe's earlier albums, as the album *The ArchAndroid* contains a song about Cindi Mayweather titled "57821." Monáe continues to develop and add depth to the character across her different albums, and viewers see Cindi Mayweather shift through a number of different gender representations throughout the story.

Female Android Hackers and Femme Camouflage

As Anonymous demonstrates, the ability to shift between informatic opacity and spectacular visibility is useful for a contemporary political movement to enact change within a neocolonial regime facilitated by global digital networks. Monáe's Cindi Mayweather character demonstrates this ability to shift from spectacular to invisible in many ways. One way is that, over time, her gender presentation shifts among android gender on the cover of *Metropolis: The Chase Suite*; butch or masculine female on *The ArchAndroid*; and femme on *The Electric Lady*. In the narrative described, she is "the Alpha Platinum 9000 [on *The ArchAndroid*], a droid optimized for rock performance, often cloned but never equaled. Cindi is on the run, having fallen in love with the human millionaire Anthony Greendown—a pairing that, in Metropolis, is against the law."[49] Yet on *The Electric Lady*, Monáe is exploring the history of Black feminists such as Assata Shakur, living in hiding, supported by movement of people not in hiding who are in solidarity with her. In the video for "Primetime," we see Cindi Mayweather, both an android and a programmer of androids, hacking Black female androids and presenting a femme gender appearance. One might describe this as a kind of femme camouflage, exploiting the perception of femmes as ineffective or unimportant to hide her revolutionary anti-droid-slavery agenda. Cindi Mayweather's femme disturbance of the logics of visibility and representation recalls Keeling's black femme function. Still, Cindi Mayweather's android gender seeps through in the wide-eyed gaze Monáe performs in photographs, a kind of gender presentation that exceeds racialized expressions of masculinity or femininity.

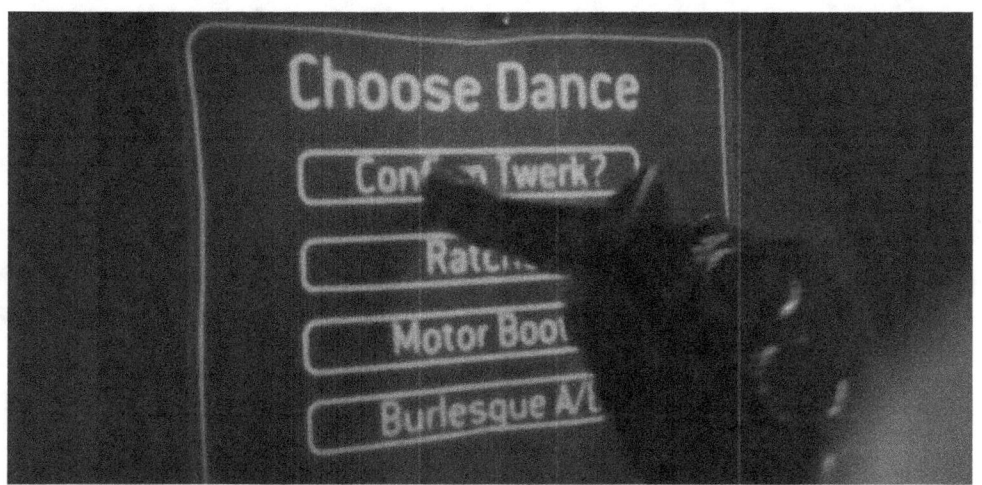

3.3 Excerpt from the video for "Primetime," by Janelle Monáe.

Monáe states, "The lesbian community has tried to claim me, but I only date androids."[50] Her embodiment borrows from Little Richard, another Black, queer, gender-non-conforming figure central to developing the style of rock and roll that Monáe's music follows at times. Given how her performance of an android is at times presented as her own life story, Monáe's gender presentation can be seen as a form of Taquiyya, a Shia form of what Nandita Biswas Mellamphy calls "hypercamouflage" that advocates complete invisibility through living among the enemy.[51] Cindi Mayweather's underground life in *The Electric Lady* follows this pattern.

In the video for "Primetime," Cindi Mayweather programs her android go-go dancers via a translucent interface that appears on the surface of their skin (figure 3.3). Offering a possible reimagining of the idea of *This Bridge Called My Back* as "This Interface Called My Back," the backs of these androids are interfaces for their types of movement, and the interfaces are translucent, able to be hidden or made visible in an instant. Throughout the video, translucent interfaces hover around the performers. While these interfaces have been made popular through films such as *Minority Report*, Monáe's use of them materializes a future that sees Black people as the skilled operators of ubiquitous computing devices. Cindi Mayweather's control over the transformation of her own body, through algorithmic digital processes of iteration, imagines the Black trans person with the ability to shift their shape and color outside of gender norms as the paradigmatic example of a futurity beyond the racialized optics of android hunting. This apocalypse is brought on by android intelligence surpassing that of humans, the singularity that, Monáe says, is her vision of the future.[52] In an interview with io9.com, Monáe articulates that her goal is not just to create speculative fiction, but to prepare people to be able to survive the impending future where android intelligence will surpass that of humans.[53] To do so, *Metropolis* relies on histories of slavery, colonization, and Black feminism to create models for resistance in a future in which computing devices not only surround us and surveil us but are on our backs. In Metropolis, algorithms constitute us. *We are algorithmic.*

Considering Sarah Kember and Joanna Zylinska's writing on intra-action of fields of mediation and identity, I propose that shifting brings to life their usage of the concept of originary technicity, the idea that the human is defined from the original moment of using tools such as flint to create fire or cave paintings to extend memory.[54] Responding to Bernard Stiegler, they say, "We are media."[55] They explain, "*What is important for us is . . . the acknowledgement of the mutual co-constitution of 'media' and 'us' along both cultural and neural lines, that is, the intertwined process of media coproduction.*"[56] The ability to shift makes a body into media. Shifting is a form of communication, of media, as anything that can change state can carry information. Further, the transformation of bodies is often facilitated by the addition of technologies to a body, such as administered hormones or lipstick. Emerging trans politics must account for more than visibility. They must also account for the forms of communication that visibility makes possible through shifting, including movement, shape-shifting, aurality, tactility, and texture.

The "temporal fluidity of media" and the "ontological (and semantic) indeterminacy" described by Kember and Zylinska are both made evident in the moment of shifting seen in Monáe's video for "Many Moons," in which Cindi Mayweather's skin color and body shape change in a moment.[57] Slowing the clip in video editing software makes clear its temporal fluidity, as it can be viewed at different speeds. Further, it portrays a body transforming, so the perception of time by that body may be seen as changing, or fluid, with respect to that of the viewer. The difference in before and after states, Cindi Mayweather's white and brown skin, allows the viewer to see the effect of a cut. In this case, one can consider the cut enacted by Cindi Mayweather's act of shifting as an ethical cut in that it allows for the potential of safety for a gender-non-conforming person of color. In the narrative, Cindi Mayweather's brown human skin of a Black woman masks the white skin of a hunted android, calling attention to the everyday racism that adds to gender-non-conforming people's precarity by inverting the values assigned to skin colors in our own time.

Digital Identity

The operation of shifting seen enacted by Black gender-non-conforming people in digital media allows a rethinking of the limits and potentials of contemporary feminism. Any feminism today that does not explicitly address the violence faced by transgender women of color is incomplete in that it reproduces that violence through exclusion. How can a trans of color feminism, a form of praxis that includes theory, activism, and cultural production, be created today to account for the historical lack of trans women in women of color feminism and the continuing fact that trans women of color are among the most common targets of violence among LGBTQI people in the United States? How can this movement be built in a moment being described as postidentity, postracial, and postfeminist? Any claims of "post-" rely on an imposition of temporality in which these categories might be able to be described as only in the past, as over: identity is over; racism is over; feminism is over. Keeling calls attention to the multiple temporalities of possibilities of queer and trans of color lives without violence when she asks, "Firmly rooted in our time, might we nevertheless feel, even without recognition, the rhythms of the poetry from a future in which M— might be? Might we allow those rhythms to move us to repel the quotidian violence through which we currently are defined without demanding of the future from which they come that it redeem our movements now or then?"[58]

To account for some of these claims of "post-," one can look to Keeling's work to reconcile women of color feminism with the contemporary regime of the digital image through the equation "I = Another." Advocating a digital identity politics, Keeling states, "'I = Another' does not jettison identification as a political strategy but introduces difference into the equation. . . . [T]his formulation of identity as difference captures the sense of transformation, rather than rupture, that characterizes many liberation movements in their contemporary configurations and describes the processes of identity and identification facilitated through the media that sustain, educate, challenge, and recollect those movements."[59] Keeling's equation can be seen as a simple form of algorithm, which are made up of a series of instructions, including variable declarations and flow control statements. Her description of the formulation points to the digital media that is constitutive of both individual and collective identities today.

Shifting can be seen in digital technologies in the fundamental operation of a bit shift. A bit is a single tiny switch inside a microchip that software interprets as a number: 0 or 1. A row of bits creates larger numbers, so eight bits allows numbers from 0 to 255 to be represented. A bit shift occurs when a numerical value is changed by turning the voltages in a given row of bits on and off to move each bit's value one down the row of bits. There are operators for shifting bits, called bitwise operators. In the C language, the left shift operator << moves all bits in a given number to the left, effectively multiplying that number by two without having to do any calculations.[60] For this reason, bit shifting operations are extremely fast operations, which is why they are frequently used in algorithms for computer graphics, compression, and cryptography. In addition, as these shifts are fundamental operations generated by compilers when human readable code is reduced to assembly language instructions, they are at the core of the algorithms of computer-generated imagery that render the frames that allow viewers to see Cindi Mayweather's skin changing from white to brown.

The operation of the shift can be seen as a basic element of algorithms, such as when bits are shifted to compute mathematical operations or when the contents of memory are shifted from one location to another in assignment statements. Circuits can also be used to embody algorithms, either with analog electronic components, such as wire and logic gates, or stitched conductive thread. While the cut, the shift, and, in the next chapter, the stitch are operators I propose as elements of a trans of color poetics, the algorithmic is an aspect of contemporary identities that both is within them and emerges from them. Algorithms constitute the media that inform how subjects and movements are formed and are created by those subjects on a daily basis as they form heuristics about how to interact with the world.

There are many dangers to consider when using an algorithm as a model of identity or as a description of a strategy for avoiding violence. Certainly, one does not want to be become an emotionless android who simply follows a program. Further, the danger of internalizing the very tools being used to control populations by contemporary governments seems clear. My aim in introducing the algorithmic as a concept to model movement, identity, and oppression is to take advantage of mental models available in order to theorize and strategize with them. While I recognize that the algorithm is a tool that can be used for oppression or for liberation, it is still a model available for thought, like mathematics, physics, or physical metaphors. As I elaborated in chapter 1, algorithms can be useful models outside the realm of the digital when one considers the similarity of algorithms, recipes, and rituals.

Code Poetry Library

Algorithmic methods are useful model sfor mentally modeling phenomena in which a single object or function can include multiple variables that change their values over time. To make algorithmic analysis more concrete for readers unfamiliar with coding, I offer two algorithms in the form of poetry. Perhaps the clearest intersection of algorithms and poetics, code poetry is a genre of poetry in which the author uses the format of computer programming languages to evoke the multiple meanings at play in poetry. I see code poetry as emerging from the strands of new media art that are concerned with exploring the materiality of digital media through artistic experimentation. For example, Jodi.org, the art collective made up of Joan Heemskerk and Dirk Paesmans, created artworks such as their website, which uses the conventions of HTML code to question modes of representation, as the artwork looks like random characters in a browser but displays a diagram of a nuclear weapon when one views the source code of the page.[61] Artists such as Mez Breeze, whose work I discuss in *The Transreal* as an example of performativity of multiple simultaneous identities, has created her own poetic language, called Mezangelle. She has been writing poems using the conventions of programming language to experiment with new ways of enfolding layers of meaning in her work since 1993 and has won numerous awards in literature and virtual reality.[62] Some code poetry is actually executable by machines, but Breeze's is not. Recent books such as Ian Hatcher's *Prosthesis* also use conventions of code to create poetry that meditates on glitch aesthetics through language. Denis Jaromil Rojo is an artist who writes executable code poems, such as this code for a fork bomb, which, when run in an ASCII command line shell can disable a computer by forking, or making copies of itself, and quickly consuming all of its memory:

```
: (){: |: & }; :
```

This poem has been exhibited as a new media artwork at festivals and in museums, including at the Transmediale festival at the Haus der Kulturen der Welt in Berlin.[63] In one sense, this line of code is considered poetry because of its virtuosity, an elegant compression of a powerful action. Poems such as these can be considered experimental concrete poetry, where the spacing and layout of the text adds to its meaning. In a poetic mode I have described both Keeling's black femme function and Monáe's ability to dance between identities through code poetry in my performance of "Femme Disturbance" at the Hemispheric Institute of Performance and Politics' symposium "Digital Humanities: Creative Activism in the Age of Digital Technologies."[64] The artist who most inspired these poems was Zach Blas, whose Transcoder library imagined fictional names for functions based on theorists such as Michel Foucault and Jack Halberstam. My code poems follow. One can read them as literal code or as one would read poetry, without expecting to understand the full meaning of every symbol or space:

```
femmeDisturbance.keeling.blackFemmeFunction () {
    delete visibility;
    if( commonSense.disrupt(racist) &&
       commonSense.disrupt(sexist) &&
       commonSense.disrupt(heteronormative) )
    {

        //once these forms of commonsense have been disrupted
        //exit this entire computational paradigm and
        //split off into a new imaginary computational system
        //yet to be defined
        fork(blackFemme(revolutionary, anticapitalist));
    }
}


femmeDisturbance.janelleMonae.flickerBetweenRealities(){
    //initialize
    delete race;
    delete gender;
    delete humanity;

    //flicker
    while ( perform(androidNotHuman) ) {
        miscegenate( human );
        //literally
        go(insane);
        danceDefyingGravity();
    }
}
```

In these two short poems, I use the syntax of C++ code, or Java code, poetically to express concepts from the work of Keeling and Monáe. At the risk of explaining away the poetry, I will describe a bit of the algorithmic poetics at work. The poems are described as a library, referring to libraries in programming languages, named groups of functions and classes. The poems have the syntax of a class declaration, used to create objects in C++ or Java. While the code could compile, given the proper header file inclusion, its meaning comes from the names I assign to variables and functions more than from what it would do as code. I elaborate each poem as a function. The first plays on Keeling's notion of the black femme function in *The Witch's Flight*.[65] Both poems use the C++ operator "delete," which is used to delete objects from memory and automatically call their destructor functions. Java has no such operators, as memory reclaiming (called garbage collection) is handled automatically. The first operation of the black femme function, as I have poetically programmed it, is to delete visibility. This refers to Keeling's statement that the black femme exceeds what is possible for cinematic representations to make visible. The poems also call functions of my own imagining, such as danceDefyingGravity(). As the function declaration is not part of the poem, the reader is left to imagine the computational translation of this performative act seen in Monáe's "Many Moons" video. Code poetry performs the indeterminate aesthetic of poetry through the multiple temporalities of the algorithm. The poem can be read in order of execution as a textual poem or as a structural concrete poem.

These two code poems provide an example of how one might code a poetic algorithm for shifting. The functions blackFemmeFuction and flickerBetweenRealities are two gestures of trans of color poetics, inspired by how Black gender-non-conforming people disrupt normative regimes of visibility, including the Black queer femmes who exceed normative femininity, described by Keeling, and Monáe's performances that defy masculine/feminine distinctions. Shifting here has multiple simultaneous levels of meaning and action. The deletion of variables and the comparison of truth values at the executable level of code literally cause bits to shift. The theoretical gestures poetically described, such as disrupting racist claims to common sense, involve shifts in perception and conceptions of reality. In the video, the android Cindi Mayweather is performing for a cheering audience at the site of an android auction, which has the appearance of an augmented reality catwalk at a fashion show, with overtones of a slave auction. Monáe's gravity-defying dancing is a form of movement that depicts the experience gender-non-conforming Black people have of escaping a violently racialized and gendered social environment through dance.[66]

Conclusion

By considering the operation of shifting, seen in trans of color media, the possibilities of algorithmic analysis unfold. Looking to an algorithmic model of identity that can represent shifting, we can extend "I = Another" with "I = x." Here "x" is a variable that can change over time, iteratively, perhaps being replaced with possibilities Keeling offers, such as "you," "us," or "I."[67] This simple algorithm can be understood to describe the multiple possible futures described by Keeling. By focusing on the moment of shifting, as made visible by Monáe, the algorithmic moment of changing identities and embodiments replaces any static identification. One could look to the assembly language instructions that might make up a line of C code, such as "x = 1," to see the inner workings of this moment of identity, or the voltages that make up lines of assembly language that Wendy Chun uses to point blur the distinctions of analog and digital.[68] Or one could look to the pixel color and location-blending algorithms of software that create digital video morphs such as those in Monáe's video, or the video compression algorithms in the code of the Netflix player that create the illusion of smooth movement in Cox's scenes in *Orange Is the New Black*, or the JavaScript code that makes the media in the online companion to this book play in the browser.[69] Or, in an effort to decolonize technology, one could understand an algorithm for shifting between identities to be a series of steps, describable in any number of languages, as a prayer, a ritual, or a game. Doing so provides a path toward a decolonial strategy for identity shifting that can evade the colonial logics of necropolitics.

Through the example of Janelle Monáe's science fiction concept album *Metropolis*, the music videos that accompany the album, and my own code poetry, I have proposed the shift as a form of movement that trans and gender-non-conforming people of color use for safety. The shift is a material/conceptual operation to add to the operations of the cut and the fold. These modes of being between visible and invisible have particular relevance for contemporary necropolitical situations, which seek to restrict movement to ensure death for trans people of color. Learning from science fiction in digital media, one can see into the moment of shifting, which offers multiple possible futures. By looking at shifting over time, I articulate an algorithmic model of analysis that can be abstracted to have uses beyond digital technologies.

Toward the end of "Many Moons," Cindi Mayweather begins to list forms of social violence directed at her communities:

Civil rights, civil war
Hood rat, crack whore
Carefree, nightclub
Closet drunk, bathtub
Outcast, weirdo
Stepchild, freak show
Black girl, bad hair

The listed items range from broad structural issues to the personal manifestations of anti-Black hatred. She begins to dance harder and harder until she ascends into the air. Her algorithm is malfunctioning, and the audience is confused. She floats in a moment of transcendence while the audience looks up at her. She slowly floats down to the floor. The last image of her shows her eyes flickering with electricity, then she falls still. The words of the song state:

And when the world just treats you wrong
Just come with us and we'll take you home
Shan, shan shan shan-gri la.[70]

Cindi Mayweather uses the shifting of her skin color from white to brown to build a community and inspire social action. Rather than simply hiding herself, she is performing on the stage of a rich media ecology, calling her audiences to rebel against the forms of violence they face, even though the performance causes her to go beyond her own limits and fall. The softness of the sound of her voice singing those last lines, over electronic sounds that seem to come from a future place free from violence, are inviting and caring. The video ends with the quote, "I imagined many moons in the sky lighting the way to freedom," attributed to Cindi Mayweather. Here Cindi Mayweather is imagined as an android Harriet Tubman of the future, leading people to freedom by moonlight. Monáe's shifting shows crucial aspects of trans of color poetics, where trans and gender-non-conforming people of color share survival strategies of modulating visibility with their communities, imagining futures of liberation that learn from histories of struggle against racial and gender oppression.

THE EXPERIENCE OF SHIFTING FOUR

YOU WAKE UP IN THE MORNING. You are a tiny pixel art avatar of a Black woman in her bedroom. Around you are small, simple pixel representations of a bed, a bookshelf, a dresser, and a table. Your viewpoint of the scene is from overhead, and you can see the other rooms in your apartment, including the bathroom, the living room, and the kitchen. You can use the arrow keys to move up, down, left, or right and the spacebar to interact with objects. Now you have to decide: What will you wear today? Will you put on makeup? Heels? You remember that you have plans to see a friend for coffee. What route will you walk to get to the coffee shop? *Mainichi* is a digital game made by Mattie Brice (figure 4.1) that places the player in this scenario from Brice's life, using algorithms to enact a trans of color poetics.[1] The representation of her morning is intimate and nuanced. You learn that she does not like the cold. She comes up with an idea for a video game while shaving her legs in the bathtub. In *Mainichi* you can play video games before going out for coffee. If you do, she makes a comment about Fenris, a gay character from the game *Dragon Age* for PlayStation 3 who was an example of queer representation in games.[2] Depending on the choices you make of what to wear and how to walk to the coffee shop, you may encounter people who scream racialized, transphobic comments at you. You can experience small moments of being misgendered by a barista. You can talk to your friend for support. Then

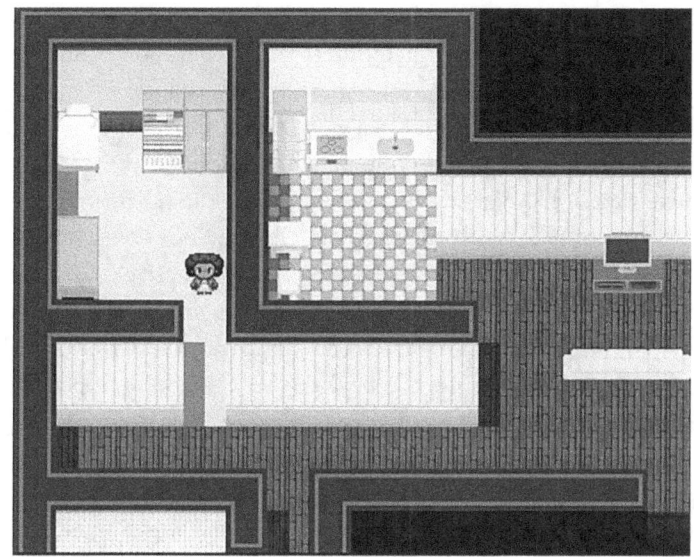

4.1 Game screen shot from *Mainichi*, by Mattie Brice.

the game's looping narrative ends, and you wake up in the morning, again. Depending on the choices you made, it is possible that yesterday you experienced racialized, gendered violence as you were walking down the street to get coffee. What choices will you make today? Will you be able to avoid violence? There are many layers of first-person experience in this moment. Brice created the game to depict her first-person experience of violence. Her intended audience was a friend who Brice wanted to better understand her experience. Further, I am writing about *Mainichi* because parts of it resonate with my own experiences of gendered violence in public spaces. In addition, the player experiences the game from a first-person narrative perspective where they are in control of the avatar.

This chapter considers two digital games by trans women of color: Brice's *Mainichi* and my *Redshift and Portalmetal*, by myself. Both take personal experiences of shifting and transform them into poetic algorithms that reach beyond voyeuristic empathy toward acts of solidarity. Shifting is an operation of trans of color poetics, as I discussed in previous chapters, where a person changes their appearance, form, or location for safety and survival. Changing one's appearance to feel, or be, safe is a daily experience for many people, including many trans women of color. *Mainichi* invites players to have an experience of how choosing to wear different clothing or accessories can change one's daily experience of violence. *Redshift* allows players to consider how migration, shifting one's location, may also increase or decrease one's safety and has deep implications for decolonial struggle. Both of these games describe the experience of shifting, which differs from seeing someone else shape-shift, as in the videos by Janelle Monáe described in chapter 3.

The experience of playing a character in a game differs from, for example, watching a character in a novel, play, or film, in which the audience watches a character make decisions. Narrative games can take digital forms, like Brice's game, but are not necessarily digital. The "Choose Your Own Adventure" series of books that I read as a child also create an interactive narrative. Interactive narratives can be simple text-only games, graphical games such as *Mainichi*, or elaborate AAA video games with massive production budgets. The interactive quality of games can be thought of as a kind of performance, where the player is invited to perform a character. This is not unique to games, though, and there are many other interactive forms, from Theater of the Oppressed to interactive films such as *Bandersnatch* on Netflix. Games change the nature of experience: having agency in a game allows one to feel closer to a first-person experience of a given phenomenon. Games use experience as a medium, not only crafting visual images, sound, and text, but also using time-based poetics to craft an affective experience. Trans of color artists such as Brice and I use digital games to bring players into first-person experiences of transphobic violence that we have lived through. In these works, trans of color poetics are a method of transforming first-person experiences into digital artworks that allow players to feel, to a far lesser degree, the acts of violence we have experienced, as well as the methods of survival we have learned. Theories of first-person experience from trans, queer, and feminist scholars can shed light on how these layers of code and media form a poetics.

First-person experience can be a useful starting point for designing digital games as practice-based research in ways that go beyond empathy, a fraught goal for artists and designers, toward solidarity, which demands concrete action. Through the experience of shifting one can gain knowledge; thus, shifting can be a method of practice-based research. A central premise of practice-based research is that by experiencing an act, one can learn something different from what one might learn from reading about it.[3] Numerous fields have interrogated the practice of theorizing first-person experience, including phenomenology, transgender studies, and digital humanities. I first consider *Mainichi* to think about the limits of the ability of games to create empathy. Brice's performance of "empathy machine," using *Mainichi* in an intimate performance, crystallizes this critique. I then describe my game *Redshift*, which uses transreal aesthetics to protect the artist from intrusive viewers, eschewing empathy in favor of acts of solidarity, both in the performance of the work and in what is asked of the players.[4] In this chapter, I focus on media that depicts shifting in the lived experience of trans women of color. Continuing this book's method of algorithmic analysis, I look at how artists are creating algorithms to perform the repetition of violence and methods of surviving violence.

To create an algorithm, one can start by listing the components involved in the phenomena being considered, then list how those components interact. The components are like variables in software—spaces in memory that change over time, *shifting*. The components' interactions can be described through lines of code that are *stitched* together by rules of syntax. The act of creating algorithms is both analytic and creative. Writing an algorithm can be poetic. There are many ways that one can choose to represent a particular phenomenon as an algorithm. Different algorithms can represent different aspects of a phenomenon at different levels of granularity and detail.[5] Intersectionality describes one kind of relation between parts, the co-occurrence or simultaneity of existence of two or more elements in the same person. Algorithms extend this possibility, allowing one to list components and then describe the relationship among them as a series of steps or decisions. Taking heed of the concerns of Black feminists such as Brittney Cooper, my intention is not to move on from intersectionality or displace Black women's academic contributions.[6] Instead, I am proposing this model to contribute to the ongoing dialogue about the relationships among digital technologies, race, and feminism developed in the work of Black feminist scholars such as Simone Browne, Jessica Marie Johnson, and Kara Keeling.[7] That dialogue has arisen, in part, in response to the violent context of digital games online.

The genre of personal experience games was described by game studies scholars before it came to public attention. One can see the idea described in the essay "Videogames of the Oppressed" (2004), in which Gonzalo Frasca writes, "I claim that video games could indeed deal with human relationships and social issues, while encouraging critical thinking. . . . I explore the possibilities of non-Aristotelian game design, mainly based on the work of drama theorist Augusto Boal."[8] In *Gaming: Essays on Algorithmic Culture*, Alexander Galloway points to this essay by Frasca as the beginning of a new theoretical project for game studies to move beyond representation: "Game studies should follow these same arguments and not turn to a theory of realism in gaming as mere realistic representation, but define realist games as those games that reflect critically on the minutiae of everyday life, replete as it is with struggle, personal drama, and injustice."[9] Galloway posits realism as linked to an attention to oppression when he defines realism as "a documentary-like attention to the everyday struggles of the disenfranchised, leading to a direct criticism of current social policy."[10] Frasca goes on to describe online communities dedicated to people telling stories about the forms of oppression they face in their everyday lives through games, and others modifying the games or making games in response. Frasca presciently describes a situation much like the Twine game community that has emerged since 2012. Twine is open source game creation software that has supported the creation of the genre of personal games and has been used to powerful effect by such transgender game designers as Brice, Merritt K, and Anna Anthropy.[11] Twine is designed for creating simple text-based games, which are interactive narratives. Game designers have used its features to create branching stories, animated text, and beautifully written poems, with many endings from which to choose. Using Twine, authors can employ a graphical interface to create algorithmic media, including games and interactive literature. The Twine interface allows one to create interactive branching narratives with a limitless number of choices. In addition, Twine includes a simple programming language that the authors I discuss use to create dynamic systems such as inventory systems, or choices that change based on players' previous choices. Twine is similar to RPG Maker, the software Brice used to create *Mainichi*, in that its purpose is to make game creation more accessible to more people.

Depictions of personal experience were at the heart of the personal game genre that came to popular attention around 2012. Anna Anthropy, a trans woman game designer, published her book *Rise of the Videogame Zinesters* in 2012, in which she described her own games created about personal narratives such as *Calamity Annie*, a game she made in 2008 about trying to get her girlfriend to stop drinking. In the book, she advocates for a proliferation of small, inexpensively made games, like the photocopied zines in her title, to allow for many more viewpoints to be depicted in the games industry, which, she claims, had very narrowly depicted the interests of a mostly homogeneous group of white heterosexual men.[12] In April 2013, the game critic Leigh Alexander wrote an article about a panel at the Different Games conference that included both Anthropy and Brice.[13] Alexander described the "personal games movement" as a new and exciting way to understand expression and design.[14] Many of these games, including *Dys4ia*, by Anna Anthropy; and *Depression Quest*, by Zoë Quinn, use simple aesthetics of plain text and pixel art to share very private, personal struggles with the player.[15] This genre brings together the feminist, trans, and queer approaches that value personal experience with the performative affordances of digital games.[16]

Dys4ia describes the personal experiences of a trans woman. It includes intimate details of moments of discrimination in doctors' offices, conflicts with people who should be allies, tender moments of connection, and bits of conversation between girlfriends. These games are powerful emotional experiences. *Mainichi* adds a trans of color experience to the genre, considering the intersectionality of oppression of trans women of color, while *Redshift* adds embodied performativity through performances on video.

As I was writing this book and creating the games I describe here, the #GamerGate movement was spreading (and continues to spread) hate online, including rape and death threats, doxxing, and swatting of game developers and critics who are female, people of color, queer, and trans.[17] The year 2014 saw the digital games community attacking female game developers online en masse, and these acts continue in 2020.[18] Much of this is a hateful response to the increasing diversity of digital games, an attempt to stop the growth of new stories in games about queer people, trans people, and people of color. Zoë Quinn, an early target of the #GamerGate movement, has linked its online hate campaigns to the election of Donald Trump. Similarly, the journalists Erin Carson and Ian Sherr make that link, describing how some of the same people involved in #GamerGate were later more visibly involved in what has been called the "alt-right," the rise of neo-Nazis and white supremacists emboldened by Trump's election.[19] These examples show the importance of deeply considering the intersections of race, gender, and algorithms that are present in digital games.

Mainichi—Beyond Empathy

Mainichi allows the player to simulate the experience of shifting that trans women of color experience every day, choosing how to modulate their visibility by choosing how to adorn their body. Unlike mainstream video games that often take tens of hours to complete, *Mainichi* is a short game that takes about fifteen minutes. Brice says *Mainichi* is like a "zine," the short, photocopied, do-it-yourself publishing form popular among feminists and punks referred to in Anthropy's book.[20] She also says that she does not see her work in the indie game genre, describing herself as "an independent, medium-agnostic game designer."[21] In the first stage of the game, as I described at the opening of the chapter, the player must choose how to get ready in the morning. The first stage results in the character—a small, pixelated Black female avatar—having a certain appearance based on the player's choices: wearing earrings or not, wearing high heels or not. These choices, the small details of shifting one's appearance about which trans people make decisions every day, have consequences for the next stage.

The second stage of the game takes the player out to the street, walking to meet a friend for coffee. This is where the decisions made in the first stage come into play. Other characters comment on your appearance. They turn their heads to look at you. The experiences you have walking down the street are both racialized and gendered, as when a nonplayer character asks to touch your hair. Brice identifies herself as a Black trans woman, and the avatar in the game shares her name.[22] In addition, as the game description states, it is a depiction of daily experiences from her own life. She goes on to state, "It stands as a commentary of how we currently use game design for broad strokes of universal experiences instead of the hyper-personal, and often exclude minority voices."[23] In the third stage, the player enters a coffee shop and continues to try to make decisions to avoid the violence of transphobia, such as whether to use cash or a credit card.

Brice's *Mainichi* game is an example of theory in practice that brings to life concerns that have been expressed by transgender studies for decades. In *Invisible Lives*, Viviane Namaste says of queer theory that "the field's neglect of the social and economic conditions in which transgendered [sic] people live makes it of questionable political import."[24] In contrast, she argues for theory based in the lived experience of transgender people. She states, "This approach is not a naive appeal to an untheorized or unproblematized category of 'experience.' It is, rather, a recognition that theory needs to emerge from the everyday social world and that it must be practically relevant to the people about whom it speaks."[25] Thus, we can understand transgender studies as theorizing from lived experience, but in a complex way that accounts for histories of feminist inquiry, queer theory, sociology, and ethnography. Recent scholarship in transgender studies has begun to account for both the whiteness of the origins of the field and "its geographic and historical location as the product of a largely North American settler culture."[26] Part of that project "highlights the multiple legacies of the European colonial project globally as they apply to gender-nonconforming knowledge and *life*."[27] I see the emerging transgender studies in strong relation to fields such as Black studies, women's studies, and ethnic studies that build from the experiences of people affected by structural violence. Similarly, I see trans of color poetics in the tradition of Augusto Boal's Theater of the Oppressed, which uses experiences of oppression as a ground from which to find agency in transforming the world through poetic practices. While one response to queer theory was to develop a transgender studies that was more engaged in activism to improve lives, another response was to account for the lack of consideration of the lives of people of color in queer theory itself.

Authors writing queer of color critique have theorized Black trans women's experiences of shifting. Roderick Ferguson's discussion of the "transgender mulatta" is an example of "polymorphous nonheteronormative formations," which "in the 1930s, . . . were racialized in terms of urban black racial and cultural difference."[28] Ferguson discusses how a mixed-race trans woman is seen as the strongest example of the potential of migration to disrupt heteropatriarchal gender and sexual norms. His discussion of how Black gender and sexuality are seen as non-normative resonates with Che Gossett's claim that Black studies, trans studies, and Indigenous studies are inseparable, in that Black expressions of gender challenge white Western gender binaries in ways that trouble the concept of trans.[29] Distinctions between trans and drag become racialized when one considers that low-income Black queer people have less access to hormones, surgery, therapy, and academia, all of which make identifications such as transgender safer for white people. Ferguson's description of a scene of a party in which a mixed-race trans woman is seen singing and her song makes space for other acts of gender fluidity is a depiction of how trans of color performances of shifting can transform a room, making space for other acts of gender transgression.

Queer of color critique engages with performance studies in important ways that inform trans of color poetics. José Muñoz describes disidentification as a kind of shifting: "Disidentification . . . understands that . . . a politicized agent must have the ability to adapt and shift as quickly as power does within discourse."[30] Focusing on disidentification may lead one to think less of those who value identification, but Muñoz states that identification is part of disidentification and that the everyday identification required for survival is itself a brave and fierce act. Discussing the drag performer Vaginal Davis, Muñoz writes, "Both modalities of performing the self, disidentification and passing, are often strategies of survival. (As the case of Davis and others suggests, often these modes of performance allow much more than mere survival, and subjects fully come into subjectivity in ways that are both ennobling and fierce)."[31] Disidentification, like shifting, privileges movement over fixity, focuses on tactical identifications over rigid identity categories. Trans of color poetics learn from disidentification by starting with identities that shift, flicker, and morph. The character in *Mainichi* shifts her appearance depending on the choices made by the player. If the player chooses to put on makeup, heels, and nice clothes, some interactions with non-player characters change. These interactions include being properly gendered and receiving compliments on your appearance, but they also include unwanted advances from strangers on the street. Yet there is no way to prevent the man from screaming that you are a man if you get too close to him. Through multiple play throughs, you learn to avoid people in the street, shifting your walking route, if you do not want to experience violent harassment.

Trans and queer responses to phenomenology are particularly useful for a consideration of games about personal experience by trans game designers who are people of color. Brice describes *Mainichi* as "an experiment in sharing a personal experience through a game system. It helps communicate daily occurances [*sic*] that happen in my life, exploring the difficulty in expressing these feelings in words."[32] *Mainichi* has a phenomenological level of detail. The game play consists of moments many would consider minute, inconsequential. As I described at the beginning of the chapter, the initial scene is the interior of an apartment, with a table, bed, dresser, bathtub, and mirror. The scene could easily recall Sara Ahmed's discussion in *Queer Phenomenology* of the role of tables in philosophy.[33] Describing her experience of writing, Ahmed begins by describing the table at which she is sitting. Phenomenology is a branch of Western philosophy that has attempted to systematize the transformation of individual experience into knowledge.

The experience of shifting can be a learned response to external forces of structural violence that are disorienting. Ahmed writes, "Phenomenology can offer a resource for queer studies insofar as it emphasizes the importance of lived experience, the intentionality of consciousness, the significance of nearness or what is ready-to-hand, and the role of repeated and habitual actions in shaping bodies and worlds."[34] She describes Frantz Fanon's decolonial interventions into phenomenology in ways that resonate strongly for trans of color lives: "Disorientation involves becoming an object. It is from this point, the point at which the body becomes an object, that Fanon's phenomenology of the Black body begins."[35] For trans people of color, the disorientation of becoming an object may begin with the experience of a racialized life and be further confounded by the process of living through gender dysphoria, identifying as transgender and becoming a medicalized subject, an object of study to be evaluated for disorder by a therapist, endocrinologist, or police officer. Ahmed goes on to say, "By implication, we learn that disorientation is unevenly distributed: some bodies more than others have their involvement in the world called into crisis."[36] The uneven distribution of crisis calls to mind the contemporary #BlackLivesMatter movements for justice for Black people murdered by police, or the disproportionate number of deaths of Black people from COVID-19.[37] The fact that Black trans people have been the number-one target of murder in the United States among LGBTQ people for years demonstrates the widespread "involvement in the world called into crisis" that Black trans people experience as the threat of murder on a daily basis, from both police and civilians. Gossett sees the violence of colonialism, transphobia, and anti-Blackness as inextricable, saying, "Terms like 'cisgender' ultimately lack the explanatory power to account for the colonial and anti-Black foundational violence of slavery and indigenous genocide through which the gender binary itself was historically instituted. For me, trans studies begins in/as Black and Native studies."[38] Gossett points to the importance of acknowledging lived experience, saying, "Rather than leaving anti-blackness and the scholarship that attends to it, as well as black/ African Palestinian lived experience, in the 'position of the unthought,' it seems to me that political solidarity can only be strengthened by grappling with these topics."[39] Gossett's work links the lived experience of violence that Black trans people experience to the structures that support those forms of violence, including the prison-industrial complex, necropolitics, and colonialism.

The experience of violence that results in a multiplicity of being afflicts trans people of color, and one can see that multiplicity in the acts of shifting offered to the player of *Mainichi*. Shifting is one way to represent identity as multiple, in process, and in movement. In one moment of the game, as the player is walking down the street, a man nearby steps into your path and begins to flirt with you. First, he says "What's up, pretty?" Then he steps backward and yells, "Holy shit, YOU'RE A MAN! FUCK!" (figure 4.2). The moment echoes a scene similar to the murder of Sakia Gunn, discussed in the chapter 3, but with a trans woman game character instead of a butch lesbian, as Gunn has been described.[40] Fortunately, you can walk away from the man. He does not physically assault you but continues screaming "THAT'S SOME-ONE'S *SON* . . . DID YOU SEE IT!? WATCH OUT FOR THAT MAN!" Before this moment, it is possible that the player might not have known that they were playing a trans woman. Ahmed states, "We learn about the experience of disorientation, as the experience . . . of being shattered, of being cut into pieces by the hostility of the white gaze."[41] This description aptly describes the experience of racialized transphobic violence, in which one's racialized gender expression is not accepted as valid or real by an onlooker who directs violence toward oneself, and one's response is to feel outside of oneself and one's body. The moment of not passing always involves the interplay of gen-

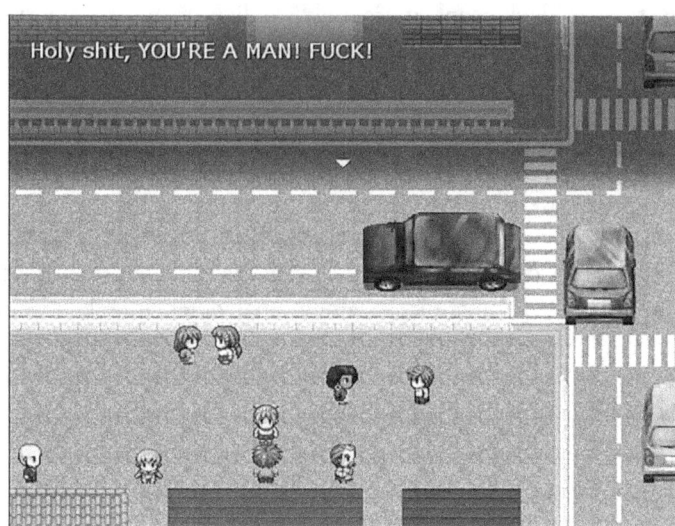

4.2 Game screen shot from *Mainichi*, by Mattie Brice.

der and race, as gendered attributes are racialized and are historically and geopolitically specific. To recognize and register the violence directed against one's gender expression, you must imagine the opinion of the other that does not accept your gender identity, or you must hear it spoken to you, or feel it taken out on your flesh, and any of these experiences requires one to be outside of the immanent moment of living your gender as presented through your racialized embodiment. Being violently torn out of one's reality can be felt as disorientation. In a blog post, Brice describes her racial identification as complex, a kind of "double-bind": "I think it's a mistake, especially with blackness, to not see the identity itself in a diaspora, spread far and integrated, surviving, in different ways."[42] Both of her parents were from the Caribbean, she states. "Enough people bothered me enough that my lineages became a chant of sorts: 'Jamaican, Indian, German, Trinidadian, Palestinian, and Venezuelan.' Did I really feel like I was from any of these countries? No, not really, I described myself as distinctly American, which I didn't understand meant assimilating with a particular white, middle class-ness."[43] Brice's Caribbean heritage, in diaspora, recalls Édouard Glissant's poetics of relation, which see the network of islands in the Caribbean and the resulting cultures and diasporas from it, as a basis for a poetics of mutually coconstituted entities.

Like Brice, I am multiracial: my mother's ancestry is from Ireland, and my father's is from Colombia. In the moment of playing *Mainichi* and experiencing violence I felt a splitting into many feelings at once, including a mix of fear and sadness, a feeling of connection with the author at having similar experiences, and a deep resonance in realizing that this game was depicting experiences I had had so many times that I had never seen before in a game. My own experiences of racialization cause a further splitting of my experience, as my father is from Colombia, but I am often perceived as white. While I refuse to cede my own *latinidad* to the perceptions of ignorant people, it does mean that I experience a great deal of light-skinned privilege, which makes my lived experience very different from Brice's experiences in *Mainichi*.

Scholars working in transgender studies have introduced valuable ways of holding the complexity of the lived experiences of trans people. Moving from experiences of disorientation to experiences of uncertainty, Gayle Salamon sees the work of phenomenology as useful for transgender politics. She states, "I seek to challenge the notion that the materiality of the body is something to which we have unmediated access, something of which we can have epistemological certainty, and contend that such epistemological uncertainty can have great use, both ethically and politically, in the lives of the non-normatively gendered."[44] Her work extends the work of both phenomenology and psychoanalysis to thoroughly complicate any simple conception that knowledge can be transparently and directly gleaned from experience. She challenges claims by trans people of the truth of their "felt sense" of their bodies by claiming that "the body itself is, finally, a mixture or amalgam of substance and ideal located somewhere between its objectively quantifiable materiality and its phantasmatic extensions into the world."[45] Her analysis powerfully calls into question what it means to feel one's body and the ways we make meaning of those feelings through language. Similarly, Sandy Stone's "The Empire Strikes Back" advocates the value of experience, but in ways that can account for its complexity, its splitting and multiplicity. Stone describes the history of trans people wanting to pass and, to do so, constructing fictional life stories that match their current gender, rather than their actual experiences of growing up assigned a gender that did not match their feelings. Describing the perils of erasing trans people's life histories, Stone says, "What is lost is the ability to authentically represent the complexities and ambiguities of lived experience, . . . the *intertextual* possibilities of the transsexual body."[46] The intertextuality of the trans body may come from the way that it can reflect different narratives over time, the way that shifting from one narrative about the body to another opens up a network of meanings. She also refers to "the chaos of lived gendered experience" as an important foundation for the field of transgender studies.[47] Stone's account speaks a great deal about the kind of knowledge that can be gained from experience,

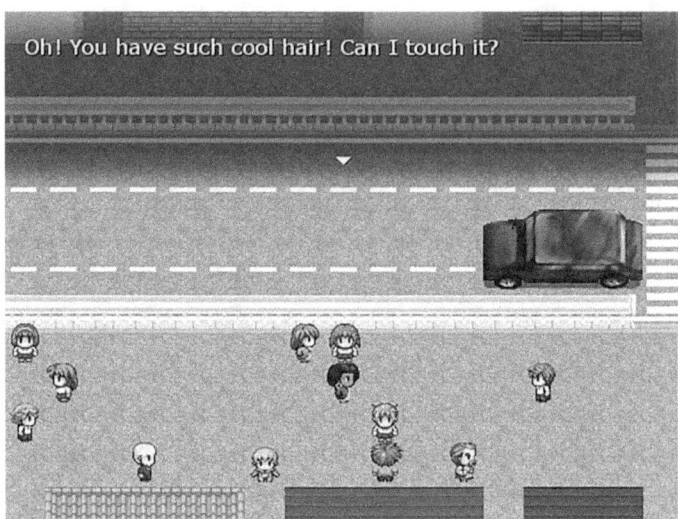

Oh! You have such cool hair! Can I touch it?

4.3 Game screen
shot from *Mainichi*,
by Mattie Brice.

the kind that is complex, ambiguous, chaotic, and intertextual, which may
lend itself to forms of expression such as performance and poetry, which can
hold these qualities without flattening them out into singularity, clarity, and
order. Stone speaks of the value of the "multiple contradictions of individual
lived experience," which are made visible in the moment of shifting, such as
the desire to choose to dress as one chooses in *Mainichi* versus the need to
avoid violence (figure 4.3).[48]

Brice describes the importance of using a game as her medium to communicate her experience to players. She states, "I knew that current attempts of
doling out social awareness just through story devices plainly didn't work. I
had to choose methods of design to communicate the feelings of my experience to the player, because otherwise I could simply point them to an essay
I've done. I would say *Mainichi* lets someone feel rather than tells them what
to feel."[49] Brice distinguishes between linear narratives, which tell stories,
and the interactive narratives of games, which, she says, allow the player to
feel some of what she feels when having these experiences.

Can algorithms bring about empathy? The artist and game theorist Celia
Pearce complicates the question of how games create empathy, saying games
"replace the classic Aristotelian techniques of mimesis and empathy with the
game specific technique of agency by giving the player 'avatars' that serve as
representatives for his or her own actions."[50] She contrasts games with other
forms of media, saying, "Empathy/mimesis requires the development of
highly constructed and authored characters with which viewers develop an

empathic bond."[51] She sees this in contrast to agency in games, which "creates a container for players to inhabit. Avatars must by definition have a certain level of ambiguity in their characters in order to allow the players to transpose or project themselves into them."[52] Where Pearce differentiates between empathy and agency, Brice claims that through agency players can gain empathy for the avatar. The question of how to bring a player or viewer into an experience in order for them to feel something similar to a character through empathy is linked to how players experience agency in a game. Even with some degree of agency to make choices, one is still told a story in *Mainichi*, and one's agency is fairly limited. The player cannot choose, for example, to not be transgender. The rarity of this underscores the importance of *Mainichi* in a massive field of digital games that almost never offer users a choice to be transgender. *Mainichi* escapes the very logics and conditions of possibility that shape most digital games—namely, the demand to profit from appealing to as large an audience as possible. Brice's work is an example of how artists can follow lines of inquiry that are less subject to the demands of capitalist markets and create novel and powerful experiences.[53]

Artists and scholars have raised strong concerns about how empathy is taken uncritically as a goal in games. Jonathan Belman and Mary Flanagan have done detailed research on the design principles involved in fostering empathy in players, focusing on efforts to reduce racism and sexual assault. They state, "Games are well-suited to this because they allow players to inhabit the roles of other people in a uniquely immersive way."[54] Using the language of Belman and Flanagan's study, *Mainichi* can be described as a game designed to induce parallel cognitive and emotional empathy, with low-involvement inductions, through a perspective-taking exercise. Cognitive empathy involves learning skills, while emotional empathy involves sharing feelings. Methods for creating agency are referred to as inductions, and low-involvement inductions include those that last for short periods of time. In contrast, the face-to-face workshops over a period of years involved in my project *Local Autonomy Networks (Autonets)* can be said to be fostering parallel empathy through high-involvement inductions. Parallel empathy is a kind of emotional empathy that describes when the observer—or player, in this case—expresses feelings similar to the feelings being observed. Both high and low involvement inductions have been shown to have a significant effect on empathy.[55] Live performances with audience involvement and three-hour workshops based on *Redshift* can be seen as having more involvement than playing *Redshift* online. *Mainichi* can be seen as an example of Belman and Flanagan's design principle of encouraging both cognitive and emotional empathy, as players have to figure out how to avoid violence while learning about the kinds of feelings trans people of color experience daily. Yet Belman and Flanagan's study raises serious concerns about empathy. They observe that if players are not encouraged to empathize—what they call an empathy induction—then when they are presented with stories of suffering they may find them entertaining.[56] They also describe how efforts to bring about empathy can backfire: if the player feels too much identification with the subject of a story—for instance, in a story about a person contracting HIV—it can cause even more negative attitudes toward the subject.[57] In addition, they describe a study that shows that "some bullies have superior perspective-taking abilities" and use that form of cognitive empathy, without emotional empathy, to cause further psychological harm to their targets.[58] There are many reasons to be cautious when trying to design games for empathy. As these studies deal with gendered and racial stereotypes, as well as stereotypes about people with HIV, they are particularly relevant for any poetics attempting to bring about a reduction in harmful acts taken toward trans people of color.

The poetic gesture I see in *Mainichi* goes beyond empathy. What the repetition of the game points to is the incomprehensibility of the violence that trans women of color face, particularly for audiences that do not share that identification. It simply restarts once the player has gone far enough in the game. The violence is potentially infinite, repeated *every day*, which is the English translation of the Japanese word *mainichi*. The player's only choice is to walk away and go back to their own life. There is no reward. Thus, *Mainichi* foregrounds the structure of game play rather than making it transparent. At the moment that the game restarts, the player is forced to acknowledge that their current attempt is over and that their choices had consequences. In addition, the game's starting over is a moment of noncorrespondence over interactivity. The player's choices have only slight influences on what happens in the game, but regardless, the game starts over at the end, and another day begins. Here one sees a formal choice in the game that highlights the inescapable situation of trans people of color: by making the player eventually decide to stop playing, *Mainichi* highlights the fact that the player *can* stop playing—they have the privilege to simply walk away. While this may build empathy, Brice has made clear that her desire for the work goes beyond that. She is more interested in audiences feeling the responsibility of being in relation with her as a person.

The most important part of the game is the ending, or the lack thereof. When the scene in the coffee shop ends, regardless of what choices you have made, the game begins again. Another day begins, and you have the same choices. Should you shave? Should you wear makeup? Should you dress nicely or casually? How should you walk down the street? In this process the player learns what choices to make to affect the outcome of the daily experiences that follow. The experience involves the teaching, learning, and shaping of an algorithm for trans of color safety in the mind of the player. Using digital media in the form of a game the player is invited to repeat the same choices over and over, much like the lives of transgender people of color, who face choices every day about how to shift their bodies to avoid violence, how to make their appearance look, how to move their bodies, what forms of interaction to choose with others. Both the iterative repetition and the digital form make *Mainichi* a very powerful example of an algorithmic model of oppression. *Mainichi* may be the clearest example of trans of color poetics, using the looping affordances of digital games to bring the player into the everyday acts of shifting in daily life that Brice has experienced, which can allow one to avoid racialized, gendered violence.

The possible endless repetition of *Mainichi*'s poetics brings us back to the asterisk operator that I discussed in the introduction. As I discussed in the introduction, in the word *trans**, the asterisk signifies potential, using a command line syntax meaning "trans anything." Similarly, after playing *Mainichi* a few times, one understands that it operates on a loop. In this way, the algorithmic form allows for a way to reference a process that is potentially limitless, having no end. Unlike static forms of media that have a set meaning, the algorithmic poetics Brice uses reflect the potential for the player to fill in their own actions in many ways. Similarly, "trans*" has come to reference the many forms of gender expression referenced by the word *trans*, which continue to find new forms and terminology daily. The operation of shifting holds space for these multiple and changing expressions of gender identity.

Brice followed up *Mainichi* with a performance titled "empathy machine," in which she projected *Mainichi* on a wall and created wearable conductive fabric sensors that required players to use her body as a game controller to control the main character. She describes the performance as a challenge to claims that virtual reality is an "empathy machine" and that games made by queer people are "empathy games," pointing to how audiences want to hear from marginalized people only when they are describing their pain and their trauma. In the performance she used objects from her home and performed the daily rituals seen in the game in an "endless loop," talking to players about their experience as it unfolded, rejecting objectification, and highlighting the performative nature of games. One can see a poetics of relation at work in Brice's performance, in the intimate relation Brice is initiating between the player and herself. Brice states that with "empathy machine" her ultimate goal is "to bring the use of play to an activist setting through performance," emphasizing how trans of color poetics can be a form of activism that challenges the limits of the audience's empathy through embodied ritual.[59]

Mainichi and "empathy machine" create a performative situation in which players can experience the repetitiveness of violence, from direct attacks to microaggressions, that transgender people of color face every day. Players experience the process of learning an algorithm for performing identity. In writing about her motivations for creating the game, Brice explains why she chose the digital medium: "I only know life with computers and video games in them. My father is a programmer and shared a love for technology with his children. I grew up surrounded by games and, naturally, wanted to make them."[60] Brice explains that she chose a program to create the game that did not require her to write code; many game authoring programs are geared toward people who can code, which she attributes to "the privileged, tastes and wants of the hegemonic man."[61] Access to knowledge about algorithms, coding, and programming languages is highly gendered, raced, and classed.[62] The historical bias against women and people of color in science has extended to computer science. Brice describes how she created the game without knowing how to code, making an example for others to be able to create games about their experiences regardless of their level of education or access to technology. Brice describes how the choice of what tools one uses to author games is "political," due to the privilege some tools assume users have, as well as the communities of knowledge sharing that form around the tools.[63] This is particularly important for trans people of color, who are often excluded from educational and professional settings, resulting in even less access to technology. Brice's *Mainichi* demonstrates how trans people of color create algorithmic and digital media about their experiences of shifting despite the ways they have been excluded from technological and scientific communities.

Algorithmic analysis is inspired by trans women of color's use of digital media, such as Brice's *Mainichi*, which allows the player to experience the repetitiveness of racialized transphobic violence. Brice's game is repetitive in a way that is both algorithmic and performative. Judith Butler writes about the performativity of gender: "As in other ritual social dramas, the action of gender requires a performance that is repeated. This repetition is at once a reenactment and reexperiencing of a set of meanings already socially established; and it is the mundane and ritualized form of their legitimation."[64] The repetition in *Mainichi* adds meaning to each of the gendered acts that a player can choose in the game, and its focus on daily rituals of self-care gesture to the idea that these acts performed in the game will be repeated endlessly. Algorithms in games can help imagine and open possibilities of trans of color life in contemporary mediated environments. National borders are highly technologically mediated places that trans people of color have to navigate daily. In what follows, I describe *Redshift*, an online game I created based on my experiences of crossing the US-Canadian border. I describe how I used practice-based research to go beyond trying to get audiences to feel empathy for trans people of color and move toward building solidarity through workshops and performances.

Redshift and Portalmetal—Toward Solidarity

I remember when the ice storm came. I had been living in Toronto for only a few months, having lived my whole life in warm cities: Miami, San Diego, Los Angeles. I had never even heard of an ice storm, and now I was living through one. A heavy rain was followed by a sudden drop in temperature, which left the power lines, trees, and homes covered in crystalline icicles. But ice is heavy, and the result was downed power lines and falling trees. While walking down the street, I leaned in close to look at seeds on a tree covered in ice; they looked like perfectly spherical ice planets. In an effort to cope with the many difficulties of this time, I started writing poems. I began to add movement pieces to the poems and eventually combined them into an online digital game using the Scalar platform. After years of collaborations in *Autonets*, where I shared full authorial control of the performances with workshop participants, I wanted to shift my work and write my own story.

Redshift and Portalmetal, which can be played at scalar.usc.edu/works /redshift-and-portalmetal, uses a science fiction narrative about space travel to consider how transgender people who are settlers on native land can work for decolonization. *Redshift* is a transreal experience that I presented through performances, workshops, and the interactive online game. One could think of *Redshift* as a resistant algorithm—that is, an algorithm designed to resist the logics of borders. *Redshift* explores the following questions: What is the feeling of migration and settlement for trans people of color? How can a commitment to decolonization inform a trans of color digital praxis? As climate change forces us to travel to the stars and build new homes, how do we not reproduce colonization? How do we build home and family on this land where we are settlers while working to undo colonization? How do we understand our chronically ill, trans, femme, nonwhite, queer bodies as resilient enough to cross galaxies?[65]

The online game component of *Redshift* consists of a series of poems and performances presented through interactive digital video and text on the web. The player must make choices to decide how to proceed through the story. The story is inspired by feminist, queer, and decolonial science fiction — particularly that of Octavia Butler, Nalo Hopkinson, and Tracy K. Smith.[66] The main character of Butler's novel *Parables of the Sower*, Lauren Olamina, is a gender-non-conforming Black person who often passes as a man in order to survive a trip across California to escape fires and violence and build a new community based on her own spiritual writing, which she calls earthseed. In the book, Lauren experiences regular pain from hyperempathy, which I understand as an expression of real-life forms of chronic pain. Her character is a powerful example of the trans of color poetics of shifting, using her ability to shift between genders to escape the violence made even more rampant by the loss of social order. *Redshift* similarly depicts Roja, a trans Latina woman leaving her planet to escape climate catastrophe and using her ability to shift her appearance to find safety. Hopkinson's book *Brown Girl in the Ring* imagines a future set in Toronto swimming in Caribbean culture and a young woman who learns to use magic to protect herself from the violence of inequality. *Redshift* imagines practices of femme adornment such as wearing jewelry related to one's culture of family as a form of magic that allows Roja to teleport across time and space. Smith's Pulitzer Prize–winning book of poetry *Life on Mars* was a significant inspiration in her imagining of space travel as a way to come to terms with the loss of her father. In *Redshift*, I similarly wrote about my experience of the near-death of my mother, due to illness, through the image of Roja's dying planet.

Redshift uses space travel as a lens through which to understand my experience of being a Latina trans woman who migrated to the unceded Mississauga New Credit territory known as Toronto. It describes my feelings about being an arrivant who wants to work for decolonization. *Redshift* continues my work developing transreal methods of storytelling, which blend truth and fiction, real and virtual, by learning from my own experiences of crossing borders and mixing them with a science fiction narrative.[67] I did this partly to protect my privacy, but I also did it to make the story not just about me. *Redshift* uses algorithmic media to ask questions about my experience of crossing of national borders in a time of climate catastrophe. *Redshift*'s algorithm can be thought of as a simple one: it takes inputs in the form of user selections of actions and presents the web pages associated with those choices. Yet there are numerous algorithms at work to make that process appear simple. *Redshift* is an algorithm that also requires the algorithms of the Scalar web platform—as well as those of web browsers, including the HTML, CSS, and JavaScript parsers—to perform.

My engagement with the algorithms of digital games builds on feminist approaches to digital humanities, extending those claims into trans studies and queer theory. My claim builds on and extends Tara McPherson's call for digital humanists to consider the code behind the images they are describing. McPherson writes:

> I would argue that to study image, narrative, and visuality will never be enough if we do not engage as well the nonvisual dimensions of code and their organization of the world. Yet to trouble my own polemic, we might also understand the workings of code to have already internalized the visual to the extent that, in the heart of the labs from which UNIX emerged, the cultural processing of the visual via the register of race was already at work in the machine.[68]

McPherson deftly articulates the inseparability of code and racial logic while calling on digital humanists to expand their fields of study to include feminism and critical race theory. Similarly, I extend McPherson's argument about code to say that it is important for scholars of race and gender to consider algorithms in their analyses of media. Code describes algorithms, but algorithms are the repetitive processes that code is describing.

The primary question that motivated my work on *Redshift* was to explore the intersections of climate change, gender, and decolonization through a digital game online. The poems in *Redshift* consider how trans of color subjects can also be implicated in ongoing processes of colonialism. I wanted to explore the tension between being a Latinx person who was actively in the process of settling in Canada while working for decolonization. Scott Morgensen points to the writing of Jodi Byrd of the Chickasaw Nation, which articulates the idea that people of color may be thought of as arrivants instead of settlers. "By using 'arrivant,'" Morgensen writes, "Byrd signals that racialized non-natives inhabit Indigenous lands while experiencing colonial and racial subjugation, and that her accounts of their participation in colonization and their responsibilities to Indigenous decolonization call for a term distinct from white people."[69] These theories address the questions I considered in *Redshift* in a textual, analytical register, while my project seeks to work through the poetics and affect involved in these entanglings of gender, race, and colonialism.

Games can be one way of using algorithms to model social phenomena to help reveal their complexity and their layers. By considering *Redshift*, one can see ways that national borders can be thought of as algorithms that include multiple assemblages. In a 2015 book on mobile robotic sensor networks, Andrey V. Savkin and his colleagues propose a formula for how to cover an entire national border with a single network.[70] They propose an algorithm for total border surveillance. In texts using assemblage theory to describe the complexity of national borders, algorithms are described as one part of an assemblage.[71] I perceive an inverse relation, in which an algorithm can describe a border as an assemblage. In *Redshift*, the player is faced with the possibility that they may not be allowed to cross the border and return home. A border is a sorting algorithm, sorting millions of people into those who can stay and those who cannot. Algorithms include subroutines, smaller portions of logic that can be repeated to complete a larger decision-making process. A border has many subroutines for sorting along lines of race, class, gender, nationality, religion, and ability. These routines are embodied into logical decisions made by border enforcement agents, software, and devices. These decisions become automatic through code and microprocessors as much as through the muscle memory of the border patrol.

The algorithms of the border surround us, shaping our everyday lives and decisions, as described in a poem in *Redshift* about how one cannot run from the sensor networks of contemporary borders; they are distributed throughout the nation and no longer appear only at geographic borders. As Gloria Anzaldúa states, describing Border Patrol agents taking undocumented people out of their workplaces to deport them to places farther away than they have ever lived, "Those who make it past the checking points of the Border Patrol find themselves in the midst of 150 years of racism in Chicano *barrios* in the Southwest and big northern cities. Living in a no-man's-borderland."[72]

The border is an algorithm designed to prevent entry, whose force also prevents escape, day after day. Describing the "neo-Copernican leap," the challenge of understanding one's self outside of the epistemology of Western colonial racism, Sylvia Wynter quotes Michel Foucault saying, "What I am trying to do is grasp the implicit systems that *determine our most familiar behaviour without our knowing it*. I am trying to *find their origin, to show their formation, the constraint they impose upon us*; I am therefore trying to place myself at a distance from them and to show *how one could escape*."[73] Such a project, of escape from the imprisoning logics of borders and carceral regimes, today would need to examine the algorithms that shape our everyday activities.

For many people, the life-threatening danger of crossing borders is a daily experience. National borders are a primary site where national governments sort those deemed human, and who therefore deserve to live, from all those deemed less than human, to be left to die. Wynter points to the urgent need in the face of climate change to shift from how "the human" historically has been defined, as a means to exclude historically oppressed groups such as immigrants, to a new "referent—we in the horizon of humanity," referring to all human beings.[74] In conceptualizing the US-Mexican border as an algorithm, I hope to remind readers that *algorithms can be hacked*, either by reverse engineering them to find their vulnerabilities or by creating counter-algorithms, resistant algorithms, or decolonial malware. By creating algorithms that act in resistance to national borders, activists and artists can work toward the survival of all people, regardless of their immigration status.

Redshift depicts shifting in the form of more commonplace embodied transformations such as the adornment of makeup and jewelry, as well as larger shifts such as transnational migration. Writing about *Redshift* was one of my first moments of realizing that the shift is an operation of trans of color poetics. One poem in the game reads,

> We have found
> ways to shift the light in the air around us,
> so at times we can be completely invisible
> going through border checkpoints,
> and sometimes in our own communities,
> at other times we shift the light to see each other
> beaming with color
> redshift
> plumshift
> blueshift
> two femmes of color hunting non-transfer lipstain
> building knowledge
> so we can colorshift into our full spectral brilliance
> and hold our individuality, in relationship,
> each moving at different velocities,
> each radiating their own hue,
> moving in shared orbits.

The game presents this poem layered on top of a video of a landscape covered in ice as part of the narrative thread about the ice planet. The poem gathers together experiences related to wearing lipstick, both for pleasure

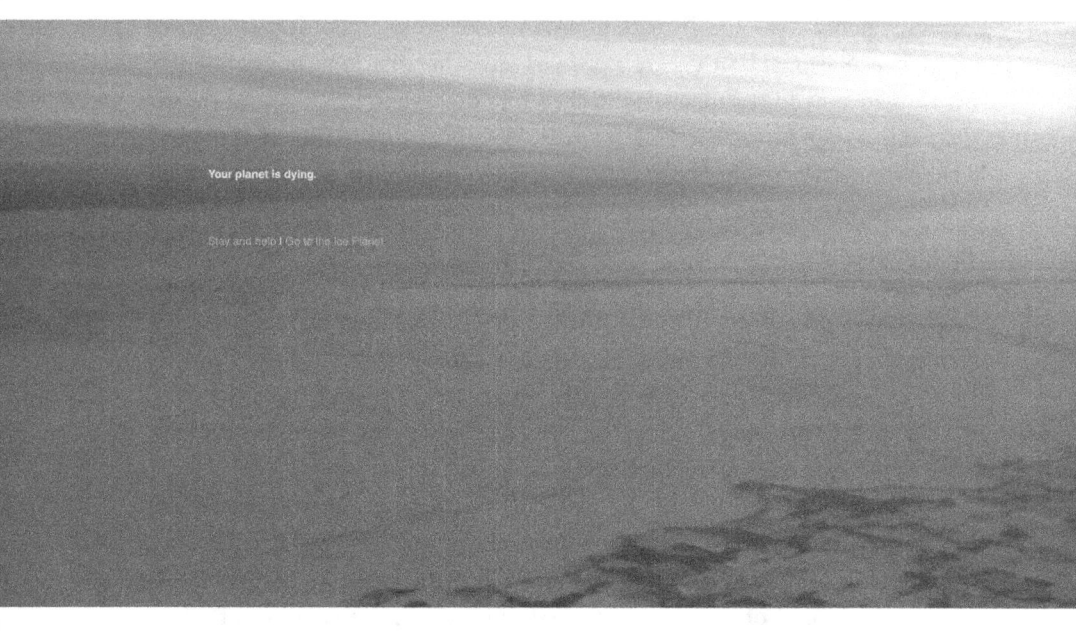

Your planet is dying.

Stay and help | Go to the Ice Planet

4.4 "Home Planet," game screen shot from *Redshift and Portalmetal,*
by micha cárdenas.

and as a survival strategy. These acts are a form of knowledge building, a
form of femme science I have used to avoid violence on a daily basis. In the
poem, I play with the idea of redshift from astronomy, how color is used to
determine the movement of a body and create images related to that operation. The act of shifting the color of my body to change the perception of a
border guard, or of members of my community, to avoid violence gave me
the idea of abstracting the operation of shifting and to look for it in other
trans artists' work.

The primary audience for the game is other queer and trans people of
color who are having similar experiences, but the form of an online game
about space travel may appeal to audiences of digital games more broadly.
In the development of *Redshift,* I wrote poetry and developed performances
for four different planets that the player can visit in the story: the dying
home planet (figure 4.4), the ice planet, the ocean moon (figure 4.5), and the
planet with no rain. While using scenes familiar to players of mainstream
video games such as traveling between planets, computer hacking, and cast-
ing spells, I depict them through a deeply personal lens. The scenes include
unexpected elements such as the interplanetary border checkpoints that one
must pass through to get to any of these planets. In *Redshift,* trans of color

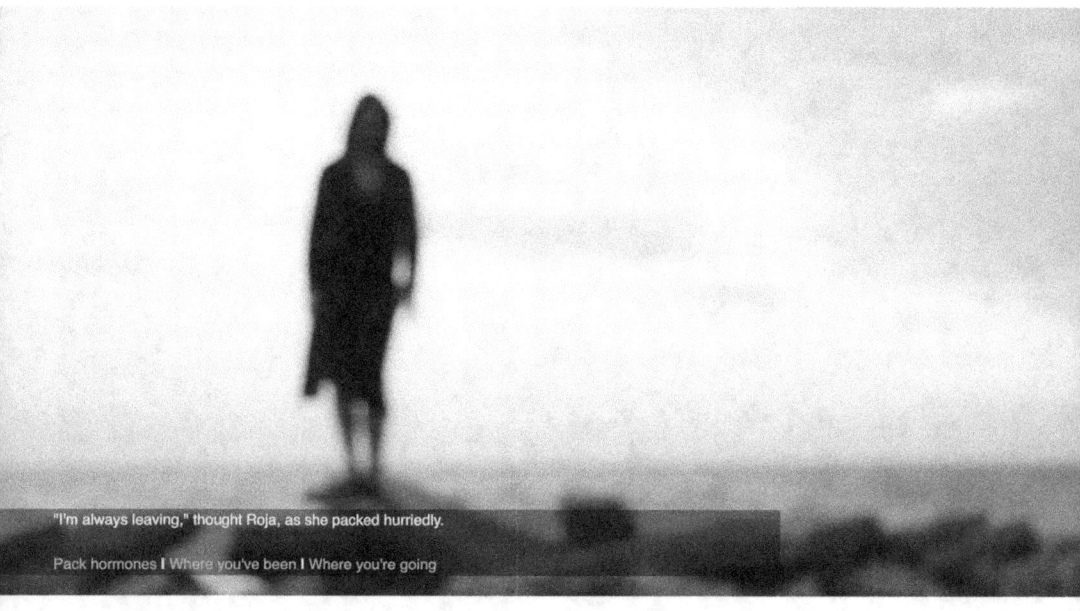

"I'm always leaving," thought Roja, as she packed hurriedly.

Pack hormones I Where you've been I Where you're going

4.5 "Ocean Moon," game screen shot from *Redshift and Portalmetal*,
by micha cárdenas.

poetics encode algorithms of survival into digital media poetics for my communities while still speaking on a different register to cisgender and white
audiences.

I presented *Redshift* in live performances in front of audiences in Toronto,
Montreal, Winnipeg, Philadelphia, and Blacksburg, Virginia, allowing them
to choose which path to take through the story and performing the text and
movement that goes with each poem. I noted audiences' reactions to the border checkpoints throughout the game, which are described through stories
of my own experiences crossing borders. One prose poem states

> You get stopped by the Interplanetary Border Guard on your way to the
> shuttle. Inside his little tower, the guard's black hair is in a fresh crew cut,
> he's white, fit, seems eager, a parody of a masculine soldier. You hand him
> your passport, he looks at it and says "wait here, please" and walks away,
> into an office where more border guards are talking. . . . Minutes pass.
>
> You pray. You are so afraid. You think of your lover, and if you'll be kept
> apart from her. You look off at the horizon, trying to appear calm, and
> wonder if this stress is worth it, or if you're just not taking care of yourself.
> Are you being committed or reckless? It's hard to tell. You wait.

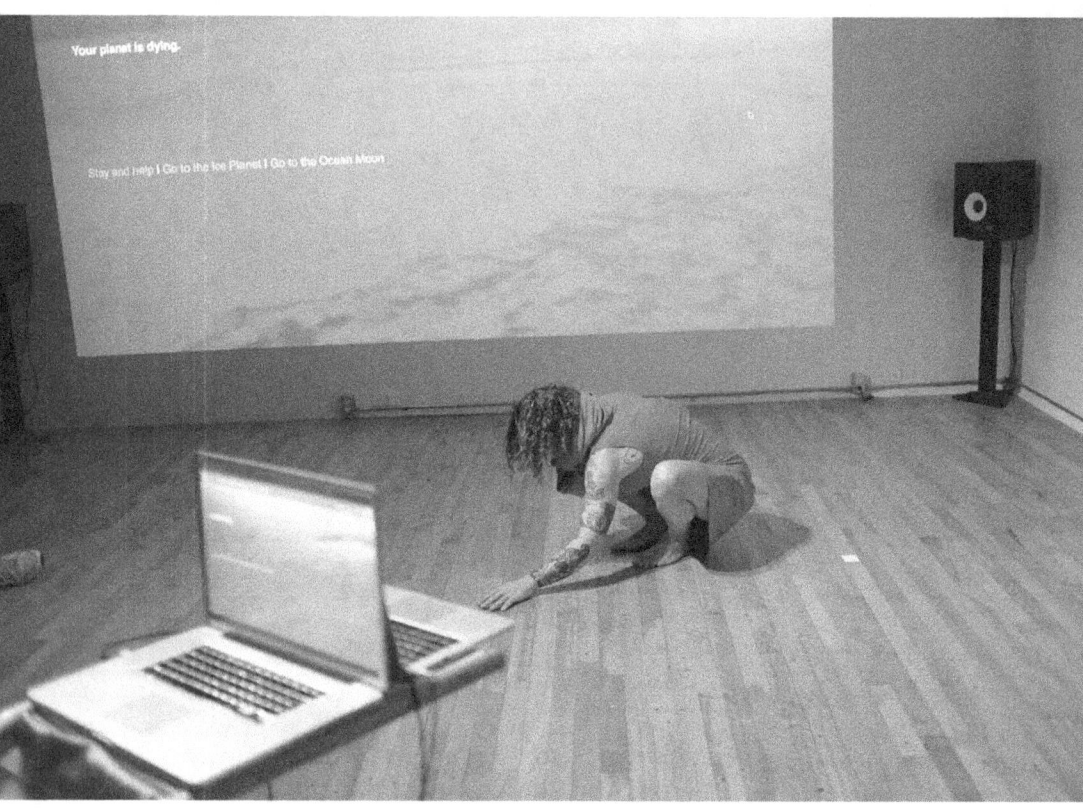

4.6 Live game play testing of *Redshift and Portalmetal*, performed at the HTMlles Feminist New Media Festival, Montreal, November 2014. Photograph by Võ Thiên Việt.

Below the poem, the players, or the audience, are given these two choices: "Wait, Quietly and Hope" or "Run." *Redshift* uses trans of color poetics to bring the audience in as coperformative witnesses of moments of violence and resilience.[75]

At a performance of *Redshift* at the HTMlles Festival of New Media in Montreal, the audience, which included transgender and cisgender people of many ethnicities, could not come to agreement as to which of these choices to make. I had the honor of performing *Redshift* on the opening night of HTMlles 11, in November 2014 (figure 4.6). The theme of the festival was "Zero Futur(e)," with the curatorial statement claiming that "the future is obsolete." HTMlles is one of very few—or perhaps the only—feminist new media art festival in the world. Acknowledging that the festival took place in "Montreal/stolen indigenous land,"[76] the organizers speculated on the value of rhetorics of "the future" in the face of neoliberalism's emptiness by look-ing to Afro-futurism, cyberfeminism, and queer futurity. On opening night, with the cold Montreal wind howling outside, the gallery at Studio XX on Rue Berry was filled with people. Described as a live playtest performance, *Redshift* was presented with two projections of the game on walls that met at a corner, and two laptops, one facing the audience and one facing me. I began the performance with a movement piece exploring themes described in the first poems of the game. From a position curled in a ball of grief, I slowly rose up to *relevé*, with arms extended overhead. I then read the first line, "Your planet is dying," and offered the audience choices, asking, "Do you stay and help or go to the ice planet?" I then paused and stood still. After a quiet mo-ment, the audience began to discuss the choices. When the audience arrived at certain screens in the game, I performed additional movements, exploring themes in the poems such as a ritualized version of the gesture of putting on a necklace repeatedly, with one foot back and one foot forward, moving my arms slowly in large and small arcs. The movement made the use of the fic-tional portalmetal—a portmanteau I invented to express the idea that femme adornments such as necklaces can connect people to their ancestors and to future generations through shared objects and rituals—visual.

As the game progressed, I noticed that the Montreal audience was one of the most engaged to which I had presented *Redshift*. Many people were will-ing to speak up and engage in debate about the choices presented to them. When given the choice of what to do at the border checkpoint, some audi-ence members argued for running as an act of resistance, while others argued for waiting as the best route to be able to proceed. The interaction raised is-sues about both privilege and experience, who thought which tactic would work best based on their experience of border crossing, and their familiarity with danger in these moments.

In the fall of 2014, I posted an open call for play testers for a beta version of *Redshift* on HASTAC.org, an online community engaged in digital human-ities, as well as on my personal website. I received responses from ten play tes-ters, including cisgender and transgender people, settlers, native people, and people whose native/settler status was nonbinary, in many different cities in Canada and the United States. The only players who said they identified with the transgender main character in *Redshift* were the play testers who were themselves transgender. This is likely due to the narrative structure or the aesthetic choices in the game, but it is an outcome worth noting. One cisgender player said, "I felt like I could switch between being myself and identifying with the character, which was a good balance." Another said, "I felt some identification with the character. There was a feeling of being overwhelmed by external factors and an attempt to feel true to oneself." These responses raise for me the question of the effect of putting the player in the position of the shifting trans person. Through *Redshift* I sought to give players a small experience of the challenges I face in my life navigating national borders and gender borders simultaneously, yet my primary goal is to demonstrate that the survival strategies that trans people use are a form of science and knowledge.

The ending of *Redshift* demonstrates an effort to go beyond empathy, toward solidarity. In an effort to allow it to have a more concrete impact, the online game ends with a statement honoring the Mississauga, New Credit, and Grassy Narrows people, including a link where players can learn more about their political campaigns, make donations, and get involved. While this is a small gesture on my part and the part of the player, it is the logical conclusion of the project, pointing players away from the game and toward taking actions in solidarity with Indigenous peoples. This ending for *Redshift* reflects the overall poetic strategy in the project of aiming at more than empathy from a sympathetic viewer, toward sharing concrete strategies of survival, such as the femme science of shifting the color of one's lips or navigating border checkpoints to be close to loved ones.

In *Redshift* I use algorithmic media to allow players to perform and experience acts of shifting that I experience in my daily life. The act of authoring the game can be understood as stitching together multiple scenes of video, lines of code, and gestures of solidarity. One of the goals is affective, like Mattie Brice's goal, to share with a larger public of players on the internet, and in person, some of the feeling of my daily experience of violence. There is another act of shifting in *Redshift* that can inform trans of color poetics: the act of writing my experiences into a science fiction narrative. I choose to shift out of the narrative framework where players will assume that these are my real, everyday experiences by presenting them through a story of time and space travel. This level of poetics is intended to subvert the common voyeuristic attitude that audiences have when viewing art made by transgender people. By blending truth and fiction, my daily reality with an imagined future reality, a method I have called transreal, I hope to disorient the player into being unsure which elements of the story are fictional and which are real while still allowing them to have some experience of them.[77] This shifting happens through different poetic choices, including word choices, visual and textual dissonance, and movement performances. The performances in *Redshift* do not depict the story narratively but make reference to affective moments. The format of digital games provides a rich space of opportunity for an audience that expects science fiction stories about masculine tropes to be invited into postcolonial, transgender science fiction stories that propose futures based on solidarity and decolonization.

The last performance of *Redshift* took place on October 8, 2015, at the YYZ Artist Run Centre in Mississauga of the New Credit territory known as Toronto, a perfect location for the project to culminate. The exhibition, *Voz-à-Voz*, was curated by Julieta María and María Alejandrina Coates and included seven media art projects dealing with relations among land, geography, and bodies, using technology and tradition to move from colonization to solidarity. The curatorial statement states, "Inspired by the conversations that took place during the symposium on *Decolonial Aesthetics from the Americas*, which was organized by e-fagia in collaboration with FUSE Magazine in 2013, this project critically addresses settler colonialism from the point of view of Indigenous and im/migrant artists and activists, particularly within the boundaries of what is now called Canada."[78] The show included Skawennati, a Mohawk artist who lives in Mohawk territory known as Montreal.[79] Her piece in the show used digital images of Second Life avatars to envision Mohawk people in the future.[80] The exhibition included invited articles on the website Vozavoz.ca. In one article, titled "The Colour of Spatial Infinity Is Red," the writer, editor, and curator Nasrim Himada writes, "*Redshift* weaves the poetics of lived experience as struggle for life. *For life* meaning the practice of everyday decolonization as ethical habitation."[81] Himada goes on to state, "In creating *Redshift*, cárdenas, in cultural practice communicates this urgency. To be reminded that, as settlers, our position is one of non-belonging."[82] In my place of non-belonging, I invited a local Indigenous artist to perform the main dance performance in the show: my former dance teacher Ravyn Wngz.

I remember being in a ballet class when Wngz came up to me and gently told me to adjust one single vertebra in my upper back, lightly placing her hand on the part of my back she was referring to. Doing so lifted my shoulders, straightened my back, and opened my heart. In early transition I learned to look at the floor to avoid the eyes of people who might see me and react violently. Years of fear, combined with actual incidences of assault, had caused my physical shape to grow in a way that hunched my back and curled my shoulders in. Perhaps Wngz saw this, or she knew the feeling herself, but her precision and gentleness as a dance instructor helped me learn more than dance. It helped me grow courage and self-confidence. I studied the longest and learned the most from the ILL NANA/DiverseCity Dance Company in Toronto, whose teachers included Ravyn Wngz, Sze-Yang Ade-Lam, and kumari giles, all gender-non-conforming dance artists. They understand dance as a political project. In their classes, which were "pay what you can" and specifically for queer and trans people of color and disabled people, they repeatedly told us to be taller, be bigger, take up more space. I cried in or after many of their classes. Over the years they did incredible community-building work in the Toronto QTPOC community. Wngz describes herself as an "African/Black, 2Spirited Being who loves herself. She is an empowerment movement storyteller, based in Toronto. She is dedicated to the liberation of Trans, Queer and Self-Identified people by sharing her journey of healing in this lifetime."[83] I was profoundly honored to perform alongside her in the last performance of *Redshift*.

After more than an hour of interactive performance of *Redshift* in Toronto, in which I read poems and the audience navigated their way to and across the ocean moon, the audience came to a choice: "Go to the ice planet | Spell for Decolonial Time Travel." They chose to cast the spell. The two projection screens updated and displayed a dark image with an orange moon behind strings of clouds in the upper-left-hand corner, reflecting on the surface of what appeared to be an ocean. The text read:

~~Spell~~
~~Code~~
~~Study~~
Prayer for decolonial time travel.
In whatever form you find best,
draw a clock that indicates,
time of death,
time of rebirth,
time of transformation,
time of love,
time of relationship conflict,
time of loss,
time of prayer,
time of dreams,
time of moonlight on water,
time of green sunlight through leaves,
time of the dream of a new child.

At this moment, Wngz slowly emerged from the crowd and stepped into the open area of the gallery in front of the two projections. She wore a long blue-and-white dress, and orchestral music started to play, rising in a cinematic arc of excitement.[84] She began with a slow *rond de jambe*, drawing a semicircle on the floor with her foot and slowly raising her arms overhead. As she continued, lowering her body and raising her arms in a "V" shape, what was striking was how she danced with the text. Wngz is a practiced professional dancer. In the spirit of openness of performance art, we had not rehearsed. The poem, with the dark scene behind it, became projected on her body and moved across her as she moved. As the poem states, it is simultaneously code, spell, prayer, and study: an algorithm. Though some of those words existed with a strikethrough, they were still clearly present for the viewer. What unfolded was the appearance of her body intertwining with the algorithm. Wngz continued, and the music transitioned to the Alabama Shakes song "Sound and Color." The light melody of the vibraphone gave a feeling of the weightlessness of space travel. As the singer melodically sang, "A new world hangs / Outside the window," Wngz seemed to be lifted into the air, head back and one arm raised. This was not trans woman of color as image of death but a visionary poetics of trans of color potential: the potential to travel to other worlds, to conjure new time-spaces, to create future families. Wngz began to sway, back arched, both arms outstretched, a moment of floating in freedom. As the song progressed, she began to swing her arms wildly in circles, in which I saw the speed of interstellar travel. As the song ended, repeating "sound and color" more and more softly, Wngz held her arms out to the sides and looked up at the sky. Only the ends of the longer lines of the poem ripple across her dress:

> ial time travel.
> you find best,
> indicates,
>
> mation,
> ship conflict,
>
> ght on water,
> sunlight through leaves,
> eam of a new child.

With her movement, Wngz create a redacted version of my original poem. Through her many acts of shifting throughout the dance, she made visible some of the stitching of our bond over years, when we danced together and she taught me the beginnings of ballet, modern dance, and what she calls street styles, including voguing and waacking. We share some struggles, though to vastly different degrees. Yet in this collaborative performance, we acted together to envision new potentialities for trans women of color by combining algorithmic media with dance. As Wngz moved, she interacted with my code and my poetry, and even with a digital double of my body projected in the scene on the walls, moving at slightly different times, in effect creating two dancing partners for her moving performance of interstellar decolonial time-space travel.

Trans of color poetics in games use the experience of shifting not only to share stories of survival strategies, but also to challenge players' understandings of concepts such as race, gender, games, and activism. The cut scenes in *Redshift*, which in conventional games are used to show high-end graphic scenes rendered in 3D that advance the plot, are used instead to convey video of experimental movement performances. In these moments, the narrative is suspended, and instead of representing the actions described in the text through performance, I chose to engage in affective explorations of the environments described in the poems. On the ocean moon I focused on the precariousness of dancing on large, unstable stones in front of a large body of water. In the desert, I am seen navigating the edges of an outcropping of rock and shielding myself from the sun with a hood. In these moments, in contrast to *Mainichi*'s effort to share a narrative, I chose to challenge the player's desire for narrative closure and instead open up a space of trans of color poetics by showing a person in a hostile environment. In *Redshift* I rely on the potential of poetics to create change, rejecting the usual dichotomy of expression or effectiveness that is placed on socially engaged art.

While *Redshift* is in one sense an algorithm, its trans of color poetics exceed the algorithmic, just as *Mainichi*'s do. The moment when *Mainichi*'s poetics are most clearly effected is the moment when one walks away from the endless loop of the algorithm. The moment when *Redshift*'s poetics are most strongly at work is when players feel that they are part of the network of relations created by the game. Following Glissant's poetics of relation, one is constituted through relations with others in a decolonial imaginary. *Redshift* considers the main character Roja's responsibility to those she is in relation with as an arrivant working for decolonization. An algorithm is useful for visualizing or modeling phenomena while accounting for the unknown. The network of relations invoked by the transnational, transgender, and multiracial concerns evoked by *Redshift* involve such far-reaching connections as to be incalculable. One might ask where the poetic does its work. In the trans of color poetics of *Redshift*, the poetics operate in the liminal space of relation, between the author and the reader, among lands, bodies, and planets. Glissant argues that "the opaque is not the obscure. . . . [I]t is that which cannot be reduced."[85] For Glissant there is no relation without opacity, no ability to connect without an ability to individuate. In *Redshift*, Roja acknowledges her responsibility to the native people of the land on which she lives, acknowledging their opacity and her own, not trying to merge the two or come to an ultimate understanding between them. Asking their permission to make a home on their land, she proposes a provisional ethics of in-betweenness, of surviving in a temporary state, between planets whose continued habitability is uncertain.

The poetics of digital games are performative in that they exist in the movement of electrons that happens only when an algorithm is run. Games exist in the liminal space of play during which a player is making choices. They exist between the movements of bodies on-screen and behind the keyboard or game controller. In between the coding of an algorithm and the conclusion of the game—when the code is run, its output is perceived, and the player reacts to it—is where the poetics happen. Fred Moten describes the poetics of the undercommons as "a social poetics: a constant process where people make things and make one another, or to be more precise, where inseparable differences are continually made."[86] Like Glissant's network of opacities, the poetics of the undercommons resonates with trans of color poetics seen in digital games, which bring differences into play. Unlike empathy, which relies on a claim of similarity, trans of color poetics rely on acknowledging difference, which is where solidarity begins. Players and characters in processes of shifting are temporarily stitched together by algorithms that enable poetics to crackle loudly, or ripple gently, across the space between bodies in motion.

An important part of algorithmic analysis involves finding the limit of the algorithm, and its excess. While attempts to model the border may include elements such as sensor networks, laws, and weapons, the violence that is the effect of the border is in excess of these logical descriptions. The violence of the border occurs at scales from the everyday to lasting trauma. The Trump administration's border policies of family separation affected thousands of families; the effects of this violence, for years to come, are so vast as to be incalculable.[87] The poetics of crossing borders, the unfolding affects and meanings stirred by the movement across the network of opacities touched by borders, is also in excess of the sorting algorithm of the border. On this connection between opacity and poetics Glissant writes, "The poetic force . . . is the opacity of the diverse animating the imagined transparency of Relation."[88] Poetics are an excess that animates relation and requires opacity. In *Redshift* one can sense this poetics in the interplay of fear, solidarity, and care.

In this chapter, I have considered two digital games based on direct experiences of shifting, created by trans women of color. Both games are examples of trans of color poetics that use algorithms to work to end racialized, transmisogynist violence. Describing *Mainichi*, I articulate how Brice's original intention may have been to bring about empathy for her daily experiences of transphobia for a friend of hers, but she ultimately questioned how players focused only on her suffering. She then created a performance of *Mainichi* in which viewers were asked to come into contact with her body in order to play, calling for a more embodied relational exchange to challenge a distanced form of empathy that simplified her complex human experience into one of only suffering. In *Redshift*, I use a transreal mode of storytelling to share my experiences of resilience with other trans and queer people of color while protecting my own privacy from voyeuristic players by blurring fiction and reality and calling players to action beyond the screen. Through workshops and performances, in collaboration with an Indigenous two-spirit dance artist in Toronto, I tried to go beyond the solidarity I could achieve in the space of the screen. In the next chapter, I find more depth in an alternative to empathy by considering how to build solidarity. Learning from women of color feminism, which is based on identity in difference, trans of color poetics can work toward building felt political connections through repeated, embodied acts of relation. Like the shift, the transreal, and the performative approaches to game design described here, the next chapter describes the stitch as a gesture of trans of color poetics that can enable networks of care and connection.

THE STITCH   FIVE

ADORNED WITH A MASSIVE HEADDRESS with an assortment of pink, red, yellow, blue, and white feathers and peacock feathers, Luis Gerardo Rosero, a Colombian dancer, enters the building of the Universidad Nacional de Colombia in Bogotá, dancing a ritual Incan dance. Rosero is dressed in elements of costumes that have been deemed masculine and feminine.[1] The scene is a cacophony of fabulousness, joyful drums, and wind instruments. Rosero is followed by Giuseppe Campuzano, who is carrying banners attached to his costume; Campuzano is followed by the Chicas Extraordinarias collective of artists in neon pink, purple, and red wigs, sequins, and lace. Rosero, trained in many dance forms, including Western forms, danced the Danza de Males, first performed in Peru before colonization and later in Colombia.[2] The dance includes subtle movements, as well as the marking of a pentagram design with his feet.[3] As I stood there, at the university my Colombian father had attended, I did not know the depth of the importance of what I was seeing. I return to this performance of *El Museo Travesti del Perú* (TMP), which I discussed in chapter 1, to elaborate the next operation of trans of color poetics, the stitch. I was attending the Hemispheric Institute of Performance and Politics to present a workshop on hacktivism as performance. I knew the significance of the drawings, objects, and performance I was witnessing in that it connected my understanding of trans people to an older lineage of Indigenous history in Peru. I did not yet know the depth of resonance I would find in Campuzano's work as I continued to study it. I went to Bogotá hoping to connect with my biological family's history, but instead I found an embodied spiritual and poetic connection to a lineage of ancestors joyously shape-shifting through dance and dress. In a performance of *TMP* at the Universidad Nacional, Campuzano subversively transformed the university's main building into the site of a large, loud, brightly colored, feathered carnivalesque performance with the drag collective Chicas Extraordinarias and Rosero, an Indigenous dancer of Andean traditional dance. I feel very fortunate to have seen Campuzano perform, and to have met him, before he passed away in 2013 at forty-four.

This chapter describes the operation of the stitch as a part of trans of color poetics, which allow artists to perform both opacity, evading surveillance, and relation, building connection and solidarity. The chapter adds another operation to trans of color poetics by putting media made by the contemporary artists Adam Harvey, Zach Blas, and the Electronic Disturbance Theater, as well as my own project *Local Autonomy Networks* (*Autonets*), in dialogue with Campuzano's *TMP*. These artworks are examples of digital media art that modulate perceptibility using stitching of materials that range from fabric to 3D models and algorithms. Through examples from contemporary art, the chapter expands the argument in this book to show how non-trans-identified artists also use trans of color poetics, and how their use differs from that of trans of color artists. The art projects in the chapter point to possible futures in which trans people may have more ability to modulate their own visibility through autonomous networks, do-it-yourself (DIY) mobile phones, camouflage, and masking while connecting to decolonial histories of related practices in the *TMP*. While the present moment is besieged by near-total surveillance at all scales, these projects show how trans people may be able, at least temporarily and in limited circumstances, to evade surveillance from the algorithms of government, police, and social media corporations. These projects offer resistant algorithms by analyzing existing technologies of surveillance and building alternative forms of visibility. In addition, stitching can be a way to build connections among people. In the second half of the chapter, I describe how the performance of *Autonets* titled "We Already Know and We Don't Yet Know" worked to build affective connections between performance collaborators and workshop participants. Solidarity and connection are important parts of the continued survival of trans people of color.

As I described in chapter 1, the performance I witnessed was part of Campuzano's project *TMP*, which has been translated as "The Transvestite Museum of Peru," despite Alvaro Jarrín's claim that the term *travesti* is untranslatable.[4] The operation of "travesti" is at times an act of shifting between genders or, as Campuzano explains, between Indigenous religions and Catholic syncretism. Travesti can also be an act of stitching in which the travesti body connects the different genders performed. As Campuzano says, the clothing, the dance, and the makeup are all a connecting stitch in the operation of the travesti.

In an interview conducted by the performance studies scholar Marcela Fuentes, Campuzano describes the way that clothes are essential to this performative ritual:

> Las danzas . . . es un cuerpo político que contiene una memoria, en la danza, en el vestido, en el maquillaje, en este performance del género que ellos hacen una y otra vez, entonces establecer este recorrido de estés dioses que crearon andróginos hasta estos danzantes de hoy, desde el rito al espectáculo también como pasar de esto. . . . Esta economía del mercado, o sea como sobrevivir también, creo que es otro ejercicio travesti, pasar de ser andrógino con una sexualidad menos fija, a ser un hombre disfrazado como una mujer, a ser un travesti, de ser una ritualista, a ser ahora una diva de carnaval de un pueblo determinado en el país, o a ser una devota de una dios prehispánico o devota de la Virgen María.

> [The traditional Peruvian and Colombian dances . . . are a political body that contains a memory, in the dance, in the clothing, in the makeup, in this performance of gender that they do over and over, so it establishes this path from these androgynous people created by deities to the dancers of today, from the ritual to the spectacle. . . . This economy of the market, or survival, I believe, is another travesti exercise, to pass from being androgynous, with a less fixed sexuality, to being a man dressed as a woman, to being travesti, to being a ritual dancer, to being now a carnival diva of a specific city in the country, or from being a devotee of a pre-Columbian deity to a devotee of the Virgin Mary.][5]

Campuzano describes how the use of clothing becomes part of a larger ritual of performance of crossing many different barriers of gender, race, and religion simultaneously. I see this as a powerful gesture of stitching, of creating costumes—whether sewing or assembling them—that is a crucial part of not only self-fashioning for trans and travesti people but also a method of daily survival and a mode of creating connections with ancestors, real and felt, as an expansive way of rewriting mythologies of nation and religion. Campuzano performs an algorithm of trans of color poetics, using the shifting body and identity of the travesti to perform rituals that transmit survival strategies and subvert colonial Western figurations of gender, identity, and secularity. Campuzano's description also references his performances of the Virgin Mary. She, Campuzano says, is "the [travesti] par excellence, with her magnificent trousseau and her performative apparitions," describing her capacity for multiplicity in her performative appearances in different places and using the word *apparitions* to conjure an image of a ghostly spirit akin to a hologram.[6]

One of the ways the stitch operates is by providing stealth through the adornment of clothing. Stealth and deception are common accusations used to justify the surveillance and harassment of trans people.[7] A simple interpretation of the operation of travesti is to understand it as "transvestism," or cross-dressing, which can be perceived as deceptive. Yet Campuzano's description of the layered poetics of the TMP reveal a complex weave of truths in rejection of the narrative of one single truth enforced by colonizers.[8] The TMP is an imaginary museum presented as a traveling installation at various artistic venues. While Campuzano describes finding some Incan artifacts depicting androgynous gods, he also describes finding and fabricating objects in the museum. Campuzano describes the project as a Trojan horse, which implies that it enters the museum through stealth. The gesture—or exercise, as Campuzano describes it—also contains a layered reference to how travesti do have to use stealth to survive in environments in which the unitary rigidity of heteronormative gender binaries are violently enforced. Yet the stealth is not a simple act of deception but a deep transformation. Campuzano describes the example of a transformation from a dancer in an Indigenous ritual to a Carnival diva as a travesti exercise, neither of which is hidden but both of which center travesti embodied movement in large, important social rituals.

Indigenous histories of resistance to gendered violence also contain an ancient gesture of algorithmic media, in which *quipus* (knots in Quechua) demonstrate that stitching algorithms has long been a part of trans of color poetics. Quipus are an ancient form of writing and computation that use a system of knots tied in string at different lengths, and in succession across strings, developed by Inca people and peoples throughout the Andes regions.[9] Campuzano describes the gesture of Indigenous people using their fingers to read the quipus while being interrogated as being "like copying on an exam."[10] She adds that this exercise of travesti is seen in the moments in which androgynous Indigenous people were interrogated by *sacerdotes*

(Catholic priests); they used quipus to share the correct answers to the many questions they were asked.[11] Here Campuzano brings together a decolonial reading of histories of trans people of color using the material of thread in embodied algorithmic performances of acts of daily survival. Through Campuzano's reading of these moments, and her performance and installation of the *TMP*, I describe the operation of the stitch of trans of color poetics.

A later act of sewing in Europe—in England in the early 1800s—ties the stitch of trans of color poetics to contemporary digital computing devices. To realize his dream of calculating mathematical tables using steam power, Charles Babbage invented the Difference Engine to mechanically calculate logarithms. In 1826, he invented mechanical notation to symbolically represent the operation of machinery. He realized that he could control the order of operations using the same punched cards that the Jacquard loom used to weave fabric. He later described the Analytical Engine, a more general-purpose mechanical computation device, to Ada Lovelace and suggested that she write her own ideas about the engine in a paper. In July 1843, Lovelace published a translation of Babbage's paper on the Analytical Engine and added her notes. The notes included what some consider the first computer program—an algorithm for using the Analytical Engine to calculate Bernoulli numbers. In the paper she stated, "The Analytical Engine weaves algebraical patterns just as the Jacquard-loom weaves flowers and leaves."[12] The connection among stitching, weaving, and computation goes back to the origins of modern computing devices.

Shifting provides the variables, elements in movement and transition. Stitching provides the mechanism for holding variables together in lines of code, grouping instructions into cohesive units. In the sense of code, a compiler is a piece of software that takes lines of code and converts them into machine-readable files, stitching together the necessary connections between code libraries and symbol files. This chapter builds on the previous two chapters about shifting by describing a new operation that adds complexity and form to trans of color poetics. The stitch extends trans of color poetics beyond an individual experience to a network of relations.

The stitch is a material and conceptual operation, similar to the cut (discussed in chapter 2) and the fold discussed by Gilles Deleuze. Deleuze considers the work of Gottfried Wilhelm Leibniz, which combines calculus and philosophy to elaborate the operation of the fold in ontology, art, and media. Deleuze states, "The world must be placed in the subject in order that the subject can be for the world. This is the torsion that constitutes the fold of the world and of the soul."[13] In *The Fold*, Deleuze considers Baroque art through Leibnizian terms such as the *monad*, the soul, and God to elaborate elements of his own process ontology, such as the multiplicity and the assemblage, building on the mathematics of objects in motion in calculus. Like the fold, the stitch is an operator that connects two elements, but a fold entails two entities that are already part of a singular entity. The stitch is an operation that involves using one entity to connect two formerly separate entities.

The stitch is intended to resonate for transgender people who choose to undergo surgery, like the cut as I described in chapter 1. Many trans people, for many different reasons, choose to modify their bodies surgically. All of these surgeries involve cutting, shifting, and stitching. The stitch, in the case of surgery, is a necessary part of healing, a temporary object that holds parts of the body together to allow the body to find its own sustenance in a new form. The stitch brings the affect of pain into this consideration of creation and facilitates a change in shape, a shift. Often, stitches received by transgender people today are temporary augmentations; they are dissolvable stitches that hold the body together during a time of healing and then fall out when they are no longer needed. Stitches may be used to augment a form such as a body or to create forms out of fabric. The basis for the idea of the stitch is an experience of stitching wearable electronic garments, yet the idea can be seen in many creative practices, including fashion, media, and art.

Originating out of a material practice of making objects by sewing, the stitch is part of a poetics of object making, as well as part of a process of making new concepts. As described by Deleuze and Félix Guattari in *What Is Philosophy*, "Philosophy is not a simple art of forming, inventing, or fabricating concepts, because concepts are not necessarily forms, discoveries, or products. More rigorously, philosophy is the discipline that involves creating concepts. . . . To create concepts is, at the very least, to make something."[14] Their claim is very relevant to the aims of this book, which are not only to analyze and critique, but also to generate new concepts and to do so through making, which is at times called by different names: practice-based research, design research, digital humanities, and research creation.

Stitching looks to women of color feminism and feminist science studies for inspiration. As sewing is a technique of making that has been used primarily by women throughout history, and continues to be primarily a task of women in sweatshops in the global South, this proposal of the stitch as a material and conceptual operation can be seen as a feminist proposal, a way of generating new concepts by learning from people who have been subjected to material inequalities because of their gender, race, and geographic location. The stitch can be thought of as a gesture of feminist making, which values the forms of knowledge practiced daily by oppressed people as they make their lives in the face of violence. The operation of creating relations through the stitch, of finding means to connect groups of people who formerly were separated, can be seen as a continuation of the work of women of color feminism, which sought to bring together women across racial lines. In this way, the stitch can be a way of imagining the community-building work necessary to create community-based responses to violence, as demonstrated in my project *Autonets*, in the collaborations between Campuzano and activists in Bogotá and Lima, and in the Electronic Disturbance Theater's collaborations with activist groups.[15] Trans of color poetics are also a contribution to queer and feminist approaches to technoscience in that they seek to use numerous kinds of technology—from digital technology to more low-tech approaches—for transfeminist ends. Through an articulation of the algorithmic operations in trans of color poetics, this book begins with trans of color survival strategies in the understanding of digital media art, in sharp contrast to the many studies of digital media that do not even regard trans of color experiences as relevant to the field.

A stitch can be understood as not just a form of movement but also a tool. In her widely influential essay "The Master's Tools Will Never Dismantle the Master's House," Audre Lorde refers to "those of us who stand outside the circle of this society's definition of acceptable women."[16] In the essay she refers to "those of us who are poor, who are lesbians, who are Black, who are older," but I read an opening here for trans women of color in women of color feminism, and an opening for a trans of color feminism.[17] Lorde is referring to the tools of racism, sexism, and homophobia, yet her formulation is deeply important for anyone setting out to make technological tools in the service of social justice. The artists and designers I discuss in this chapter create tools with the intention of transforming oppressive social relations.

When artists and designers work for social justice by creating tools, art and design overlap. While one stream of the history of art is founded on the idea of artistic autonomy, another group of artists has been motivated by a desire to change societal relations. The art historian Kristine Stiles describes how Clement Greenberg was the most influential art critic of the post-1945 period in the United States. Greenberg described modern art in ways that valued abstraction as a move toward the universal, encouraging art practices such as gestural and geometric abstraction, which were "bereft of social and political engagement."[18] These ideas in modernism are a continuation of the objectivity of rational liberal humanism advocated by the Enlightenment to center European whiteness as universal. Grant Kester, also an art historian, writes about how the figure of the singular artistic genius, autonomous from social demands, first emerged from Immanuel Kant's theory of the artistic genius and is still prevalent today in much art criticism and curatorial practice. Kester describes, in contrast, a multitude of politically engaged art practices in the twentieth century, from the Situationists to feminist art collectives and "the remarkable profusion of contemporary art practices concerned with collective action and civil engagement."[19] Art movements since the 1990s, including tactical media, new media, and relational aesthetics, have sought to create art that can change social conditions. Recent movements in design, such as speculative and critical design, contestational design, and design justice, share these goals. Some contemporary art theorists question the viability of creating objects to change social relations, such as Rita Raley, who refers to the term *tactical gizmology* to deemphasize the objects and, instead, emphasize tactical media as performance.[20] In the next section I consider artists' attempts to create objects to attempt to transform social relations, connecting Campuzano's curated museum objects to the work of Adam Harvey, Zach Blas, the Electronic Disturbance Theater, and myself. These artists explore the possibilities for escaping surveillance by stitching clothing, masks, and mobile phone applications.

Countersurveillance beyond the Visual

The forms of stealth that travestis and trans people of color use for survival on a daily basis are also concerns of cisgender artists who see the right to privacy as a political issue. The cloak, as an object of clothing that gives both stealth and protection, recurs in Campuzano's writing and performance. "Museo embozado, cuyas máscaras—la artesanía, la fotocopia, la gigantografía, el <<banner>>, esos sistemas de producción en masa—no ocultan, sino, al contrario, muestran. No camuflan, sino travisten" (Cloaked museum, whose masks—the crafts, the photocopy, the *gigantografía*, the << banner >>, those systems of mass production—do not hide, but, on the contrary, they show. They do not camouflage, but they travesti), writes Campuzano.[21] The wall text in an exhibition of the TMP, beside a rich dark cloak embroidered with silver flowers that was a large part of Campuzano's costume for her performance of the Virgin Mary, states, "Cross-section of the androgynous-transvestite sacredness: Virgin—under her cloak the memory of our hermaphrodite gods."[22] Here Campuzano describes the cloak not only as a part of transformation brought about by a costume, but also as a protective gesture, a gesture of hiding the underlying histories of Indigenous gender fluidity that were outlawed by colonizers and were then incorporated into syncretic rituals that combined Catholic images with Incan practices. The exhibition is a restaging of *TMP* from the São Paulo Biennial at the Gallerie de L'Erg in Brussels. Yet, as Campuzano points out, he was not the first travesti to perform the Virgin Mary, and other artists have created cloaks for stealth.[23]

Trans and queer communities' concerns about modulating visibility need to be considered in light of the widespread use of surveillance technologies. Many artists and designers reacted to the news about widespread surveillance by the US National Security Agency (NSA) with tactical responses aimed at stopping that surveillance. In 2013, Edward Snowden, an analyst at the NSA, released millions of documents to corporate media outlets around the world detailing how the NSA was monitoring the communications of millions of Americans, as well as many people in other countries.[24] Mass public outrage followed. Many people saw this practice as unconstitutional, in violation of the Fourth Amendment's protections from unwarranted searches. One of the main documents described how a warrant was issued to the NSA to obtain metadata from Verizon on millions of phone calls of people in the United States, a warrant that was later decided, after Snowden's revelations, to be unconstitutional.[25] The facts of this widespread spying, released by Snowden and broadcast in the media, started a public dialogue over the concerns of increasing surveillance facilitated by major corporations, including Google, Facebook, and Microsoft.[26] Adam Harvey and Zach Blas have created artworks that specifically respond to these issues. I see these projects as related to projects I have worked on—the *Transborder Immigrant Tool* (*TBT*), by the Electronic Disturbance Theater, and *Autonets*. These projects all take a similar political approach to changing social relations by creating new technological objects using various kinds of stitching.

The cloak, the object of clothing, is synonymous with the idea of stealth. Adam Harvey, an American artist who lives in Berlin, has created numerous anti-surveillance garments, including a cloak to protect the wearer from the thermal imaging systems used by the unmanned aerial vehicles known as drones. The biography on his website states that he is an American artist; his racial, gender, and sexual identifications are not mentioned there or in the articles I read, but he appears to be white and male.[27] Harvey, in collaboration with the fashion designer Johanna Bloomfield, uses fabric with metal woven into it to disrupt thermal imaging used by drones in a project titled *Stealth Wear*. The website describes *Stealth Wear* as "a vision for fashion that addresses the rise of surveillance, the power of those who surveil, and the growing need to exert more control over privacy."[28] In an interview with Joanne McNeil of Rhizome.org, Harvey describes how his interest in challenging surveillance technologies emerged from seeing how the Uniting and Strengthening America by Providing Appropriate Tools Required to Intercept and Obstruct Terrorism Act of 2001—better known as the USA PATRIOT Act—effectively turned cameras into "enablers of surveillance societies."[29]

Stealth Wear makes visible the ways that bodies are increasingly monitored by algorithms that determine who is to be the target of surveillance, or violence, such as the algorithms of a drone. Harvey states in interviews that these projects are intended more to generate conversation than to be practically functional. The project includes another religious garment (like Campuzano's Virgin Mary costume); in this case, however, the garments are a burqa and a hijab. Discussing the project in a TEDx talk, Harvey says that the project is concerned with asking, "Is there a way to disappear?"[30] His only justification for showing the burqa is to be "deliberately provocative," he says. "Instead of providing a separation between man and God, [the burqa is intended to] provid[e] a separation between man and drone."[31] While Harvey's project seems to be motivated by the good intention of providing safety for Muslim people unjustly targeted for violence by the algorithmic warfare of the "war on terror," there is no evidence that he is speaking from his own experience or that he has had conversations with affected communities. His anti-drone garments—a hoodie, a hijab, and a burqa—are priced between $475 and $2,500. (His website also offers more affordable aluminized mylar blankets.)[32] While such prices are out of reach for many people, they are low compared with the cost of objects created through current military research into creating invisibility cloaks, as I described in chapter 3. Researchers at the University of Texas, Dallas, have also demonstrated that transparent carbon nanotube sheets can be used to create a mirage effect, potentially hiding the wearer or even a large-scale area.[33] Harvey's *Stealth Wear* project is thus an act of stitching that enacts a cut in the field of surveillance by drones.

Methods of transformation, or concealment, that trans people targeted by violence use include not only clothing, but also makeup. Harvey's anti-surveillance artwork began not with *Stealth Wear* but with *CV Dazzle*, a series of hair and makeup designs intended to defeat computer vision (CV) algorithms in a way similar to how stealth wear defeats thermal imaging. These designs are futuristic and often not practical; some cover the face, draw shapes or additional eyes on the face, or use hair to disrupt the face's geometry. The facial appearances in *CV Dazzle* are very gender-non-conforming; they were created through a process of algorithmic analysis that I see as an act of stitching. In his TEDx talk, Harvey describes how he created the looks by testing them with the kind of CV algorithms that were commonplace in 2019 in smartphone camera applications and digital cameras.[34] These CV algorithms are in themselves a form of colonial violence embedded in the everyday lives of technology users and of people subjected to CV surveillance in cities around the world. The idea that you can determine someone's gender by looking at them is violent. The imposition of only "male" and "female" labels is violent, erasing the lived experiences of people throughout history. Artificial intelligence (AI) systems for CV are based on the colonial assumption that a white male observer is objective and can see the interior truth of a person, turning them into an object, which is based in, and reinforces, white supremacy. Here the decolonial strategy of a poetics that is not only visual becomes a strategy for cutting into the field of mediation of algorithmic surveillance technologies. Visual strategies are not enough to escape the contemporary algorithms of surveillance. One must take the specifics of algorithms of surveillance, from CV to mobile phone networks, into consideration to avoid detection.

The creation of these designs is a collaborative performance with the algorithms of CV: the looks must be created, then processed by the algorithm that gives a confidence value for the presence of a face. Then the design must be modified and retested. Through this process, an algorithm for how to style one's hair and makeup is created around the decision contours of the CV algorithm. The CV Dazzle looks contain multiple gestures across one's face and hair. The process of designing them is an act of stitching, like Campuzano's DNI (De Natura Incertus) project (see the introduction), in which a material object is created in response to an algorithm, thus embodying the limits and boundaries of the algorithm in a material object. In this case, the object is a face decorated with makeup and hair shaped by the limits of the algorithm.

Like the quipu, garments can encode resistant algorithms. Harvey has created other stitched fabric garments in collaboration with Hyphen-Labs, which includes Black and Latinx women of color, in the project HyperFace.[35] For the Hyphen-Labs project Neurospeculative AfroFeminism, presented at the Sundance Film Festival in 2017, Harvey created a textile print that can defeat CV algorithms. The collaboration included Carmen Aguilar y Wedge, Ashley Baccus-Clark, Nitzan Bartov, J. B. Rubinovitz, and Ece Tankal from Hyphen-Labs, who worked with Harvey to create "an Afrocentric countersurveillance aesthetic." The resulting fabric confuses neural network algorithms for facial detection by including many false faces within it. Thus, a camera pointed at a person wearing the fabric will detect a multitude of faces.

A face mask made of mesh with blue eyeshadow, red lips, and long, curved eyelashes sits atop the cloak of the Virgin Mary costume in the TMP installation in Brussels. The mask is a style used in the Chonguinada and Tunantada dances in Peru, and many of such masks are included in Campuzano's book.[36] The dances involve Indigenous people in the regions of Junín and Juaja wearing masks and dancing in ways that satirized the Spanish colonizers. The dances are recorded as far back as the seventeenth and eighteenth centuries. While masks are an ancient method of transformation, in the TMP the masks facilitate a layered poetics of transformation, gender subversion, and decolonial performance.

The contemporary artist Zach Blas creates masks that seek to unseat the colonial assumption that the aesthetics of a face can be a way to read a person's character. His *Facial Weaponization Suite* (FWS) is another project with the intent to disrupt surveillance. Blas is a first-generation Puerto Rican cisgender male queer artist currently residing in London with whom I have collaborated on numerous projects, including performing in videos for his *Face Cages* series of works.[37] The FWS project, exhibited from 2011 to 2014, consists of a series of masks designed to disrupt biometric surveillance by digitally scanning the faces of multiple people and stitching them together in 3D modeling software.[38] The resulting forms are beautiful and strange. The masks have been exhibited in museums and galleries, including the Museo Universitario Arte Contemporáneo (MUAC) in Mexico City, Eyebeam in New York, and HTMlles in Montreal.[39] They are perfectly smooth objects, digitally fabricated. Richly pink, blue, gray, and black, they shine with a plastic sheen, as if they were wet. Blas created four series of masks; the pink "Fag Face" masks (figure 5.1) were the first series, a response to a study at the University of Washington that claimed to have developed CV software that could detect homosexual people's faces, calling both the assumptions and the uses of such a study into question.[40] The bright pink, bulbous "Fag Face" masks were made from scans of multiple queer men's faces. Other series of masks in different colors were based on scans of faces of workshop participants. The black masks focused on the racism behind biometric technologies' inability to detect Black faces. The blue masks considered feminism's relationship to visibility in consideration of French laws regarding wearing hijabs. The gray masks highlighted biometrics at the Mexico-US border.[41] Blas articulates how biometrics such as facial recognition discriminate along lines of race, gender, and sexuality, reinforcing normative notions of identity as fixed and transparently legible through visibility.[42] Those notions are Western colonial impositions that trans of color poetics, as seen in Blas's work, actively resist.

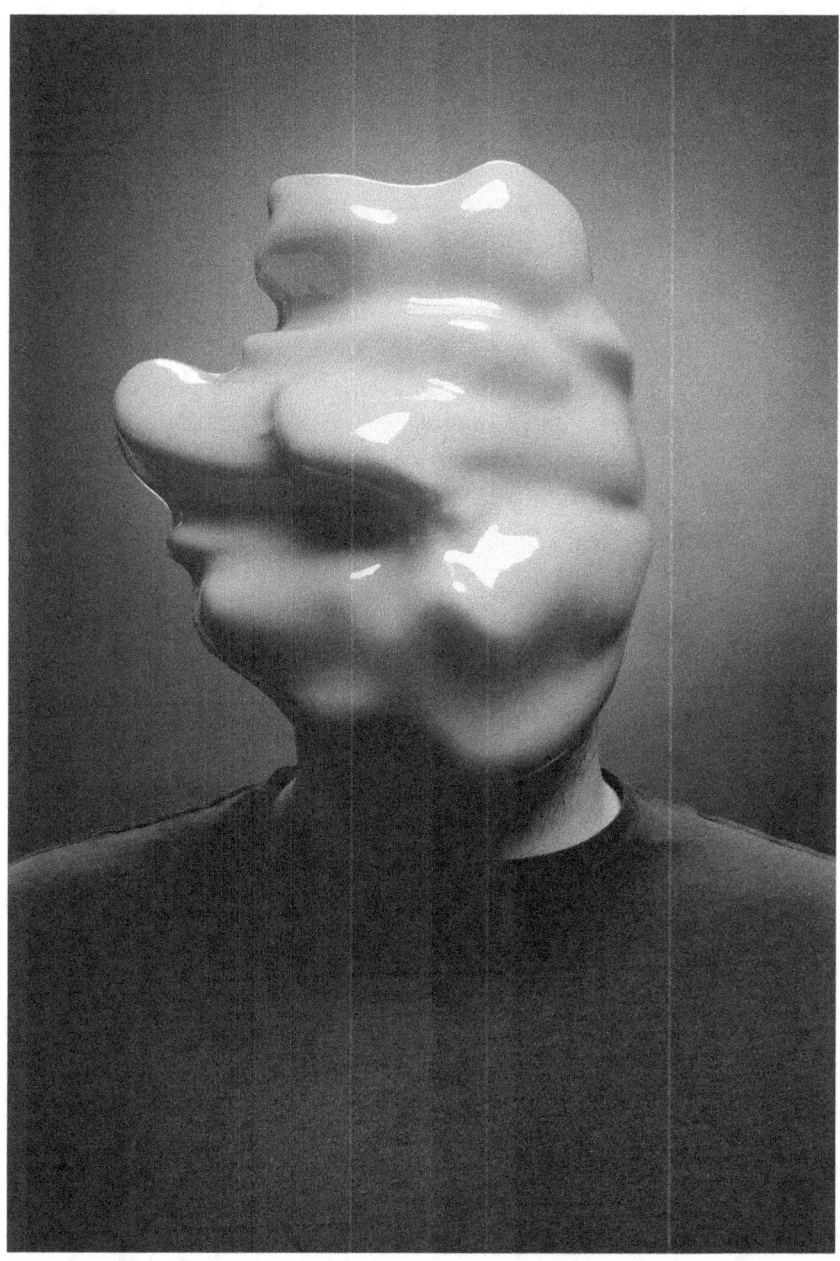

5.1 "Fag Face" mask, *Facial Weaponization Suite*, by Zach Blas.

Eschewing visibility as a political strategy for queer people, people of color, and feminists, the FWS focuses instead on a politics of opacity informed by Édouard Glissant's writing. Blas's website describes the collective aspect of the project as "making 'collective masks' in community-based workshops that are modeled from the aggregated facial data of participants, resulting in amorphous masks that cannot be detected as human faces by biometric facial recognition technologies."[43] In an interview with *Newsweek* magazine, Blas points to the ways that biometric tools such as facial recognition software "are being developed by police and the military to criminalize large chunks of the population."[44] In another article, Blas describes his concern as focusing on "queer people, people of color, transgender people, broad sets of minoritarian populations."[45] In earlier chapters, I argue that trans of color poetics focus on movement over position, modulation of visibility more than inhabiting a space of visible or invisible. Blas's work on the harm caused by visibility for queer people helped me theorize this argument. Blas sees the FWS project as "speculative proposition and practical experimentation, . . . an opaque practice, producing variations on how to become informatically opaque."[46]

Blas's FWS is performing a trans of color poetics in that it uses the gestures of stitching and shifting to work toward the survival of trans people of color. As discussed in chapter 3, Blas's essay is based on Glissant's idea of opacity. "Glissant's aesthetico-ethical philosophy of opacity . . . is paradigmatic," Blas writes. "His claim that 'a person has the right to be opaque' does not concern legislative rights but is rather an ontological position that lets exist as such that which is immeasurable, nonidentifiable, and unintelligible in things."[47] In chapter 2, I discuss the value of opacity for the trans of color poetic gesture of the cut, in which an act of cutting of connection can be an important gesture of protection. Blas is more concerned with algorithms of capture than surveillance in general, stating that "humans write capture algorithms, and that means that human bias is often found in the very technical architectures of capture."[48] In the algorithmic stitching of data Blas uses to create masks that disrupt the mediation of bodies by biometric surveillance, one can see the act of stitching used to enact a cut in a field of mediation.

Blas's project operates in the mode of speculative design, as only a few masks were designed as prototypes; they are not sold for practical use. Speculative design is a field in which designers create objects as theoretical experiments, not limited by the constraints of practicality or marketability. Anthony Dunne and Fiona Raby are two well-known figures in the field, which is taught at universities in game design and media design programs.[49] Speculative design has been critiqued by the Brazilian theorists Luiza Prado and Pedro Oliviera for "willingly ignor[ing] struggles other than those that concern the intellectual white middle classes."[50] Blas's work, however, is an example of speculative design that does not fall under their critique. As he stated, Blas is designing these masks in part for trans people, and he has collaborated with trans artists in performances of the FWS. Similarly, another artist group, the Electronic Disturbance Theater 2.0/b.a.n.g. lab (EDT) describes its work as speculative but differs from much speculative design in that it works from a commitment to safety for trans migrant people as a central component of its project.

The dance in the performance of TMP in Bogotá was an act of border crossing in many ways. Campuzano states, "Este es un cuerpo político que continua una memoria, en la danza, el vestido, el maquillaje" (This is a political body that continues a memory, in the dance, the dress, the makeup), gesturing with his hand toward his chest.[51] While the performance challenged colonial notions of gender, it was also a literal act of border crossing, with Campuzano traveling from Peru to Colombia, as well as an act of transnational collaboration in that Campuzano chose to work with a dancer, as well as an activist collective, from Bogotá. Similarly, the *Transborder Immigrant Tool* (TBT) is a project that centered the act of border crossing as an act of creating art.

The TBT had the goal of providing physical and poetic sustenance to people crossing the Mexico-US border by creating an app for inexpensive recycled phones that would allow the user to find water in the desert (figure 5.2). The project has been described by one of its founders, Ricardo Dominguez, as "speculative disturbance" and "contestational design."[52] The artist Tad Hirsch has defined contestational design as "design activities that engage in advocacy work in collaboration with and/or on behalf [sic] particular players in adversarial political processes."[53] While speculative design often adopts more of a stance of free-floating autonomy from the realities of gendered and racialized violence, contestational design begins from a standpoint of opposition to an existing power structure. The TBT is a combination of cell phone and software that intends to provide both physical sustenance, in the form of water, and poetic sustenance, in the form of recorded audio of spoken poetry, to people attempting to cross the Mexico-US border. The project began with the research question, "Can sub-$20 phones be made useful for emergency navigation"?[54] As the Mexico-US border is one of the most contested geographies in the hemisphere, Dominguez's description of the project as contestational design holds true. Trans of color poetics are a method aligned with

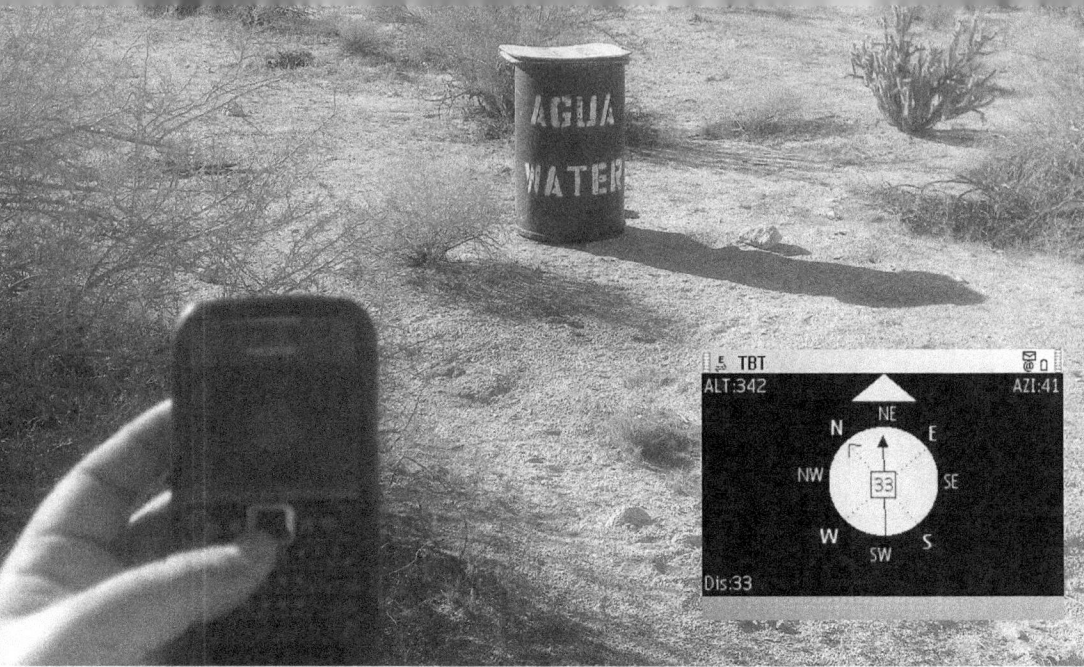

5.2 Concept for *Transborder Immigrant Tool*, by Electronic Disturbance Theater, showing working tool and screen shot from a Nokia e71 cell phone, 2011.

contestational design as poetics that begin with a standpoint of resistance to the white supremacist cis-heteropatriarchal norms that inflict violence on trans people of color daily.

While one goal of the TBT was to develop a way for people crossing the border to access global positioning system (GPS) service without being tracked by cellular networks, performing a cut into that field of mediation, the project performs the stitch in the form of collaboration, writing software, and building solidarity. While the cut is an act that uses interruption to create opacity, stitching is an act in which time is used to create relation. To interrupt surveillance from both the border patrol and anti-immigrant vigilantes who patrol the Mexico-US border, Brett Stalbaum wrote a custom software application to run on the phones that was able to receive GPS signals from satellites but did not send out any cellular transmissions. This interrupted efforts to monitor outgoing cellular radio transmissions from the phones. The phone worked by mapping water caches placed in the desert by Border Angels and Water Stations, Inc., humanitarian aid organizations based in San Diego. Creating the software involved a collaborative process of going into the desert alongside members of those organizations to place water while recording coordinates to create a GPS map of the caches. Organizers with Border Angels told us about their concerns about anti-immigrant groups getting hold of our GPS map of their water caches, so the application used encryption to store the map data securely. The only way to access the GPS coordinates in the *TBT* was to use the tool and walk to each water cache individually. Collaboration was central to the project both within and outside the EDT. In addition, because it is a J2ME Java application, the code can be seen as an act of stitching that combines many code libraries to function. Finally, my writing on the *TBT* pointed to an affect shared by transgender people and migrant people: hope of being somewhere else, whether that place of inhabitation is another country or another body.[55] Highlighting this shared affect is intended to build solidarity between immigrant justice movements and gender justice movements, which are often separate, despite the continued detention of transgender migrant people, such as Marichuy Leal Gamino, a trans woman who was held in a detention center near Phoenix for more than a year and was sexually assaulted while in custody.[56] The links among these movements are manifold, and the poetry seeks to bring those layers of connection to life.

Algorithmic Poetics

The *TBT* has been described by the Electronic Disturbance Theater/b.a.n.g. Lab as transforming the GPS run by the US military into a *global poetic system*, to use a term created by Laura Borràs Castanyer and Juan B. Gutiérrez.[57] Consider the following excerpts from "net.walkingtools.Transformer," a poem I wrote as part of the *TBT* project. I first performed it in a performative lecture about the *TBT* at the Catalyzing Knowledge in Dangerous Times Conference at the University of California's Berkeley Center for Race and Gender and later published it in the article "Operation Faust y Furioso" with the Electronic Disturbance Theater:[58]

```
package net.walkingtools;

import info.QueerTechnologies.TransCoder;

public class Transformer extends java.lang.Object
implements java.lang.Runnable
{
/* Fields */
private java.lang.String lifeLine;
```

```
private boolean maleOrFemale;

private boolean citizenOrMigrant;

private java.lang.String genderDesired;

private java.lang.String genderGiven;

private java.lang.String oldName;

private java.lang.String newName;

private java.lang.String birthPlace;

private java.lang.String destination;

private java.lang.String attributes;

private java.io.File uploadMyBody;


private net.walkingtools.j2se.walker.HiperGpsTransformerShifting nepantla;

private net.walkingtools.j2se.editor.HiperGpsCommunicatorListener listener;

private volatile boolean walking;

private volatile boolean running;

private volatile boolean dancing;

private volatile boolean transforming;

private volatile boolean danger;

private byte[] me;


publicAndPrivate TransCoder theSoftBody;


/* Constructors */

public

Transformer(net.walkingtools.j2se.editor.HiperGpsTransformerShifting ,

java.lang.String) {


    if(genderGiven != genderDesired || birthPlace != destination)

    {

        walking = true;


        /* attempt to enter into a queer time and place via the

        transcoder library */


        while(theSoftBody.qTime(GogMagog)){


        dancing = joy;

        transforming = hope && pain && fear && fantasies &&

            uncertainty;
```

```
//is the assignment operator, that of identity, binary
    in itself?
//try some other methods like becoming serpent through
    poetry

nepantla.open(imaginedWorld);
nepantla.shift(towardImaginedBody);
uploadMyBody &~& resistLogicsOfCapital!

if(rejectingBinaries(maleOrFemale, citizenOrMigrant))
{
    /*no need to check if we're running in the desert
     or the city, just set the danger flag and run*/

    danger = high;
    running = true;

    /*multiply identities here, but we'll need
    support to do that, the code won't be enough */
    lifeLine *= love [[& care] & community] & solidarity + resistance;

}

else
{
    /* perhaps its best for us to just escape logic
    and western rationalism altogether
    thirst and desire already do this for us */

    oldName = newName = null;
    exit();
}

}
 }
 }

}


// end class Transformer
```

The poem uses the actual code of the *TBT* and stitches into it a poetic meditation on the intersections of transborder and transgender. While following the format of Java source code, the poem exceeds the bounds of computational logic that would allow it to function. It uses the syntax of the algorithms that control mobile phones to express emotional experience, in the tradition of cyberfeminist poetry. I describe elements that can be regarded as constituting an identity, such as name and birthplace, with variable declarations, creating a place in memory for those elements. Then I place those variables into an algorithm in which one can see specific ways that different parts of an identity can be parts of decision-making logic for trans people of color and migrant people.

Multiple levels of meaning are sewn together through these algorithmic poetics. The poem opens with a long list of declarations of variables, which is standard in code. Yet when these declarations are read as a poem—particularly when they are read aloud—there is so much repetition that it hints at the ritual space of performance, or a poetic degree of repetition. The poem uses standard Java keywords such as *private* and *public*. To describe the body, though, an invented category is used: "publicAndPrivate." Some variables here refer to parts of an identity, such as "genderDesired," which can reproduce a problematic modularity, which Tara McPherson has described as an element of racial logics.[59] Yet variables are dynamic processes in memory, maintained by electrical charges, performative in that they exist only at run time. If one considers open source algorithms, such as the algorithms of Scalar that run the digital components of this book, they are available in a public repository and can be modified to suit one's particular uses. Perhaps the danger of modularity of code can be offset by its mutability and potential for collaborative editing. The code of a computer program is also a body, and that body exists in process, in transition. In her review of *Troubling the Line: Trans and Genderqueer Poetry and Poetics*, Frances Richard describes my poem as potently performing "the act of transing" through "tropes of the poem as a transmittable body, a private 'lang. String' rendered 'public class.'"[60] Richard describes how the body described in this poem not only is stitched together from lines, but also connects the poet and the reader, an act of transmission.

My poem "net.walkingtools.Transformer" shows that there can be both precision and poetic ambiguity in an algorithm. Flow control statements in the poem are used to express commonalities between transgender and immigrant experiences. The line

```
if(genderGiven! = genderDesired ||
    birthPlace! = destination)
```

reads, for readers who know Java or C-derivative languages, as "if gender given is not equal to gender desired, or birthplace is not equal to destination." The code that follows inside the parentheses is executed if this "if" statement evaluates to true for the subject in question. This line imagines elements of my life experience, as a trans person, encoded into computer code in the Java programming language. One could also imagine such an algorithm being used within a video game about transgender migration, or a Transportation Safety Administration algorithm for deciding outcomes for airline passengers. In addition, the poem plays with programming conventions such as "flags," or variables used to control the logical flow within a program. In the poem I set the danger flag variable to high to indicate a high level of danger. Other lines in the poem depart from coding conventions and imagine code libraries that execute the functions of Chicana feminism. These lines were inspired by Blas's transcoder library, which includes functions based on theorists such as Donna Haraway, Judith Butler, and Michel Foucault.[61] Lines such as

```
nepantla.open(imaginedWorld)
```

call an object that is not described here but left to the imagination of the reader. The nepantla object refers to Gloria Anzaldúa's usage of the Nahuatl word *nepantla*, referring to a space in between worlds, a space of transformation, a liminal space often accessed through ritual. Anzaldúa described "nepantla" as the ability to shape-shift, allowing one to access different kind of knowledge. She states, "The writer, as shape-changer, is a *nahual*, a shaman."[62] She wrote extensively about the experience of shape-shifting as central to her writing process, providing an important example of shifting as an operation of poetics.[63] Yet in this imagining, the nepantla space is part of a code library that can be accessed when needed by a function call. One may imagine this as a decolonial usage of code, attempting to stitch Aztec traditions passed down through Anzaldúa's queer, disabled, trans of color feminist writing together with trans subjectivities that operate today through Java code on mobile devices. After working on the *TBT* for four years, I decided to start a new project to increase safety for groups of which I felt more a part: transgender people, women, and trans women of color.

Solidarity is an act of stitching. Perhaps the largest impact the *TBT* had was to start conversations—many, many conversations—opening the possibility for connecting people separated by borders through the trans of color poetics of stitching. In our publication *Sustenance: A Play for All Trans[] Borders*, the EDT describes the *TBT* as a conversation piece.[64] Grant Kester has described contemporary art practices that provide space for dialogue, engage publics in dialogue, and emerge from collaborative practices "conversation pieces."[65] While the *TBT* created a functional prototype, it was not used by many people besides the artists. It did, nevertheless, generate hundreds of news articles around the world, prompting a great deal of conversation about the ethics of giving someone water in the desert, particularly if that desert is an international border. The piece also prompted conversations about the ethics of artists attempting to work for survival for immigrants and trans people. These conversations led me to use the strategy of creating art as a means of working for the safety and survival of oppressed peoples for my next decade of artistic creation. The conversations we had with activists putting water near the border were acts of stitching, building solidarity by finding our shared goals. The conversations we had with one another in the collective also created bonds among us. Conversation, when used to build bonds of solidarity, is an act of stitching. It is my hope that the conversations people had in response to the media articles also allowed them to find common ground in the ethical gesture of providing sustenance for those in need. Yet my own practice led me to want to focus more on safety for the community of trans people of color, which led to my creation of *Local Autonomy Networks* (*Autonets*).

Autonets was directly inspired by the prison abolition movement, which was a part of many conversations in QTPOC art and activist spaces in Los Angeles. Many of my collaborators were part of the Coalition to End Sheriff Violence in Los Angeles Jails. I originally built prototypes of *Autonets* in the form of a line of clothing and accessories with conductive thread and wireless transmitters that were capable of forming autonomous mesh networks. I made hoodies, bracelets, and a dress in black and gray, in collaboration with fashion designer Ben Klunker. The initial hoodies had circuit boards and silver conductive thread sewn on the outside of the garment. After feedback from workshop participants in Detroit, I made the garments more discreet, sewing the circuits into the seams of the hoodies. The hoodies had LED lights around the hood that, when activated, would light up and slowly pulse on and off. The dress also included a hood and was draped with many folds that came down to below the knee.[66] The bracelets were straps of black leather that contained batteries and the wireless transmitters, with mesh network-ing circuitry; they were the simplest version of the devices. I used the Lilypad Arduino platform to stitch the electronics into the garments. Mesh networks route traffic among devices locally instead of sending all data through phone companies and international domain name system (DNS) backbones. Thus, they may offer one of the few ways to avoiding the NSA's surveillance nets, which capture all internet traffic at the DNS level of communication.

Autonets demonstrates a struggle over forms of communication that is far older than digital networks used for surveillance today. Colonialism controls the forms of communication that the colonized are allowed to use. In the Spanish colonization of the Americas, embodied communication was deval-ued, even outlawed, to enforce the written word as the only legitimate form of communication, and thus to reinforce Spanish rule over the Indigenous peoples of the Americas.[67] Moving knowledge away from the body to priv-ilege the mind is part of a larger project of Enlightenment philosophy that privileges the unitary Western male subject as pure objective mind, mirror-ing the form of God, able to go anywhere.[68] In contrast, Indigenous peoples, non-Western peoples, and women and gender-non-conforming people were all relegated to the base realm of the material body, with no access to higher knowledge, and thus no right to power.[69] Walter Mignolo argues for a decolo-nial geo-body-politics that accounts for this history, grounding knowledge in bodies in specific places.[70] These histories of struggle over the site of knowl-edge and the forms communication can take continue in today's landscape of the internet. Rosi Braidotti has linked this Enlightenment subject of colo-nialism to the fantasy of the internet as "cyberspace," reinforcing patriarchal imaginations.[71] Lisa Nakamura cites Ziauddin Sardar, who "regards cyber-space as a medium that can only transmit imperialistic ideologies," but con-trasts him with Jeebesh Bagchi of the Raqs Media Collective, who sees the in-ternet as a potentially liberatory space: "Envisioning and using the Internet in visual rather than primarily textual ways can be a radically empowering move for nonliterate groups."[72] Nakamura states, "As the Internet becomes richer in moving images, it may have more to offer users whose cultural ver-nacular encompasses video and signboards, visual cultures of movement and signification, rather than text."[73] Nakamura sees a parallel between these ar-guments and postcolonial debates over maintaining cultural authenticity through language. I argue that what is at stake is the distribution and repro-duction of power through communication mediums, reproducing epistemol-ogies that limit political possibility.

Digital communication through the internet, for example, is not a transparent transmission of language or images. Each packet of data—whether it is a pixel or a character—is encoded into the Internet Protocol Suite, commonly known as TCP/IP, and contains multiple layers of information including routing and hardware information.[74] This communication standard was created by the US Department of Defense, but is now maintained by the Internet Engineering Task Force under the auspices of the Internet Society, a nonprofit organization with headquarters in the United States and a board of trustees who are also mostly in the United States.[75] Communication standards such as HyperText Markup Language (HTML) are largely defined by US-based corporations. Theorists such as Ngũgĩ wa Thiong'o have considered the question of how language, the medium of communication, limits and shapes possibilities of thought and expression. While Thiong'o claims that African literature can be written only in African languages, Glissant is more invested in a decolonial reappropriation of French.[76] These two differing strategies, in light of decolonizing digital communication, invite a much deeper consideration of the limitations and possibilities of encoding systems in general. Trans of color poetics, as embodied in *Autonets*, take up these debates but work to find practical solutions to finding safety.

One performance of *Autonets* titled "Local Autonomy Networks: Find Each Other" took place at the international ZERO1 Biennial in San Jose, California, in September 2012.[77] The performance used speculative design prototypes of wearable networked clothing in performance in the public space area of an international art biennial with participants from Gender Justice LA (GJLA).[78] The performance built on months of Theater of the Oppressed workshops in which participants worked with prototypes of networked *Autonets* garments I had produced and discussed how they might use them for safety. In these workshops, held in Los Angeles, people used both verbal dialogue and embodied gestures to express how safety and violence felt in their bodies. As I described in the introduction, practice-based research intersects with transgender studies as described by Susan Stryker, who states, "Transgender studies considers the embodied experience of the speaking subject, who claims constative knowledge of the referent topic, to be a proper—indeed essential—component of the analysis of transgender phenomena."[79] In this performance, trans people of color are not the objects of study, but the subjects of knowledge creation. Together we created the gestures in this performance: a visual, embodied, affective research outcome of the question of how to use technology to reduce violence against trans people.

The "Find Each Other" performance of *Autonets* in September 2012 included Ezak Perez, a two-spirit performer, who put in years of work stitching community together with Gender Justice LA. Focusing on the work of Campuzano is one way to listen to the specific desires and demands of travestis. Another important decolonial formulation of gender nonconformity is embodied by two-spirit people. Perez organized a theater of the oppressed group within Gender Justice LA that met every two weeks. I met with them for more than a year, building friendship, relation, and solidarity and watching them foster confidence, joy, and connection among our communities. We performed together at the GJLA annual fundraiser weeks before the performance of "Find Each Other."

Performing "Find Each Other" with GJLA was a way to support that group's continued work of building safety for the community of trans, gender-nonconforming, and low-income people in Los Angeles. We drove together from Los Angeles to San Jose for the performance, on the sunny Highway 5, through the wide agricultural spaces of central California, listening to music, talking, and laughing. It was an important time of connection for all of us. In the afternoon before the performance, we held a Theater of the Oppressed workshop to develop gestures that embodied ideas and feelings of protection and resistance. The imperative of the title "Find Each Other" speaks to the impulse behind the performance: to find a community that can provide safety. As a trans woman of color living in Los Angeles, I felt isolated from numerous queer communities, and I felt my vulnerability daily. The performance, and the process of collectively building networks of safety, helped to give me a feeling of connection to trans people, two-spirit people, and people of color that I needed to feel happy and safe. In the workshop, we discussed how to keep one another safe without calling the police. We discussed questions such as, "Can I call you if I get assaulted?" We talked about who could be a buddy for someone else when walking home at night. Participants in the workshop had experience with violence from police. We felt that we needed to rely on one another to keep us safe, because no one else would. So questions arose about whom to call instead of the police; what to do once violence had occurred; and how we could protect one another.

For the public performance we collectively decided to do an evening performance in which participants would practice the skill of dispersing and coming together when signaled by the electronic garments. In a busy outdoor art festival environment in downtown San Jose, with hundreds of audience members, loud music from other installations, roving police, and spontaneous performances, our performance group was made up of cisgender and transgender people, white people and people of color, straight people and queer people, and we all wore *Autonets* hoodies or bracelets. Three of the participants were professionally trained dancers and performance artists. Two were scholars pursuing graduate degrees. Three were organizers with Gender Justice LA who were part of a group that met regularly and offered trainings in Theater of the Oppressed. Using the hand-stitched garments, we practiced embodied methods for modulating our visibility in public space. After blending into the crowd, one member of the group would turn on their garment and make a physical gesture, developed in the workshops, that expressed the participant's ideas and feelings about the prompts "protection" and "resistance." Some gestures were very concrete, and some were very abstract. One gesture involved the performer spinning in a counterclockwise circle, ending by extending their right arm with fingers up and palm forward and screaming, "Stop!" In another gesture, a performer first reached their right arm up in the air, fingers splayed wide, then brought that arm was in front of them at eye level; the left hand was placed on top of the right, interlacing the fingers. The performer would then lower their hands a few inches and bend their knees, three times. When they saw that the hoodies had been enabled and the gestures were beginning, other members of the group would join, mirror the gesture being performed, then begin their own gesture for others to mirror. This technique, borrowed from dance, is called flocking.[80] The performance used the flocking technique to stitch our movements together into an expression of solidarity.

The performance had many motivating intentions, including mine and those of the participants. One shared goal was to bring some of the feelings of violence felt by the participants into the space of an international art biennial, to exceed what was expected of a comfortable, affluent audience looking for entertainment. The participants were highly aware of the power differential between them and the art audience and curators, and of the multiple levels of mediation into which they were entering as trans people, people of color, and gender-non-conforming people, who are already hypervisible to the surveillance networks of the state. Another goal was to develop concrete skills for the participants, practicing ways of coming together at a moment's notice to respond to violence. While the speculative design prototypes made future possibilities of communication visible, the participants discussed the difficult realities of building prison abolition responses to violence that do not rely on police or prisons for safety. Ultimately, these performances were performative, speculative gestures, as the strength of bonds needed to rely on others to protect them from violence cannot be built through a handful of workshops and performances.

Autonets started with wearable electronics as speculative design prototypes but continued as a research creation project over four years, during which I discussed the prototypes with different groups experiencing violence in many different cities, including Detroit and Toronto. We collectively envisioned possible futures of building autonomous networks of communication for safety. The project centered on the research question, "Can I, as an artist, work with communities to build networks of communication that can reduce the violence that queer and trans people of color experience?" Ultimately, the wearable electronics approach proved to have too many problems to be useful, given the current state of the technology. The wearable transmitters were too expensive, and circuits sewn by hand were not reliable enough for long-term use. In addition, as with the *TBT*, battery life was a limiting factor. These concerns, raised by participants in workshops, led me to shift the focus of the project to the possibilities of building communications networks that do not rely on digital technologies, such as embodied forms of communication and movement that can be used for safety, including signaling methods and practices of dispersing and converging.

To work to end violence against trans people of color, the strategies they use to survive should be centered and valued as both knowledge and artistic production. Poetics include repertoires of gestures, similar to how an algorithm is made up of multiple operations. Learning trans of color poetics from trans of color communities provides new operations of thought and action. Proposing the operation of the stitch, I have elaborated algorithmic methods made perceptible by contemporary artists through art, design, and media, as well as through my practice-based research and art projects. I addressed the stitching work of media artists working to escape government surveillance. These examples demonstrate stitching fabric, code, and communities together. In the next section of this chapter, I return to the *Autonets* performance in São Paulo to consider how stitching can build solidarity.

The Decolonial Stitch

Theorizing travesti as an operation is an act of solidarity that acknowledges the specific lived differences of trans people of color to articulate trans of color poetics. Learning from women of color feminism—a movement founded to bring together women of different races and ethnicities, including Latinx, Indigenous, Asian, and Black—trans of color poetics also seek to build solidarity among gender-non-conforming people of many ethnicities and localities. In place of an aesthetics that would seek empathy from well-meaning viewers, trans of color poetics seek solidarity that can actually work for safety, evoking action from trans people of color and our allies who are willing to take action with us, for all of our continued survival in the face of globally rising fascism.[81] With the success of transgender studies in the academy, it is deeply important that people experiencing intense marginalization because of their racialized genders not be left out. Travestis in Brazil, for example, continue to face a lack of medical care, even when transsexual medical care has been made part of the universal health-care system. Because many travestis do not want gender confirmation surgery, they are seen as disruptive to cis-heteronormative gender binaries and are routinely denied the medical procedures they need.[82] Conditions are even more precarious for travestis in Peru than in many other countries in Latin America, as there is no national law there protecting the rights of trans and queer people.[83]

Travesti organizers in Brazil have demanded to be identified separately from transsexuals, reaffirming the importance of listening to specific groups' politics and poetics to articulate a broader framework of trans of color poetics. The Brazilian Health Ministry published a report in 2013, "National Policies for the Comprehensive Health of Lesbians, Gays, Bisexuals, Travestis, and Transsexuals," that for the first time outlined national priorities for LBGT health.[84] The report was shaped in response to pressure from travesti organizations that do not want their particular form of gender expression to disappear under pressure to call themselves transsexuals.

Identity in difference is a central operation in women of color feminism, and trans of color poetics can stitch together connections that provide safety. Kara Keeling describes in her article "I = Another" an algorithmic formulation of identity in difference. The stitch consists of an embodied gesture that binds two entities together using a third. Here I continue to bring the stitch into deeper dialogue with decolonization by returning to a consideration of my performance "We Already Know and We Don't Yet Know" (see chapter 2). To return to my earlier consideration of Glissant, the stitch can be understood as an extension of his poetics of relation. Glissant ties relation to mestizaje through the French word *métissage*. His formulation of relation here recalls the mestizaje of Chicana feminism, which used weaving as a model for solidarity, in the writing of Anzaldúa and Chela Sandoval.[85] Glissant does not use the word *stitching*, but he does refer to fabric and weaving when he says, "Opacities can coexist and converge, weaving fabrics. To understand these truly one must focus on the texture of the weave and not on the nature of its components."[86] He posits a joining of multiple entities that maintain their separateness, each still opaque but woven together. Glissant urges one to consider the "texture of the weave" of multiple opacities, which I understand as the quality of relation among people, with each person having their own right to opacity. By focusing on the texture of the fabric, and "not on the nature of its components," one can grasp the effect of solidarity, the feeling of connection, instead of simply focusing on individual experiences. With "We Already Know," the feeling we sought to sew among participants was one of safety. That safety was created by building trust over days in the workshop, but also by knowing other workshop participants were nearby. The performance was also a way of rehearsing methods of communication that might allow that texture of safety to be felt in daily life by practicing nonverbal, nondigital methods of communication.

Trans of color poetics of stitching can sew solidarity, increasing the chances of survival and safety for trans people of color. Solidarity is an affect, a feeling of connection, followed by a performative utterance, a commitment, or an action. Unlike empathy, which is thought to be a feeling that can be evoked, and is thought to be an end in itself, solidarity requires an acknowledgment of shared struggle. While artwork by trans people is often thought to have the goal of building empathy, the subject of that empathy is often cisgender people. In contrast, I am interested in building solidarity among other oppressed people who want to work together to end our shared oppression. Solidarity is saying and feeling that, although we are different, your struggle is my struggle. At the core of solidarity is a felt sense of connection.

Activists' responses to the extreme violence against trans and queer Latinx people in the Orlando Pulse massacre serve as a powerful example of solidarity as part of decolonial struggle. On June 15, 2016, the Audre Lorde Project (ALP) released a statement on its Facebook page and website titled, "Do Not Militarize Our Mourning: Orlando and the Ongoing Tragedy against LBGTSTGNC POC," stitching connections among the murders of trans and queer people of color, women of color feminism, and colonialism:

> From our experiences on the ground as an organizing center for and by Lesbian, Gay, Bisexual, Trans, Two Spirit, and Gender Nonconforming People of Color (LBGTSTGNC POC) we know that this massacre is not the exception, it is part of the economy of violence against LBGTSTGNC, Black people & People of Color, indigenous people, and immigrants. It makes explicit what the institutions of war, prisons, detention centers,

and the police teach our communities every day: that we were never meant to survive. . . . Contrary to what the media and mainstream LBGT organizations and publications are depicting: the victims and survivors are Black, Latinx, AfroLatinx, Trans, Gender Nonconforming, undocumented, and working class. These identities matter. They matter because of the US occupation and militarization of Puerto Rico and Latin/South America due to US sanctioned economic violence. . . . They matter because there is an epidemic of murder of Black and Latinx Trans Women and Gender Nonconforming people and this tragedy is part of this ongoing colonial project.[87]

The statement makes evident the knowledge construction in which QTBIPOC activists are engaged. "We were never meant to survive" is a direct reference to Audre Lorde, who wrote this phrase in her poem "A Litany for Survival."[88] Her words' usage here demonstrates how the poetics of women of color feminism continue to do work against violence inflicted on trans and queer people of color. Much of this violence is similar to the kinds of murder of women of color that Lorde wrote about, such as the police killing of young black boys.[89] The activists of the ALP are using the algorithms of social media networks to make connections between the violence against trans people of color and the roots of that violence in colonization. To understand the poetics of trans people of color in digital media, it is necessary to understand the colonial frameworks that are the foundations of the concepts of transgender and the digital, as well as to understand the formation "people of color" as a decolonial strategy. Gendered and racialized violence are global challenges of incredible urgency, and decolonization provides a global framework for responding to these challenges. Gender and race in contemporary society are inseparable from the digital technologies that define and manage them. While contemporary gender binaries and racial categories can be seen as a result of colonial processes, digital technologies also represent a continuation of global colonial logics. This chapter identifies the ways that colonialism operates through digital communications, ways that colonialism's effects can be undone, and efforts to build postcolonial futures. Decolonial acts of solidarity are acts of stitching, connecting communities across national borders and across lines of gender, racial, and sexual identification.

The stitch is a decolonial operation in transnational and transcultural collaboration. Stitching is seen here in affective, material, and conceptual operations involved in collaboratively building visions of decolonial futures. In "We Already Know," which I discussed in chapter two, the stitch can be seen in a physical practice of transnational solidarity between a group of Colombian artists/activists and myself, which led to questioning the colonial relations involved in digital media art. "We Already Know" focused on embodied forms of communication in public space both as a way of sharing affect and a means of creating safety networks that are free and do not rely on costly digital technologies. Despite the ongoing claims that digital networked culture is postracial, postfeminist, postidentity, postnational, and postcolonial, the contemporary world is still largely structured around colonial divisions of global North and South, as is evidenced by the concerns from artists in Colombia about a lack of access to digital technologies in our planning of "We Already Know." The persistence of the global colonial divide has been referred to as neocolonialism by the feminist scholar Chandra Talpade Mohanty.[90]

Decolonization provides a framework to examine the ethical and political implications of socially engaged media art in transnational, hemispheric, and global contexts—contexts that are shaped by national borders, postnational identifications, and the neocolonialism of global capital. By working with a community-based design approach in the United States, Canada, Brazil, and Germany with my practice-based research project *Autonets*, I questioned the neocolonial processes that shaped the technologies I was making. Looking to the history of colonization as a moment in which embodied communication is replaced with written communication, I propose that learning from digital networks to abstract their form and reproduce them without digital technologies is a decolonial act, and collaborating transnationally with people in the global South can be a way of decolonizing digital media. In this formulation, the operation of the stitch, of creating networks and performances by joining people across national borders, becomes a part of the process of decolonization. One can learn about colonization from analyzing digital technologies. One can analyze digital technologies by creating new ones. In what follows, I describe an example in which the creation of wearable electronic devices led to a new understanding of the colonial dimensions of digital technology.

Stitching Transnational Collaboration

The performance "We Already Know and We Don't Yet Know" was developed in collaboration with a network of artists and activists from Colombia, Brazil, and the United States. The socioeconomic status of my collaborators in Colombia and Brazil allowed much less access to digital communications technologies, largely because of the cost. As a result, the solutions that I was proposing from a US context did not appeal to these Latin American activists and had to be reimagined. The performance of *Autonets* in Brazil resists colonial violence. It brings together critical understandings of gendered, racialized, colonial violence with trans of color poetics of digital media to create artworks that challenge neocolonialism. While working on the first series of prototypes of *Autonets*, in 2009, the members of the Cero29 artist collective in Bogotá told me that their primary concern was the possibility of preventing disappearances.[91] Disappearances are a tragic occurrence throughout Latin America, and in Colombia they are a result of neocolonial drug war policies that have seen the Colombian government receiving "billions of dollars in American aid, training and equipment, making it one of the top 10 recipients of US assistance worldwide."[92] Reports stated that, as of June 2015, the Colombian military and paramilitary collaborators had killed 4,475 civilians since 1986 in a process called "false positives," in which soldiers were given financial bonuses for body counts, then murdered civilians and dressed them in guerrilla uniforms.[93] Human Rights Watch has described the "false positives" as "one of the worst episodes of mass atrocity in the hemisphere."[94] My initial proposal to Cero29 was for hoodies that contained wireless transmitters and GPS units so that, in case of a kidnapping, someone could easily activate their wearable electronic garment and be locatable. The Cero29 members' response was twofold. First, they said that they were very concerned about government surveillance and thus did not want to work with GPS units at all. And second, the garments were far too expensive to be useful to them, as I discussed earlier.

The *Autonets* performance in São Paulo still, in some ways, reproduced the dynamics of neocolonialism, which I feel are important to address. Part of the project of trans of color poetics, learning from decolonization movements, is to be self-critical and understand how one is implicated in larger colonial processes. Ultimately, we did not secure enough funding for the members of the Cero29 collective to travel to São Paulo, but I was able to attend and facilitate the workshop. As the workshop took place in an academic context, most of the participants were from the United States; only three were from Brazil, and none identified as Indigenous. In leading the workshop, though, I gave full authorial control to the workshop participants. I invited them to offer any gesture in the performance that they wanted and any words or sound. The valuation of colonial power in a given situation has many dimensions, such as the fact that many participants in my "We Already Know" workshop and performance were people of color: Black, Latin American, and mixed race (figure 5.3). As Walter Mignolo writes, "Latinos and Black Americans in the United States are demonstrating that either the margins are also in the cen-

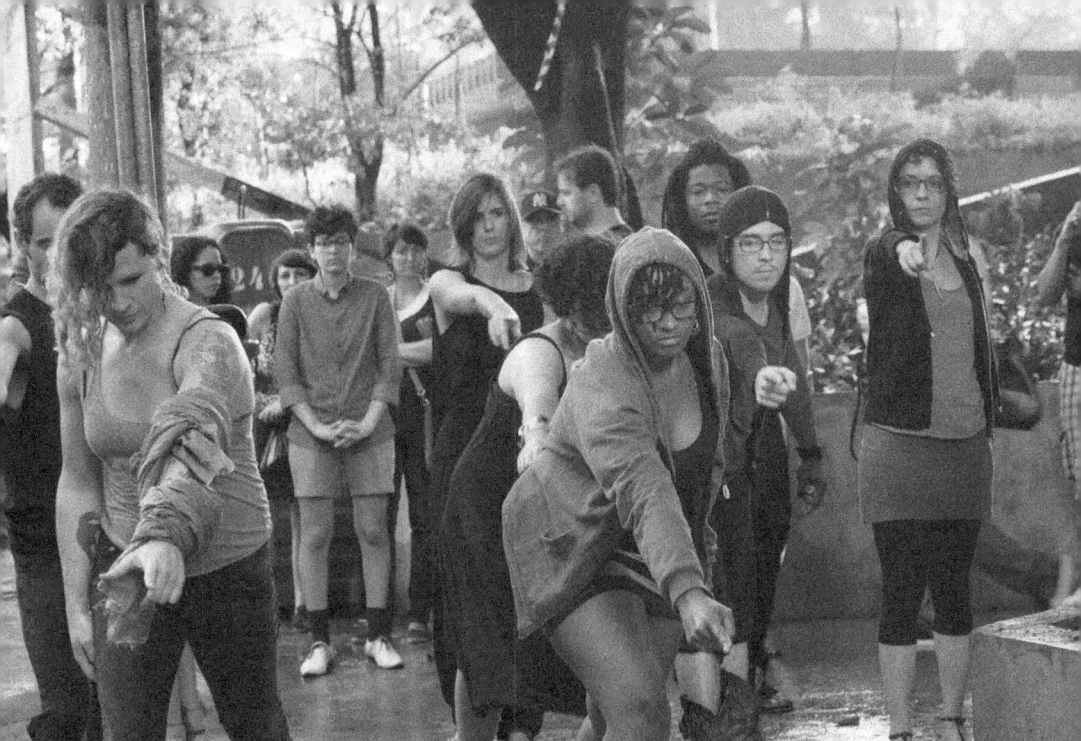

5.3 "We Already Know and We Don't Yet Know," *Autonets*, by micha cárdenas, performed at the Hemispheric Institute of Performance and Politics, Eighth Encuentro, São Paulo, 2013. Photograph by Frances Pollitt. The video is accessible at http://scalar.usc.edu/works/poetic-operations/we-already-know-and-we-dont-yet-know.

ter or . . . that knowledge and aesthetic norms are not universally established by a transcendent subject but are universally established by historical subjects in diverse cultural centers."[95] In this way, one can see how the analysis of neocolonialism across lines of global North and global South is not always perfectly binary, since there are so many differences of power within those two huge divisions. Similarly, Mohanty articulates a decolonial struggle that recognizes that people formerly considered "Third World" peoples are now spread everywhere across the globe due to neoliberal globalization, migration, and diaspora, which she describes as a neocolonial situation.[96] Thus, the stitch can be seen as an attempt to bring people together against the violence of neocolonialism, which in "We Already Know" was a response to violence against queer and straight, trans and cis, men and women of color from various sites throughout the Americas. The stitching in this performance, bringing people together across borders to build transdigital methods for preventing violence, is a performance of trans of color poetics.

"We Already Know" was a micropolitical gesture. No reviews were written about it. The audience was about fifty to seventy-five people. My primary audience for the performance, just as with "Find Each Other," was the workshop participants. The process of creating the performance together over the three-day workshop was the actual act of stitching, building trust, connection, and solidarity by discussing how we could collectively work for safety for trans people of color, women and people of color affected by transphobic acts of violence and incarceration. The most important gesture in the performance, to me, was the moment when we all stepped out of the repetition of the flocking. Part of our agreement for the performance was that anyone could step out at any time and improvise with the architecture of the street, or blend into the audience. My gesture in the performance embodied my imagination of death, falling to one side and letting my arm swing limp. At one point, I moved away from the group flocking and lay down on a long cement planter, arm dangling down. At that moment one of the performers, the Italian media artist Alessandra Renzi, walked over to me and began gently playing with my hair. Her improvised gesture escaped the algorithmic repetition and transformed the scene from one of loss to one of care. Next, another performer lay down on the planter, mirroring my gesture and adding a layer to the scene, which could be read as an act of solidarity.

When stitched together, the movements in "We Already Know" become a ritual of care. One of my main goals for the workshop was to discuss ways that we could create a performance about violence that would not reproduce violence. We sought to create art about the traumas of transphobic violence and prisons without retraumatizing ourselves, instead searching for healing. In the performance there is a gesture of arrest, a gesture of cutting, a gesture of death, a gesture of mourning, and improvised gestures of care and tenderness. We began by looking at the networked clothing I had created as a prototype. From there, we discussed how to build abolitionist networks of safety through verbal agreements and embodied practices.

Conclusion

In workshop after workshop, in city after city, when I spoke about the idea of building local networks for safety for trans people, people of color, and women, the response was the same: "We need this here." I presented *Autonets* in Toronto multiple times, including a workshop titled "Autonets Convergence" at the University of Toronto, with the goal of seeding a DIY network of hackers to produce more safety technologies for marginalized groups.[97] In

Berlin I presented a workshop at Transmediale titled "Building Local Autonomy Networks."[98] Berlin was where I experienced the worst daily harassment, ridicule, and physical assault. A trans woman there told me that it was normal; that she had been spit on, on her way to meet with me. The performance there involved choreography I created with my collaborators in which, after many instances of harassment and after I had been told that the U-Bahn, the city's rapid transit system, was too dangerous for a trans woman to take, they stood between other people on public transit and me.[99] In each city, I maintained the same horizontal collaboration ethic that I had in Los Angeles. The content of the performances was completely up to the participants. They were invited to use any gesture, sound, or words they chose to in the workshops, which we then performed publicly. At the Dark Side of the Digital Conference In Milwaukee, the title we developed for our performance was "Healing Is our Response," and the performance began with individual performers spread throughout the building, a kind of living museum in the style of La Pocha Nostra. Then we converged in the center of the space to flock with all of our gestures as a group.[100]

Autonets developed the idea of local safety networks in a post-internet future. While looking at the insidious way the NSA had surveilled people en masse, it became clear to me that the internet is a technology designed by the US military to surveil and conduct war. Part of my vision of a decolonial future of justice includes surpassing and leaving behind the internet. Mesh networks, such as networked clothing that contains its own transmitters and can communicate without phone networks or internet infrastructure, offer one possible avenue for this future. In Detroit—where 40 percent of residents did not have access to the internet in 2017, often because of the cost—organizers with the Detroit Community Technology Project are building community-based mesh networks.[101] *Autonets* is an art project that demonstrates possible uses for mesh networking and possible futures beyond the internet. Perhaps part of the future of justice for trans people of color will see the technology becoming more affordable, and we can each wear our own wireless networks, which, when linked together, can span huge distances. Yet the project also expresses my own longing for connection and safety. In a time when I still felt so much fear for my physical safety on a daily basis, I imagined, what if I could simply touch my heart, activating a pressure sensor that would inform everyone in my personal safety network that I need help? I see implications of this technology for many other communities, as well, such as disabled people. Ultimately, the focus of the project moved to more affordable strategies of building support networks, such as using text messaging in Los Angeles and using non-verbal communication in Brazil. The shift from physical safety to emotional safety, exploring the feeling of safety in workshops and performances, came toward the end of the five-year project. All of these experiences stemmed from the original act of stitching wireless transmitters into hoodies.

Mohanty's global vision of decolonization emerges from women of color feminism, and I build on that claim to extend decolonization to include trans people of color. Considering that Audre Lorde was a major figure in women of color feminism, can one reconcile her claim that the master's tools cannot dismantle the master's house with the effort I have described here of decolonizing the digital, of learning from and repurposing digital technologies? Lorde states, "Survival is . . . learning how to take our differences and make them strengths."[102] She urges solidarity across lines of difference of race, class, and gender, and the process I have described here understands transnational solidarity between trans people of color in the United States and people experiencing violence in global South countries as a step toward decolonization. Women of color feminists have questioned binary divisions between people in profound ways. Anzaldúa describes *la conciencia de la mestiza* as a mediator, saying, "A counterstance locks one into a duel of oppressor and oppressed. . . . [B]oth are reduced to a common denominator of violence. . . . [W]e will have to leave the opposite bank, the spilt between the two mortal combatants somehow healed so that we are on both shores at once, and, at once, see through the serpent and eagle eyes."[103] The operation of the stitch learns from digital technologies to move through and across multiple fields of mediation, to see from many viewpoints, and to come together to build a trans of color poetics. Building relations among people involves finding points of connection and resonance. Learning from Glissant's poetics of relation, in which each individual is composed of a network of relations, I extend the stitch to stitching relations among people.

Writing algorithms requires stitching together many shifting elements into a coherent order, into a logic, into a poetics. Proposing the operation of the stitch, I have elaborated algorithmic methods made perceptible through art, design, and media by contemporary artists, as well as through my own practice-based research and art projects. Trans of color poetics learn from the movement of trans people of color in digital media to build new models for thinking race, gender, and sexuality in digitally mediated, networked environments, with the goal of reducing violence. The media artists' work discussed in this chapter uses different design methodologies, from speculative design to contestational design and community-based design, each with varying degrees of engagement with the communities each project is intended to benefit. On many levels, this book learns from social movements, from my collaboration with Gender Justice LA and Giuseppe Campuzano's collaborations with collectives in Bogotá to the ways that *Autonets* embodies prison abolition strategies. This chapter included the Audre Lorde Project's articulation of the direct link between the ongoing violence of colonialism and the murders of trans and queer people of color.

By following the thread of the stitch, by looking for the operation of the stitch in the work of artists and activists working to reduce violence against trans people of color, this chapter has demonstrated how artists, regardless of their identities, can use these poetic operations to create opacity and re-lation. The artists working with digital media discussed here—Harvey, Blas, EDT, and myself—all demonstrate methods of modulating algorithmic per-ceptibility. By shielding the users of their tools from CV, cell phone location tracking, and internet DNS routing, these artists show that modulating per-ceptibility must take into consideration algorithmic modes of perceiving, which are not only visual. To work to modulate one's perceptibility today, a consideration of simple visual camouflage would be incomplete. Even with a perfect invisibility cloak, an object from fantasy stories, one would be perceptible to contemporary forms of surveillance if one were carrying a smartphone. That is what the *TBT* sought to prevent by writing a custom app that did not access cell phone towers. Even if one is not noticed as being gender nonconforming when walking down a street, artificial intelligence-based CV algorithms may still be identifying one's face and body as anoma-lous or as demanding further investigation, which Harvey's and Blas's work challenges. In some cases, the best strategies for modulating perceptibility to build safety involve giving up digital technologies and focusing on the physical gestures that can be used to replace digital networks, as in *Autonets*. These methods can be created in collaboration with algorithms, performing for the algorithm to test whether it can perceive you. They can also be cre-ated through an awareness of the methods of surveillance that exist as a field of mediation of algorithmic perceptibility. The trans of color poetics of the stitch open speculative moments of hope for futures of existence beyond the colonial, cis-supremacist, white-supremacist, coded gaze, as Joy Buolamwini has named it—futures in which our care for one another depend not on our sameness but on our ability to find identity in difference.[104]

Like the repetition that algorithms can perform, bonds among people are built through repeated acts of presence. Lavelle Ridley argues that the mo-ment in which Black trans women can stop and take a breath, can find a reprieve from the daily violence of transphobia to be with their friends, is the moment that allows an "imagining otherly."[105] Perhaps the most powerful moments of stitching in *Autonets* were those of providing a refuge for one another. In repurposed classrooms, backyards, and living rooms, with Ezak, Chella, and Shruti from Gender Justice LA, and all of the other participants, we held space for one another to use our bodies to imagine how we could feel safer. We laughed and reflected and shared space away from the violence of police, of misgendering, and of assaults on the street. In Brazil, we started each day of the workshop lying on the floor and breathing together, to the sounds of Alicia Keys's piano playing, feeling our bodies and making intentional space to build solidarity across lines of racialized gender. Stitching solidarity is an act often performed in moments of rest. While trans of color poetics work for broad social change, they often resonate through quotidian, intimate acts of witness, care, and solidarity.

VISIONARY TRANS OF COLOR FUTURES
CONCLUSION

A lot of heads were bashed [at Stonewall]. But it didn't hurt their true feelings—
they all came back for more and more. Nothing—that's when you could tell that
nothing could stop us at that time or any time in the future.
—SYLVIA RIVERA, Street Transvestite Action Revolutionaries

You're lucky that this is all we did. You're lucky that we are appealing to your
humanity. You're lucky that we're not asking for vengeance or revenge, because
that's easy. Our love is radical; it's abolitionist. It's a future where each and everybody has what they need, what they deserve, what they want.
—RAVYN WNGZ, artist and activist, Black Lives Matter—Toronto

ON JUNE 13, 2016, I attended another vigil for our community, a mourning
ritual for trans and queer people of color at the Black Power Epicenter in
Seattle. The event was held to honor and mourn the forty-nine trans and
queer people murdered at the Pulse nightclub in Orlando, Florida. Most of
the victims were Puerto Rican. The song, sage, and togetherness of this healing space felt nourishing, and necessary. Enacting the algorithm of mourning
again, we fill in the variables of names and pictures every time for the circumstances of each new death, but the scale of this horrific event was much

larger, requiring a different way of gathering and holding each other. Many people in Latinx queer and trans communities still ache from the Orlando massacre. The act of violent backlash against trans and queer Latinx people underscores the fact that we have begun to open queer and trans Latinx futures as a possible reality, and those futures make some people very afraid. Queer Latinx futures point to queerness as horizon, as described by José Muñoz, and as possibility. Trans Latinx futures gesture toward worlds free of colonial borders of gender, sexuality, and nationality. As the Audre Lorde Project statement discussed in chapter 5 states, these murders continue deeply troubling recent trends of escalating violence against Latinx people, and trans and queer people of color more broadly, but any recent increase should be understood as part of an older colonial history of violence. Trans of color poetics respond to these histories, revealing and challenging the ways that colonial violence continues in white-supremacist, transphobic violence by offering visionary methods of creating safety through solidarity.

Sylvia Rivera, of Puerto Rican and Venezuelan descent, was a crucial figure in advancing a movement for livable transgender lives.[1] Rivera's futurist vision sharply contrasts the way that trans women of color have been often figured as the image of death and imagines them instead as the image of futurity. While many examples exist of transgender characters in science fiction literature, trans women of color have been largely absent from science fiction films.[2] Queer theory has mobilized the figure of the Latina trans woman to represent regressive heteronormativity and false consciousness, as I discussed in chapter 3. Scholars of queer *latinidad* tell a different story. In *Sexual Futures, Queer Gestures and Other Latina Longings*, Juana María Rodríguez studies queer Latina gesture from contemporary art to daily life. She states, "Futurity has never been given to queers of color, children of color, and other marginalized communities that live under the violence of state and social erasure."[3] Rodríguez sees potential in the expressive capacities of Latinx queer and trans people to build new futures.

In digital gaming communities, conversations about violence against trans women have been advanced by queer and trans game designers. On March 10, 2015, Merritt K published an article about #GamerGate describing how the response from feminist game designers and scholars has focused on only the most privileged women. K writes, "Black and Latina trans women—mostly sex workers—have been murdered every week in 2015. . . . Collectively, we've failed these women, and we've built communities and organizations that mostly benefit people more powerful than them. And I'm worried about the same dynamic happening as we continue to resist online and offline harassment of marginalized people in games."[4] She describes the siege mentality that defined many conversations about #GamerGate, which reduced the issue to gender and focused on the safety of white cisgender women, ignoring the trans people and people of color who were also targeted by the campaign of online violence that spread offline, seeping out into politics in the United States. #GamerGate is one example of discussions of technology and social justice that fail to include the considerations of trans people of color, but there are many more. Trans of color poetics, as I have described it here, begins with the history of rituals of survival that gender-non-conforming people have used throughout history to bring a more nuanced consideration of racialized gendered violence in digital media.

The need for trans people of color to engage in creating their own futures by engaging with digital technologies is urgent, yet it has always been up to us to imagine our future through trans of color poetics. I have shown across this book how trans people of color learn forms of movement that allow them to survive, including the cut, the shift, and the stitch. Chapter 1 described trans of color poetics as a decolonial poetics grounded in the concept of poetics of relation and learning from M. Jacqui Alexander's global vision of decolonization as a project of liberation for people everywhere with histories of colonial violence. Chapter 2 showed how cutting into fields of mediation can enact opacity, disrupting colonial forms of power and ways of knowing through the performance of "We Already Know" in São Paulo. Shifting is made both visual and audible in the films of Janelle Monáe, discussed in chapter 3, showing how the modulation of visibility is more important for survival under necropolitics than any one state of visibility. Direct experiences of shifting are described through the digital games *Mainichi* and *Redshift and Portalmetal* in chapter 4, demonstrating the limits of empathy in games. While *Mainichi* was initially made from a desire to create empathy, the looping algorithmic form of the game gestures beyond, to the incomprehensibility of violence. *Redshift* uses a transreal mode, shifting between fiction and nonfiction to speak to multiple audiences on different registers, and the game ends by urging players to engage in real-world acts of solidarity with Indigenous peoples. Instead of empathy, chapter 5 calls for solidarity, which involves both a feeling and the actions that feeling inspires, by considering how the *Autonets* project used the operation of stitching to create relations among people. Yet *Autonets* also enabled opacity from internet surveillance, which the artists Adam Harvey and Zach Blas and the Electronic Disturbance Theater are all shown to enable, as well. The examples of stitching demonstrate that trans of color poetics can be enacted by anyone and are not limited to artists with particular identities. These gestures, forms of movement made perceptible through digital media, offer decolonial strategies for justice for many people who experience violence today.

When Gloria Anzaldúa writes, "If going home is denied me then I will have to stand and claim my space, making a new culture—*una cultura mestiza*—with my own lumber, my own bricks and mortar and my own feminist architecture," I hear a need for a feminism for trans Latinas and Chicanas.[5] A trans of color feminism can account for the historical absence of trans people and trans concerns in both white feminist and women of color feminist theory, activism, and art. I understand trans of color poetics as part of a larger movement for trans of color liberation. Performances and workshops of *Autonets* were created in collaboration with activist organizations working for justice for trans, two-spirit, and gender-non-conforming people of color, including Gender Justice L.A. and ILL NANA/DiverseCity Dance Company. Part of the work of women of color feminism was to stitch together communities across racial lines, which I discuss in chapter 5, and that operation can also be seen in the work of trans of color artists imagining possible futures.

My focus is on justice for trans women of color because our needs have been largely ignored and unaddressed. To work to end violence against us, the strategies that trans people of color use to survive should be centered and valued. I have described some of the necropolitical mechanisms that allow trans women of color to be murdered on a daily basis, such as new forms of controlling visibility and movement. I hope that understanding these mechanisms will aid in preventing violence against other racially gendered groups of people, as well. Violence against trans women of color can be seen as part of the global problems of anti-Black violence, violence against women, violence against Indigenous peoples, and violence against people of color. Focusing on trans people of color in digital media and art involving the digital, such as digital performance, I have used algorithmic analysis to articulate trans of color poetics to help contribute to ending these larger global crises.

As each chapter has illustrated, algorithmic analysis involves breaking problems down into components and operations. The cut and the fold are two material and conceptual operators that have been considered previously in media theory, transgender studies, and performance studies. I have proposed the stitch and the shift as operators of thought and action, learning from histories of weaving and shape-shifting in women of color feminism. The intersectional model proposed by Kimberlé Crenshaw transformed the thinking of so many people while calling much-needed attention to the specific nature of violence faced by Black women. Similarly, my hope is to extend dialogues about the intersections of race, gender, and sexuality by proposing algorithmic analysis as a method of thinking, and creating, that learns from the experiences of trans women of color.

Trans of Color Poetics amid Rising Authoritarianism

When I began writing this book in 2013, there seemed to be a moment of optimism, which was soon tempered by the continued rise in murders. Laverne Cox's *Time* magazine cover was published in May 2014, the year after I began writing. Her claim was that, even though we were making great gains in visibility, there was still a deep need to take concrete steps for the safety and survival of our communities. The first issue of *TSQ: Transgender Studies Quarterly* was also released in May 2014. In 2020, in the midst of Donald Trump's presidency, the situation was more dire as I finished this book. While violence has always been present against trans people of color, the hatred was now out in the open. The Trump administration was working toward what trans-exclusionary radical feminists such as Janice Raymond have wanted for decades: to legislate transgender people out of existence.[6] To do so would continue the genocidal violence enacted by European colonizers when they arrived in the Americas hundreds of years ago.

The questions that motivated this book are more relevant than ever. While Black people and trans people of color have been living in a state of emergency for many years, many more communities are now in a similar state. The need to manage visibility and be able to understand more shades of visibility than just invisible or visible is especially true in this age of internet propaganda wars being waged through Facebook ads.[7] The importance of creating new concepts and new forms of poetics, such as trans of color poetics, is still crucial when the urge is to simply react. It has been made public that one of the strategies of the Trump administration was to act so quickly that the opposition was left constantly reacting, never building its own long-term strategies, never resting.[8] The urgency of solidarity is as important as ever, as so many communities—trans people, Black people, immigrants, Muslims, disabled people, cisgender women, Jewish people, Indigenous people—are finding themselves increasingly under attack. The need to look closely at racial and gendered violence, and their intersections, is as urgent as ever, with a former president who said that white supremacists are "fine people" and has been accused by more than ten women of having sexually assaulted them.[9] The importance of learning from the experiences of oppressed peoples, of listening to them and centering their leadership, is crucial in this moment, when it seems that the violence of white supremacy is new but it is actually a centuries-old pillar of colonialism. Trans of color poetics center the artistic strategies of trans people of color, which builds on their experiences of survival, in the face of so much violence. By putting Black trans women, Latinx travestis, and two-spirit performance artists at the core of this consideration of violence, this book illustrates the long histories of oppression and survival that have continued to morph over time, finding ways of persisting under new digitally enabled forms of necropolitical death. Tracing the algorithms that shape so much of our political possibility today back through the rituals of gender transformation of people of color demonstrates how decolonial strategies can provide ways through and beyond the morass of contemporary regressive movements toward totalitarianism.

What the shock of Trump's election to the presidency in 2016 underscores is the increasing importance of algorithms. Trump won then even though he lost the popular vote by millions of votes, the worst loss in US history.[10] He did so by exploiting the algorithm of the Electoral College. Trump's election also largely benefited from Russian hackers.[11] Further, there is no doubt that Trump's use, and abuse, of electronic media such as Twitter played a role in his election. The importance for those of us in resistance to fascism to understand algorithms, to be able to resist their workings, is powerful, and growing. Algorithms play an ever-increasing role in people's daily lives, in the form of artificial intelligence (AI) assistants from Apple, Google, and Amazon, in the form of social media sorting algorithms and in the form of increasingly deadly drones, robots, and androids. In August 2018, the United States and Russia blocked a treaty proposed in the United Nations against autonomous weapon systems with the power to take human lives.[12] Algorithmic analysis, as scholars of algorithms such as Safiya Noble, Joy Buolamwini, Virginia Eubanks, and I have demonstrated, includes reverse engineering existing algorithms, analyzing the workings of algorithmic media, writing resistant algorithms, analyzing code (when it is available), and analyzing processes to find their components and operations.[13] I imagine many more methods of algorithmic analysish will be articulated by others.

In this book, I have shown that a focus on algorithms and algorithmic processes in digital media by trans people of color allows one to reveal some of the operations of trans of color poetics—particularly the cut, the shift, and the stitch. These operations are also used more widely by contemporary media artists. In the past three years, public awareness of the dangers of algorithms has grown immensely. Noble's book *Algorithms of Oppression* has contributed significantly to this awareness. In the book, she argues not only that

Google's search engine reinforces racism, but that the company intentionally profits from it.[14] Noble articulates powerful arguments for increased legislation of search algorithms to protect the public good. While I agree that a long-term legislative strategy is important, I believe that the current political climate in the United States is highly unlikely to produce legislation that will protect trans women of color in any meaningful way. In fact, the Trump administration made changes to law that are harming transgender people further. Given this situation, this book advocates an approach that is inspired more by the politics of direct action. Sylvia Rivera and Marsha P. Johnson did not seek funding and legislation to work for safety for trans women of color. Instead, they opened their home to other trans women and provided them with food and shelter, creating the Street Transvestite Action Revolutionaries (STAR) house to intervene directly in the problem. They organized to raise bail and legal support for trans women in jail.[15] Trans people have already been using algorithmic methods of safety for many years, and we need to continue to develop strategies in conversation with affected communities, with the knowledge and power of algorithms as one of our methods. Much as Crenshaw used law to work for safety for Black women, trans people of color can use algorithms for our own ends. Today algorithms have much of the power of law, if not more.

Academics, artists, and activists analyzing and developing algorithms can work with affected communities to develop novel interventions. In her recent article "Design Justice, A.I., and Escape from the Matrix of Domination," Sasha Costanza-Chock articulates a detailed analysis of the design of Transportation Security Administration's security checkpoints and how the technologies and methods they use harm trans and nonbinary people.[16] In the article she articulates methods of design justice from the Design Justice Network. I was fortunate to join a Design Justice Network gathering at the Allied Media Conference in Detroit on a hot summer day in 2017 and discuss the principles she outlines while sitting in a circle in the grass at Wayne State University. Members of the network, including Una Lee, have been an inspiration for my methods in this book. One of the most important Design Justice Network principles she cites is, "We center the voices of those who are directly impacted by the outcomes of the design process."[17] Using design methods such as these, artists and activists can create systems using algorithms to work to improve the lives of trans people.

Another Design Justice Network principle is, "We prioritize design's impact on the community over the intentions of the designer."[18] Principles such as this one can be very helpful for artists and designers working for justice.

It is unlikely that large corporations making millions of dollars from their algorithms will adopt these methods, unfortunately. It also seems unlikely that legislation will be able to intervene into the everyday design processes of these companies. Yet the Design Justice Network's principles provide a crucial example for those who want to use design for justice. Design justice is a set of practices that are like trans of color poetics, yet they are more focused on design of applications and interfaces for practical usage than on creating artworks. Both design justice and trans of color poetics begin from the concerns of multiply marginalized people, work directly with affected communities, and prioritize safety over profit.

As I have shown in this book, practice-based research, when performed in collaboration with communities, is a long, messy process. In my projects described here, the process has meant working creatively with limited resources, creating prototypes, failing, trying again, and iterating. Throughout the process, the experiments and iterations have been a very fruitful grounds for conversations about some of the most pressing issues in the participants' lives and mine. It is a slow process that does not always proceed in a linear fashion. Led by creativity in the face of need, this form of research takes many sub-paths, diversions, and turns, slowly spiraling forward. From there, the reflection and writing on the research shifts to another level, which also provides feedback into the processes of creation but goes off in its own direction, as well. Part of the usefulness of algorithmic analysis is to identify the limits of algorithmic effects. Both the shift and the stitch, elements of algorithms that can be sensed in trans of color poetics, have effects beyond their immediate enactment, and that is where their poetics are most felt: in the effects of the shift that remain unknown until after one has changed, in the rippling network effects of the stitch, in which one extends one's network of relations through acts of solidarity. My hope is that trans of color authors and artists, and their allies, will add algorithmic analysis as a method alongside the intersectional and assemblage models that have been so fruitful and important for generations of thinkers and activists. Above all, my hope is that I have contributed to the emerging field of trans of color scholarship in a way that adds strength to the argument that trans people of color can no longer be spoken for, erased, and excluded in theory and art. The writings and artwork of trans people of color have much to tell the world today about how to create artwork from methods of survival, how to create ideas from activism, and how to respond to violence by building bonds of community.

In June 2020, just as this book was about to go into production, the United States erupted into a massive uprising to say that black lives matter and call for an end to police. The uprising was in response to the murder of George Floyd by police, which was recorded on video and shared online.[19] Soon after this uprising of millions of people marching and rallying around the world, people added the name of Tony McDade, a Black trans man who had recently been murdered by police, to their claims for justice. While the officer who killed Floyd has been prosecuted, to date there have been no arrests in the case of Tony McDade.[20] Among the many posts online about this uprising was a re-post of a video by Northwest Tap Connection shared on Instagram and You-Tube of a 2016 tap performance to Monáe's song "#HELLYOUTALMBOUT," which I discussed in chapter 3.[21] The powerful video shows Black people of all ages tap dancing, with a cathartic passion that seems to allow them to float, to Monáe's song. The format of the song is call and response, which consists mostly of "say her name," followed by the name of a murdered Black person. The song could be described with a simple algorithm, a single shifting variable: "Say her name: X," where "X" is the name of a Black person who has been killed. Like the asterisk in "trans*," the phrase creates a placeholder filled with potential and futurity, materialized only when the ritual is performed or the algorithm is executed. The asterisk can indicate those who have not yet come or those who have not yet gone. The resurfacing of the video, with new names of Black people murdered by the police filled in every time the song is performed at protests, shows how the ritual created by the song is potentially infinite. While the George Floyd uprising was happening, Nina Pop, a Black trans woman, was murdered, and her name was added to the names recited in protests.[22] We struggle for the day that this song is no longer an infinite list but has an end because Black people are no longer murdered for their race, and Black trans people are no longer murdered for their race and gender.

On August 9, Black Lives Matter—Toronto posted a video on Instagram .com of Rayvn Wngz. It had 14,133 views at the time of this writing and had been reposted on many large social media accounts in a viral moment.[23] The video showed Wngz speaking at a press conference about the defacement of statues of the slaveholders and colonizers Sir. John A. Macdonald at Queen's Park and Egerton Ryerson at Ryerson University.[24] Wngz states,

> We've tried many different ways to get the attention and the conversation of those in leadership roles and positions. It took us having to do this to get y'all to show up. We've been writing letters, we've been creating books, photography, performance art. We've been doing every single way possible to let you know what we deserve, what we need. . . . It's in the technology

of Blackness that we find abolition and in the technology of Black women, right, that we find radical love. And intersectionality. The technology of Black trans folks in leadership roles. . . . Our love is radical; it's abolitionist. It's a future where each and everybody has what they need, what they deserve, what they want. It's raising your kid who is four years old and who is not afraid of the police.[25]

Wngz's words, reproduced algorithmically through social media thousands of times, describe the technology of Black trans folks working toward a vision of futures shaped by abolitionist love. In this book, I have avoided asking what non-trans people can do to stop the murders of trans people of color. Instead, I have focused on the brilliant technologies that Black people, Indigenous people, and people of color have created to survive centuries of genocidal efforts to end our lives. By articulating algorithmic analysis I have described many of the algorithms and algorithmic elements of trans of color poetics, keeping the focus on how trans people of color have engaged in visionary future world building using the operations of the cut, the stitch, and the shift. The movements for justice for George Floyd and Breonna Taylor, fatally shot by police in her own apartment in Louisville, Kentucky, in 2020, have mobilized millions and even mobilized unprecedented numbers of people in support of Black trans lives.[26] The importance of this moment is massive. In the summer of 2020 police cars burned across the United States; the president was forced to evacuate the White House; and calls to defund the police resulted in the city of Minneapolis saying it would dismantle its police department.[27] Still, the murders of trans women of color such as Nina Pop receive little attention from media outlets and social movements. Following the inspiration of groups such as the Combahee River Collective, my aim here is to highlight how trans people of color are saving themselves and creating beautiful, powerful artworks about their visions for their futures. Yet solidarity is still crucial for all of our survival in the face of mounting crises of climate change, pandemic, and authoritarianism. In this time when COVID-19 is disproportionately killing Black, Latinx, and Indigenous people, and poor people, necropolitics is made plainly visible. In the failure to prosecute the police who killed Breonna Taylor, the state's role to decide who must be killed is made evident.[28] There is still so much work to be done, with Minneapolis faltering on its promise to end policing and #BlackLivesMatter murals being used as cosmetic appeasements without real structural changes to policing.[29] In these new movements, continuing the work of #BlackLivesMatter, we see trans people of color, and their allies, responding to the violence of racist transphobia, the legacy of slavery, and ongoing colonialism with poetic gestures: splashes of bright pink paint, fuchsia stencils that say "ABOLISH," pink-and-black feathered costumes, new forms of networked solidarity, and new demands for cuts to police budgets as a step toward the abolition of police and prisons. In these gestures one can see shifting, stitching, and cutting combining in a ritual of resistance that is an old, old algorithm that will continue looping far into the future in new iterations and permutations. As Sylvia Rivera said, they may try, but nothing can stop us—now or any time in the future.[30]

NOTES

Introduction. Algorithmic Analysis

1. *Travesti* has been translated as transvestite, referring to a person who cross-dresses, but I, and others, argue that it has a meaning that goes beyond that, as I discuss later in this chapter. "Travesti, Miguel A. López," *Glossary of Common Knowledge*, June 2015, accessed September 5, 2018, http://glossary.mg-lj.si/referential-fields/subjectivization/travesti. For more, see the "Trans Studies en Las Americas" issue of *Transgender Studies Quarterly* 6 (2) (May 1, 2019), Durham, NC, Duke University Press.

2. Rose, "Giuseppe Campuzano's Afterlife," 243.

3. MAL, "Linha da Vida: Museu Travesti do Peru, 31a Bienal," accessed March 17, 2015, http://www.31bienal.org.br/pt/post/1543.

4. It is possible, if unlikely, that this artwork was created without digital tools, but the artist passed away in 2014, and I am unable to find documentation describing its creation. Even if the work was created in analog, its engagement with the digital algorithms of ID scanning technologies is undeniable. Campuzano's death is referenced in "São Paulo Art Biennial Will Feature Transvestite and Transsexual Artists," *Folha de S. Paulo*, June 16, 2014, accessed September 6, 2018, https://www1.folha.uol.com.br/internacional/en/culture/2014/06/1471085-sao-paulo-art-biennial-will-feature-transvestite-and-transsexual-artists.shtml.

5. Mbembe, "Necropolitics."

6. Aristotle, *Aristotle's Poetics*; Glissant, *Poetics of Relation*.

7. Stryker and Aizura, *Transgender Studies Reader 2*, 8.

8. Stryker, *Transgender History*; Stone, "The Empire Strikes Back," in Stryker and Aizura, *Transgender Studies Reader 2*.

9. Stryker, *Transgender History*, loc. 1664.

10. Stryker, *Transgender History*, loc. 159, 2256.

11. Stryker and Aizura, *Transgender Studies Reader 2*; Chen, *Trans Exploits*; Ochoa, *Queen for a Day*; Snorton, *Black on Both Sides*.

12. Graham, "Inequitable Distributions in Internet Geographies," 17.

13. Dutta, "An Epistemology of Collusion."

14. Lawrence La Fountain-Stokes, "Giuseppe Campuzano and the Museo Travesti del Perú," *E-Misférica* (blog), 2013, http://hemi.nyu.edu/hemi/en/campuzano-interview.

15. La Fountain-Stokes, "Giuseppe Campuzano and the Museo Travesti del Perú."

16. Jarrín, "Untranslatable Subjects."

17. Rose, "Giuseppe Campuzano's Afterlife," 243.

18. Lawrence La Fountain-Stokes, "E6.2—El Museo Travesti Interview," Hemispheric Institute of Performance and Politics, accessed April 17, 2019, http://hemi.nyu.edu/hemi/en/campuzano-interview.

19. Stryker et al., "Introduction," 13.

20. Field, "The Unhelpful Notion of 'Renaissance Man.'"

21. National Aeronautics and Space Administration, "How Algorithm Got Its Name," *Earth Observatory* (blog), January 5, 2018, https://earthobservatory.nasa.gov/images/91544/how-algorithm-got-its-name. See also John N. Crossley and Alan S. Henry, "Thus Spake Al-Khwārizmī: A Translation of the Text of Cambridge University Library Ms. Ii.vi.5," *Historia Mathematica* 17 (2) (May 1, 1990): 103–31, https://doi.org/10.1016/0315-0860(90)90048-I.

22. Turner, Victor W. "Symbols in African Ritual," 1100, emphasis added.

23. Aha et al., "Instance-based Learning Algorithms"; Grefenstette, "Genetic Algorithms for Changing Environments"; Monge and Elkan, "The Field Matching Problem."

24. Crenshaw, "Mapping the Margins."

25. Fisher, "Pauli Murray's Peter Panic."

26. Fisher, "Pauli Murray's Peter Panic," 95–96.

27. Puar, *Terrorist Assemblages*, 212.

28. Crenshaw, "Mapping the Margins"; Puar, *Terrorist Assemblages*.

29. Puar, "I Would Rather Be a Cyborg than a Goddess," 57.

30. Emi Koyama, "The Transfeminist Manifesto," in *Catching a Wave*, 248.

31. Heaney, "Women-Identified Women."

32. Hong, *The Ruptures of American Capital*, loc. 45.

33. Lisa Wade, "Loretta Ross on the Phrase 'Women of Color,'" *Society Pages*, March 26, 2011, accessed March 3, 2020, https://thesocietypages.org/socimages/2011/03/26/loreta-ross-on-the-phrase-women-of-color.

34. Rivera-Servera, *Performing Queer Latinidad*, 25.

35. Ecleen Luzmila Caraballo, "This Comic Breaks Down Latinx versus Latine for Those Who Want to Be Gender-Inclusive," *Remezcla* (blog), October 24, 2019, https://remezcla.com/culture/latinx-latine-comic.

36. Dutta and Roy, "Decolonizing Transgender in India," 334; Aizura et al., "Introduction," 308.

37. For discussion of the complex history of these terms, see Stryker, *Transgender History*; Valentine, *Imagining Transgender*.

38. Sharpe, *In the Wake*, 30.

39. Stryker, *Transgender History*, loc. 623.

40. Hayward and Weinstein, "Introduction: Tranimalities in the Age of Trans* Life," 196.

41. Hayward and Weinstein, "Introduction: Tranimalities in the Age of Trans* Life," 197.

42. That is the title as it reads on the copyright page of the fourth edition: Anzaldúa, *Borderlands/La Frontera* (2012).

43. Anzaldúa and Keating, *This Bridge We Call Home*, 5.

44. Anzaldúa, *Borderlands/La Frontera* (1999), 41, 99.

45. cárdenas et al., *The Transreal*.

46. Undoubtedly, such personal work takes a toll. Still, I strive for it to be healing for myself and others.

47. Ellen Nakashima and Shane Harris, "How the Russians Hacked the DNC and Passed Its Emails to WikiLeaks," *Washington Post*, July 13, 2018, accessed September 4, 2018, https://www.washingtonpost.com/world/national-security/how -the-russians-hacked-the-dnc-and-passed-its-emails-to-wikileaks/2018/07/13 /af19a828-86c3-11e8-8553-a3ce89036c78_story.html?utm_term=.843eebdd1a09.

48. "Steve Bannon: Five Things to Know," Anti-Defamation League website, accessed February 7, 2020, https://www.adl.org/resources/backgrounders/steve -bannon-five-things-to-know; David Smith, "Q&A: What Are Trump and the White House's Links to the Far Right?," *Guardian*, August 14, 2017, https://www .theguardian.com/us-news/2017/aug/14/donald-trump-steve-bannon-breitbart -news-alt-right-charlottesville; Kevin Granville, "Facebook and Cambridge Analytica: What You Need to Know as Fallout Widens," *New York Times*, March 19, 2018, https://www.nytimes.com/2018/03/19/technology/facebook-cambridge -analytica-explained.html.

49. Levi Sumagaysay, "Steve Bannon Named in Facebook-Cambridge Analytica Lawsuit," *Mercury News* (blog), April 6, 2018, https://www.mercurynews.com /2018/04/06/steve-bannon-named-in-facebook-cambridge-analytica-lawsuit.

50. Kate Crawford, "Artificial Intelligence's White Guy Problem," *New York Times*, January 20, 2018, https://www.nytimes.com/2016/06/26/opinion/sunday /artificial-intelligences-white-guy-problem.html; Joy Buolamwini, "When the Robot Doesn't See Dark Skin," *New York Times*, June 22, 2018, accessed August 14, 2018, https://www.nytimes.com/2018/06/21/opinion/facial-analysis-technology-bias.html.

51. Noble, *Algorithms of Oppression*; Eubanks, *Automating Inequality*.

52. Noble, *Algorithms of Oppression*, 171.

53. Noble, *Algorithms of Oppression*, 184.

54. Khorri Atkinson, "More Transgender People Reported Killed in 2015 than in Any Other Year," MSNBC.com, November 20, 2015, http://www.msnbc.com /msnbc/more-transgender-people-reported-killed-2015-any-other-year.

55. Alex Schmider, "2016 Was the Deadliest Year on Record for Transgender People," GLAAD.org, November 9, 2016, https://www.glaad.org/blog/2016-was -deadliest-year-record-transgender-people.

56. Emily Waters and Sue Yacka-Bible, "A Crisis of Hate: A Mid Year Report on Lebian, Gay, Bisexual, Transgender and Queer Hate Violence Homicides," Report for the National Coalition of Anti-violence Programs, accessed November 7, 2017, http://avp.org/wp-content/uploads/2017/08/NCAVP-A-Crisis-of-Hate-Final.pdf.

57. Transgender Europe, "Transgender Day of Visibility 2016—Trans Murder Monitoring Update," press release, March 30, 2016, https://tgeu.org/transgender -day-of-visibility-2016-trans-murder-monitoring-update.

58. Burton et al., *Trap Door*.

59. Burton et al., *Trap Door*.

60. Katy Steinmetz, "The Transgender Tipping Point," *Time*, May 29, 2014, accessed July 29, 2014, http://time.com/135480/transgender-tipping-point; Sarah Hughes, "Laverne Cox: 'We Live in a Binary World: It Can Change,'" *The Independent*, May 31, 2014, accessed August 28, 2017, http://www.independent.co.uk/news /people/laverne-cox-we-live-in-a-binary-world-it-can-change-9461564.html. Cox's formulation invites a consideration of the contemporary political theorist Giorgio Agamben's idea of the state of exception as it applies to human rights discourses for transgender people. To understand contemporary governance, Agamben re- lies on the French philosopher Michel Foucault's notion of biopolitics, which is based on the idea that governments maintain authority through the promise of life by managing populations' health. In response, the Cameroonian theorist Achille Mbembe describes the present situation of violence for colonized subjects as necropolitical. Populations targeted by governments today include noncitizens who attempt to cross national borders, racialized groups, and trans and gender- non-conforming people. While Agamben argues that contemporary governments operate with impunity through a permanent state of exception as the basis for their sovereignty, Mbembe extends his argument by saying that sovereignty today includes the right to kill, using the slave plantation and the colonized country as models for this form of power.

61. Mbembe, "Necropolitics."

62. Stryker and Aizura, *Transgender Studies Reader 2*. To describe trans necropo- litics, Haritaworn et al., *Queer Necropolitics*, and Snorton, *Black on Both Sides*, build on the description of queer necropolitics in Puar, *Terrorist Assemblages*.

63. Sandoval and Davis, *Methodology of the Oppressed*, 807.

64. Hemispheric Institute of Performance and Politics, "E6.1—*particle Group* Berlin Script," accessed October 6, 2020, http://archive.hemisphericinstitute.org /hemi/en/nanogarage.

65. Keeling, "Queer OS."

66. Imarisha and brown, *Octavia's Brood*, 3.

67. Allied Media Projects, "Network Principles," *Allied Media Projects*, accessed March 17, 2021, https://alliedmedia.org/network-principles.

68. I discuss the AMC's specific influence further in the conclusion. In addition, American studies is an important framework here, focusing on social movements

as a mode of theorizing and theory that works alongside and in solidarity with so-cial movements. I have attended American Studies Association conferences for many years and shared much of the writing in this book there. Both of these con-ferences are vital sources of community and inspiration where other trans and queer people of color are using technology to build new worlds.

69. Barad, *Meeting the Universe Halfway*, loc. 1392.

70. Barad, *Meeting the Universe Halfway*, loc. 785.

71. Jagoda, "Gaming the Humanities."

72. See the website for the collaborative design studio And Also Too, accessed November 27, 2018, https://www.andalsotoo.net.

73. Kester, *The One and the Many*, 10.

74. Benford et al., "Performance-Led Research in the Wild."

75. Davis, *Are Prisons Obsolete?*; Spade, *Normal Life*, 19; Colectivo Situaciones, *19 & 20*.

76. Glissant, *Poetics of Relation*, xii.

77. "How to Work with Events in a C++ Class," *CodeGuru*, posted by Slavko No-vak, November 18, 2002, accessed May 3, 2019, https://www.codeguru.com/cpp/cpp/cpp_mfc/events/article.php/c4075/How-to-Work-with-Events-in-a-C-Class.htm.

78. "Break Statement in C," TutorialsPoint.com, accessed May 3, 2019, https://www.tutorialspoint.com/cprogramming/c_break_statement.htm.

79. In chapter 1, I describe two performance art pieces about rituals of safety for queer and trans people of color that I created as part of the *Autonets* project. In chapter 2, on shifting, I describe performances of my game *Redshift and Portalmetal*. Chapter 3 on stitching considers media art projects that counter algorithms of sur-veillance by Adam Harvey, Zach Blas, and me.

80. Mattie Brice, "Empathy Machine," *Mattie Brice* (blog), July 1, 2016, accessed October 8, 2020, http://www.mattiebrice.com/empathy-machine.

Chapter One. Trans of Color Poetics

Epigraph: Esdras Parra, in *The Collected Poems of Esdras Parra*, 11.

1. Lawrence La Fountain-Stokes, "Giuseppe Campuzano and the Museo Trav-esti del Perú," *E-Misférica* (blog), 2013, http://hemisphericinstitute.org/hemi/en/campuzano-interview.

2. As I described in the introduction, I alternate pronouns for Campuzano to reflect her constant shifting between genders.

3. Peterson and Tolbert, *Troubling the Line*, 16.

4. Peterson and Tolbert, *Troubling the Line*, 488.

5. Parra, *The Collected Poems of Esdras Parra*, 259.

6. "Quizás Quizás Quizás," August 15, 2017, accessed March 22, 2021, https://desdeotromar.tumblr.com/post/164215961666/desdeotromar-desdeotromar-ill-just-say-it. The translation of Parra's poem also adds uncertainty: while Berrout un-derstands the last line to mean "to be human once more," another translation could be "to be a new man."

7. Parra, "Introduction," 4–5.

8. "Utopian Pulse–Flares in the Darkroom," press release, Museum of Contemporary Art in Krakow, January 16, 2016, https://en.mocak.pl/utopian -pulse-flares-in-the-darkroom-project.

9. Hemispheric Institute of Performance and Politics, "E6.2—The Transvestite Museum," accessed June 9, 2020, https://hemi.nyu.edu/hemi/en /campuzano-presentation.

10. Lawrence La Fountain-Stokes, "E6.2—El Museo Travesti Interview," Hemispheric Institute of Performance and Politics, http://hemisphericinstitute.org /hemi/en/campuzano-interview.

11. La Fountain-Stokes, "E6.2—El Museo Travesti Interview."

12. Ochoa, *Queen for a Day*, 23.

13. La Fountain-Stokes, "E6.2—El Museo Travesti Interview."

14. Anzaldúa, *Borderlands/La Frontera*, 2012, 48.

15. Rose, "Giuseppe Campuzano's Afterlife," 241.

16. Rose, "Giuseppe Campuzano's Afterlife," 243.

17. Rose, "Giuseppe Campuzano's Afterlife," 242.

18. For more on this, see Dutta and Roy, "Decolonizing Transgender in India."

19. Stone, *The War of Desire and Technology*, 19.

20. Driskill et al., *Queer Indigenous Studies*, 3.

21. Driskill, *Asegi Stories*, 6.

22. Moraga, *A Xicana Codex of Changing Consciousness*.

23. *This Bridge Called My Back* did include writings by Max Wolf Valero, who identifies as a trans man, and numerous women engaging in masculine gender transgressions. In many of the central texts of women of color feminism, including Moraga and Anzaldúa, *This Bridge Called My Back*; Lorde, *Sister Outsider*, and Anzaldúa, *Borderlands/La Frontera*, there are no trans women authors, or even any mention of trans women. This changed later, in *This Bridge We Call Home* (2002), edited by Anzaldúa and AnaLouise Keating, which included a trans woman and a cisgender man. The tension may have arisen from Moraga's attitudes about trans people, in contrast to Anzaldúa's desire to build bridges across difference, which she articulated in later writings.

24. Alexander, *Pedagogies of Crossing*.

25. Glissant, *Caribbean Discourse*, 120.

26. Glissant, *Poetics of Relation*, 16–17.

27. Glissant, *Poetics of Relation*, 11.

28. Glissant, *Poetics of Relation*, 34.

29. The word *métissage* is defined as crossing, crossbreeding, or miscegenation and has a clear resonance with the concept of *mestizaje*, as discussed thoroughly by Gloria Anzaldúa and many other Chicana feminists. *Mestizaje* often refers to racial mixing. In the context of Mexico and the borderlands, a mestiza is often understood to be the child of a Spanish person and an Indigenous person. These definitions invite a deepening of intersectional considerations of race and gender by considering the interactions between mixed race and transgender. Glissant also uses poetics to connect circuits and decolonization, providing another justifica-

tion for engaging in practice-based research, which continues his thinking by using circuits to create media that is both poetic and decolonial. Other interesting uses of poetics include the Caribbean philosopher Sylvia Wynter, who describes a form of autopoiesis that informs my understanding of poetics as concerned with more than language. Donna Haraway's book *Staying with the Trouble* extends this thinking with sympoiesis, a poetics of becoming-with other beings and species. Donna J. Haraway, *Staying with the Trouble: Making Kin in the Chthulucene* (Durham, NC: Duke University Press Books, 2016).

30. Glissant, *Poetic Intention*, 200.

31. Glissant, *Poetic Intention*, 17, 200. In this milieu, Glissant states, "If I now examine the Occident, I see that it has decidedly not stopped conceiving of the world first as solitude and then as imposition—of the Occident."

32. Anzaldúa, *Borderlands/La Frontera*, 2012, 90.

33. Taylor, *The Mask of Art*, 26, 31.

34. "The Story of L. A. Rebellion," Film and Television Archive, University of California, Los Angeles, accessed October 8, 2020, https://www.cinema.ucla.edu /la-rebellion/story-la-rebellion; Ashley Clark, "The L.A. Rebellion: When Black Film-Makers Took on the World—and Won," *Guardian*, April 9, 2015, http://www .theguardian.com/film/2015/apr/09/the-la-rebellion-when-black-film-makers-took -on-the-world-and-won.

35. My hybrid poetry-and-bioart project *Pregnancy* can be viewed online at https://scalar.usc.edu/works/poetic-operations/pregnancy.

36. Laurel, *Computers as Theatre*.

37. Laurel, *Computers as Theatre*, 35.

38. Soraya Murray, "The Poetics of Form and the Politics of Identity in *Assassin's Creed III: Liberation*," *Kinephanos*, July 2017, https://www.kinephanos.ca/2017 /the-poetics-of-form.

39. DeLanda, *Intensive Science and Virtual Philosophy*, 133.

40. For more on the simultaneity of past, present, and future, see adrienne maree brown and Autumn Brown, "A Breathing Chorus with Alexis Pauline Gumbs," *How to Survive the End of the World* (podcast), December 19, 2017, https:// www.endoftheworldshow.org/blog/2017/12/19/a-breathing-chorus-with-alexis -pauline-gumbs.

41. Deleuze, *Expressionism in Philosophy*, 217.

42. Thom, *A Place Called No Homeland*, 27.

43. Thom, *A Place Called No Homeland*, 8.

44. Thom, *A Place Called No Homeland*.

45. Thom, *A Place Called No Homeland*, 51.

46. Parra, *The Collected Poems of Esdras Parra*, 5.

Chapter Two. The Decolonial Cut

1. Guattari and Rolnik, *Molecular Revolution in Brazil*, 465–66.

2. Guattari and Rolnik, *Molecular Revolution in Brazil*, 465.

3. Deleuze and Guattari, *Anti-Oedipus*, 38–39.

4. Deleuze and Guattari, *Anti-Oedipus*, 325.

5. Glissant, *Poetics of Relation*, 189.

6. "Cities | Bodies | Action: The Politics of Passion in the Americas," Hemispheric Institute of Performance and Politics, 2013, accessed May 12, 2020, https://hemisphericinstitute.org/en/enc13-home.

7. The names of the performers are not listed on the web page for the performance at the Hemispheric Institute or at the 2boys.tv website.

8. "2boys.tv with Radwan Moumneh and Alexis O'Hara: Tightrope/Cuerda Floja," Hemispheric Institute of Performance and Politics, accessed August 31, 2018, https://hemisphericinstitute.org/en/enc13-performances1/item/1995-enc13 -2boys-tightrope.html.

9. Rita Moreira, *Hunting Season/Temporada de Caça*, video, posted June 16, 2012, accessed September 8, 2018, https://www.youtube.com/watch? v=rjan_YdoC5g &t=10s; Donna Bowater and Priscilla Moraes, "Brazil: Targeting Trans People with Impunity," *Al Jazeera*, April 22, 2015, accessed September 8, 2018, https://www .aljazeera.com/indepth/features/2015/04/brazil-targeting-trans-people-impunity -150413210248222.html; Sofia Utsch, "Brazilian Dictatorship and the Queer Movement," *Making Queer History*, June 4, 2017, https://www.makingqueerhistory.com /articles/2017/6/24/brazilian-dictatorship-and-the-queer-movement.

10. Yoko Ono and John Lennon, *Grapefruit* (New York: Simon and Schuster, 2000).

11. *Ulay & Abramović AAA AAA 1978*, video, Homless TLV, posted March 26, 2014, https://www.youtube.com/watch?v=KeaUOdvooBA&ab_channel=HomlessTLV.

12. micha cárdenas, "Research," *Critical Realities Studio*, accessed May 12, 2020, https://criticalrealities.sites.ucsc.edu/research.

13. Taylor, *The Archive and the Repertoire*, 89.

14. Taylor, *The Archive and the Repertoire*, 19.

15. Taylor, *The Archive and the Repertoire*, 19–20.

16. Taylor, *The Archive and the Repertoire*, 24.

17. Taylor, *The Archive and the Repertoire*, 36; Anzaldúa, *Borderlands/La Frontera* (1999), 99; Mignolo, *Local Histories/Global Designs*, xiv.

18. Taylor, *The Archive and the Repertoire*, 22.

19. Kember and Zylinska, *Life after New Media*, 23.

20. Kember and Zylinska, *Life after New Media*, 77.

21. Kember and Zylinska, *Life after New Media*, 23.

22. Haiken, *Venus Envy*; Heyes and Jones, *Cosmetic Surgery*.

23. Stone, "The Empire Strikes Back: A Posttranssexual Manifesto," *Transgender Studies Reader*.

24. Samantha Riedel, "How Sandy Stone 'Struck Back' against Transmisogyny," *Them*, October 17, 2019, accessed May 19, 2020, https://www.them.us/story /generations-sandy-stone.

25. VNS Matrix, "A Cyberfeminist Manifesto for the 21st Century," *Transmediale/ Art and Digital Culture*, 1991, https://transmediale.de/content/a-cyberfeminist -manifesto-for-the-21st-century; Plant, *Zeros + Ones*.

26. subRosa, "Stolen Rhetoric: The Appropriation of Choice by the ART Industry," in Wilding and Wright, *Domain Errors!*, 135.

27. Nakamura, *Cybertypes*, 4–5.

28. Nakamura, *Cybertypes*, 4–5.

29. Hayward, "Spider/City/Sex," 100.

30. Hayward, "Spider/City/Sex," 100.

31. American Society of Plastic Surgeons, "Gender Confirmation Surgeries," American Society of Plastic Surgeons, accessed March 25, 2021, https://www .plasticsurgery.org/reconstructive-procedures/gender-confirmation-surgeries.

32. Hayward, "Spider/City/Sex," 96.

33. Hayward and Weinstein, "Introduction," 198.

34. Transgender Europe, "Transgender Day of Visibility 2016—Trans Murder Monitoring Project," press release, March 30, 2016, https://tgeu.org/transgender -day-of-visibility-2016-trans-murder-monitoring-update.

35. Margo Apostolos, faculty webpage, USC, accessed May 26, 2015, https:// kaufman.usc.edu/faculty/margo-apostolos.

36. "Merce Cunningham and Lifeforms," *LondonDance.com*, n.d., http:// londondance.com/articles/features/merce-cunningham-and-lifeforms.

37. The lights on the garments were not relied on as signals for gestures in this performance because of the bright daylight during the performance, a hemispheric difference we had not planned for, as the performance began at 8 p.m.

38. Huizinga, *Homo Ludens*, 10.

39. Schechner, *Performance Studies*, 52.

40. Doing so resonates with claims by Teresa de Lauretis that gender is a technology and by Lisa Nakamura and Peter Chow-White and Wendy Chun that race operates as a kind of code: de Lauretis, *Technologies of Gender*; Nakamura and Chow-White, *Race after the Internet*; Chun, "Race and/as Technology."

41. Kember and Zylinska, *Life after New Media*, 75.

42. Halperin, "The Normalization of Queer Theory."

43. Juana María Rodríguez, *Sexual Futures, Queer Gestures and Other Latina Longings*, Kindle loc. 213.

44. José Muñoz, *Cruising Utopia*, 91.

45. Rodríguez, *Sexual Futures, Queer Gestures and Other Latina Longings*, Kindle loc. 213.

46. Rodríguez, *Sexual Futures, Queer Gestures and Other Latina Longings*, Kindle loc. 213.

47. Santana, "Transitionings and Returnings," 184.

48. Harding, "Outperforming Activism."

49. Claudio Altenhain, "Tropicalizing Surveillance: Implementing Big Data Policing in São Paulo, Brazil," *DataActive*, November 16, 2017, accessed February 15, 2019, https://data-activism.net/2017/11/tropicalizing-surveillance -implementing-big-data-policing-in-sao-paulo-brazil.

50. Altenhain, "Tropicalizing Surveillance."

51. "COMPSTAT Policing in Los Angeles," Los Angeles Police Department

website, accessed February 15, 2019, http://www.lapdonline.org/crime_mapping_and_compstat/content_basic_view/6363.

52. Cindy Chang, "LAPD Officials Defend Predictive Policing as Activists Call for Its End," *Los Angeles Times*, July 24, 2018, accessed February 15, 2019, https://www.latimes.com/local/lanow/la-me-lapd-data-policing-20180724-story.html.

53. Stop LAPD Spying Coalition, "Before the Bullet Hits the Body: Predictive Policing in Los Angeles," report, May 8, 2018, https://stoplapdspying.org/before-the-bullet-hits-the-body-dismantling-predictive-policing-in-los-angeles.

54. Beauchamp, *Going Stealth*, 2.

55. Spade's writing in *Normal Life* continues important groundwork laid by Viviane Namaste on the social administration of transgender people: see Spade, *Normal Life*; Namaste, *Invisible Lives*.

56. Spade, *Normal Life*, 150–51.

57. Spade, *Normal Life*.

58. Since I wrote this, the TSA has changed its technology to display generic outlines, but the process is still invasive, and how the images are created or used is not transparent to travelers: see Joel Johnson, "100 Naked Citizens: 100 Leaked Body Scans," *Wired*, November 16, 2010, https://www.wired.com/2010/11/giz-scans; Declan McCullagh, "Feds Admit Storing Checkpoint Body Scan Images," CNET, August 4, 2010, accessed May 19, 2020, https://www.cnet.com/news/feds-admit-storing-checkpoint-body-scan-images.

59. Puar, *Terrorist Assemblages*, 167, 198, 200.

60. Kember and Zylinska, *Life after New Media*, 82.

61. Tuck and Yang, "Decolonization Is Not a Metaphor."

62. Annie Lloyd, "A Brief History of L.A.'s Indigenous Tongva People," *LAist*, October 9, 2017, accessed May 22, 2020, https://laist.com/2017/10/09/a_brief_history_of_the_tongva_people.php.

63. Tuck and Yang, "Decolonization Is Not a Metaphor," 17.

64. Tuck and Yang, "Decolonization Is Not a Metaphor," 20.

65. Tuck and Yang, "Decolonization is not a Metaphor," 21.

66. Glissant, *Poetics of Relation*, 189–90.

67. Glissant, *Poetics of Relation*, 189–90.

68. Glissant, *Poetics of Relation*, 190.

69. Glissant, *Poetics of Relation*, 191.

70. Fabian, Rachel, and Hannah Goodwin, "Interview with Ricardo Dominguez," *Media Fields Journal*, accessed March 26, 2021, http://mediafieldsjournal.squarespace.com/interview-with-ricardo-domingu.

Chapter Three. The Shift

Portions of chapter 3 were published in the *Ada Journal of Gender, New Media and Technology* as "Shifting Futures: Digital Trans of Color Praxis," http://adanewmedia.org/2015/01/issue6-cardenas.

1. Here I refer to "Hacking the Black/White Binary," the title of the issue of *Ada*

Journal of Gender, New Media and Technology in which an earlier version of this chapter appeared.

2. "Tracing the Evolution of Janelle Monáe's High-Concept Music Videos," *Dazed*, April 13, 2018, https://www.dazeddigital.com/music/article/39679/1/janelle-monae-visual-aesthetic-evolution.

3. "Bio," Janelle Monáe official website, accessed July 28, 2014, http://www.jmonae.com/bio.

4. Keeling, "I = Another," 713.

5. Chris Azzopardi, "Queen Dream Janelle Monáe and Lesbian Rumors," *Rainbow Times* (blog), September 12, 2013, accessed May 3, 2019, https://www.therainbowtimesmass.com/queen-dream-janelle-monae-lesbian-rumors.

6. "Janelle Monáe Performs 'Americans,'" video, *The Late Show with Stephen Colbert*, broadcast July 20, 2018, accessed June 4, 2020, https://www.cbs.com/shows/the-late-show-with-stephen-colbert/video/EB7A2523-5FCA-7A63-F513-BA4D66B7447C/janelle-mon-e-performs-americans.

7. Deleuze and Guattari, *A Thousand Plateaus*, 3–4.

8. For example, such an algorithm in pseudocode might include steps such as:

1. Calculate position of a point in line L, using the equation defining line L in assemblage A; call this position xyz.
2. If xyz is within device size bounds, draw xyz to output device.
3. If points remain in L, return to instruction 1. If lines remain in A, change line L to next line in A; return to instruction 1.

9. Keeling, "Looking for M—," 577.

10. Galarte, "On Trans* Chican@s," 233.

11. Aren Aizura, "Trans Feminine Value, Racialized Others and the Limits of Necropolitics," in Haritaworn et al., *Queer Necropolitics*, 130.

12. Aizura, "Trans Feminine Value," 131.

13. Namaste, *Invisible Lives*.

14. Gibson, *Neuromancer*; Oshii, *Ghost in the Shell*.

15. Gao et al., "Materials Selections and Growth Conditions for Large-Area, Multilayered, Visible Negative Index Metamaterials Formed by Nanotransfer Printing," 256–61.

16. "Breakthrough in Creating Invisibility Cloaks, Stealth Technology," *ScienceDaily*, March 31, 2014, accessed February 11, 2019, https://www.sciencedaily.com/releases/2014/03/140331114430.htm.

17. This space inbetween states relates strongly to the concept of differential consciousness as described in Sandoval, *Methodology of the Oppressed*.

18. Butler, *Bodies That Matter*; Nakamura, *Cybertypes*; Wald, *Crossing the Line*.

19. Tim Murphy, "Who Cares about Islan Nettles?," *Out Magazine*, March 4, 2014.

20. Murphy, "Who Cares about Islan Nettles?"

21. Kember and Zylinska, *Life after New Media*, 186.

22. Barad, *Meeting the Universe Halfway*, 1123.

23. Barad, *Meeting the Universe Halfway*, 1180.

24. Barad, *Meeting the Universe Halfway*, 1134.

25. Keeling, "Looking for M—," 579.

26. I use the female pronoun "she" here for Gunn because that is the pronoun used by Keeling.

27. Keeling, "Passing for Human," 248.

28. Snorton, *Black on Both Sides*, 57.

29. "Janelle Monáe Brings Mothers of Slain African Americans for 'Hell You Talmbout' at Women's March: Watch," *Billboard*, January 22, 2017, accessed May 3, 2019, https://www.billboard.com/articles/news/7662606/janelle-monae -hell-you-talmbout-womens-march.

30. "Janelle Monáe Brings Mothers of Slain African Americans."

31. Janelle Monáe, Cindi Mayweather, Twitter post, January 10, 2020, https:// twitter.com/JanelleMonae/status/1215782996965355521.

32. Katherine McKittrick, *Sylvia Wynter: On Being Human as Praxis.*; Mignolo, Walter D. *Local Histories/Global Designs: Coloniality, Subaltern Knowledges, and Border Thinking.*

33. Wynter, "Unsettling the Coloniality of Being/Power/Truth/Freedom," 260.

34. Barad, *Meeting the Universe Halfway*, Kindle loc. 5625–50.

35. D. Fox Harrell, "Toward a Theory of Critical Computing," CTheory.net, May 13, 2010, accessed September 6, 2018, http://www.ctheory.net/articles.aspx? id=641.

36. Soraya Murray, "The Poetics of Form and the Politics of Identity in *Assassin's Creed III: Liberation*," *Kinephanos*, July 2017, https://www.kinephanos.ca/2017/ the-poetics-of-form.

37. Murray, "The Poetics of Form."

38. Snorton, *Black on Both Sides*, 56.

39. Butler, *Bodies That Matter*, 91.

40. Butler, *Bodies That Matter*, 90.

41. Butler, *Bodies That Matter*, 132.

42. Alexander, *Pedagogies of Crossing*; Mohanty, *Feminism without Borders*.

43. Blas, "Informatic Opacity." I return to Blas's work in detail in chapter 5.

44. Mbembe, "Necropolitics," 29–30.

45. Mbembe, "Necropolitics," 29–30.

46. Brian Anthony Hernandez, "Watch Holograms of Janelle Monáe and M.I.A. Perform Duets Cities Apart," *Mashable*, April 6, 2014, https://mashable.com /2014/04/06/mia-janelle-monae-holograms/#H4Vbe16U2GqM.

47. Brittany Spanos, "Janelle Monáe Frees Herself," *Rolling Stone*, April 26, 2018, https://www.rollingstone.com/music/music-features/janelle-monae-frees -herself-629204.

48. Janelle Monáe, *Dirty Computer—An Emotion Picture*, video, posted April 27, 2018, accessed March 5, 2019, https://www.youtube.com/watch?v=jdH2Sy-BlNE.

49. Gillian "Gus" Andrews, "Janelle Monae Turns Rhythm and Blues into Science Fiction," *io9*, accessed March 26, 2021, https://io9.gizmodo.com/janelle -monae-turns-rhythm-and-blues-into-science-ficti-5592174.

50. Christian Hoard, "Artist of the Week: Janelle Monáe," *Rolling Stone*, June 20, 2010, https://www.rollingstone.com/music/music-news/artist-of-the-week -janelle-monae-186564.

51. Nandita Biswas Mellamphy, "Larval Terror: The Globalization of Insecurity in the 21st Century," *Center for 21st-Century Studies: The Dark Side of the Digital*, 2013, http://works.bepress.com/biswasmellamphy/36.

52. Andrews, "Janelle Monae Turns Rhythm and Blues into Science Fiction."

53. Andrews, "Janelle Monae Turns Rhythm and Blues into Science Fiction."

54. Kember and Zylinska, *Life after New Media*, 17.

55. Kember and Zylinska, *Life after New Media*, 13.

56. Kember and Zylinska, *Life after New Media*, 164.

57. Kember and Zylinska, *Life after New Media*, 169.

58. Keeling, "Looking for M," 579.

59. Keeling "I = Another," 56.

60. For example: "A single left shift multiplies a binary number by 2:

```
0010 << 1 = 0100

0010 is 2
0100 is 4"
```

"Bit Shifting (Left Shift, Right Shift)," *Interview Cake: Programming Interview Questions and Tips*, accessed February 15, 2019, https://www.interviewcake.com /concept/java/bit-shift.

61. Kyle Chayka, "JODI Makes Art Online, but Don't Call Them Net Artists," *Creators* (blog), May 10, 2012, https://www.vice.com/en_us/article/8qmy73/digart -jodi-makes-art-online-but-don% E2% 80% 99t-call-them-net-artists.

62. Aria Dean, "Mezangelle, an Online Language for Codework and Poetry," *Rhizome*, December 15, 2016, http://rhizome.org/editorial/2016/dec/15/mezangelle -an-online-language-for-codework-and-poetry.

63. Denis Jaromil Rojo, "ASCII Shell Forkbomb," n.d., https://jaromil.dyne.org /journal/forkbomb_art.html.

64. See the symposium announcement for "Digital Humanities: Creative Activism in the Age of Digital Technologies," March 30, 2012, https://2012core2 .commons.gc.cuny.edu/2012/03/26/digital-humanities-creative-activism-in-the -age-of-digital-technologies.

65. Keeling, *The Witch's Flight*.

66. Janelle Monáe, *"Many Moons" Official Short Film (HD)*, video, posted April 4, 2009, accessed February 14, 2019, https://www.youtube.com/watch?v =EZyyORSHbaE.

67. Keeling, "I = Another."

68. Chun, *Programmed Visions*, 143.

69. Janelle Monáe—Many Moons." *Genius*, accessed March 26, 2021, https:// genius.com/Janelle-monae-many-moons-lyrics.

70. Janelle Monáe, "Many Moons," *The ArchAndroid*, Atlantic Records, 2010, https://urldefense.com/v3/__https:/genius.com/Janelle-monae-many-moons-lyrics

__;!!OToaGQ!5aYu2pZ3e8QmpAD_VcWQeN9Eto8SdApbazlLy8CbB77N54ih35hq
SvEq8kyuA25JltRiyHmL$"https://genius.com/Janelle-monae-many-moons-lyrics.

Chapter Four. The Experience of Shifting

1. Mattie Brice, *Mainichi*, November 6, 2012, Windows and Mac, http://www
.mattiebrice.com/mainichi.

2. Ben Kuchera, "Dragon Age 2's Gay Character Controversial with Straight,
Gay Gamers," *Ars Technica*, March 29, 2011, https://arstechnica.com/gaming
/news/2011/03/dragon-age-2s-gay-character-offends-just-about-everyone.ars.

3. Jagoda, "Gaming the Humanities," 190–91.

4. micha cárdenas, *Redshift and Portalmetal*, January 16, 2015, https://micharoja
.itch.io/redshift-and-portalmetal.

5. Consider an algorithm written in the C programming language.

```
int addend_one = 1;
int addend_two = 2;
int sum = 0;
sum = addend_one + addend_two;
return sum.
```

Such an algorithm commonly has a structure beginning with the declaration
of variables and followed by a set of instructions. This structure could model how
race and gender operate in the contemporary world. An algorithm can be written
to describe a specific curve with specific slopes at defined points of inflection, which
may be used to represent a complex understanding of specific interactions of race,
gender, sexuality, ability, and nationality unfolding over time. Using algorithms allows one to find more ways to visualize and articulate multiple locations of intersections, and combinations of elements in movement, that can add depth to analyses
based on intersectional and assemblage theories. One can create an algorithm to
model particular elements of a given scenario or examine the algorithms identifi-
able within the scenario. Alternatively, one can analyze the algorithms used in media art, digital media platforms, or biometric surveillance tools to understand how
these systems challenge or reproduce racialized gender violence.

6. Cooper, "Intersectionality," in *The Oxford Handbook of Feminist Theory*, ed. Lisa
Disch and Mary Hawkesworth (New York: Oxford University Press, 2016), 85.

7. Browne, *Dark Matters*; Jessica Marie Johnson, "Life x Code: DH Against Enclosure"; Keeling, *Queer Times, Black Futures*.

8. Frasca, Gonzalo, "Videogames of the Oppressed," in *First Person: New Media
as Story, Performance, and Game*, ed. Noah Wardrip-Fruin and Pat Harrigan (Cambridge, MA: MIT Press, 2006).

9. Galloway, *Gaming*, 1170–72.

10. Galloway, *Gaming*, 1251–52.

11. Leigh Alexander, "Four Perspectives on Personal Games," *Gamasutra*,
April 29, 2013, accessed March 19, 2019, http://www.gamasutra.com/view/news
/191406/Four_perspectives_on_personal_games.php.

12. Anna Anthropy, *Rise of the Videogame Zinesters: How Freaks, Normals, Amateurs, Artists, Dreamers, Drop-Outs, Queers, Housewives, and People Like You Are Taking Back an Art Form* (New York: Seven Stories Press, 2012).

13. Alexander, "Four Perspectives on Personal Games."

14. Alexander, "Four Perspectives on Personal Games."

15. Anna Anthropy, *Dys4ia* (ZKM | Center for Art and Media, 2012), https://zkm.de/en/dys4ia; Zoë Quinn, *Depression Quest*, February 14, 2013, Windows, Mac, Linux, http://www.depressionquest.com.

16. Alexander, "Four Perspectives on Personal Games."

17. "Doxxing" is having one's private information published online; "swatting" is calling in bomb threats against their homes and venues at which they plan to speak.

18. Chris Suellentrop, "Why 2014 Was a Troubling Year for Video Games," *New York Times*, December 11, 2014, http://www.nytimes.com/2014/12/14/arts/video -games/why-2014-was-a-troubling-year-for-video-games.html.

19. Quinn, *Crash Override*; Ian Sherr and Erin Carson, "GamerGate to Trump: How Video Game Culture Blew Everything Up," CNET, November 27, 2017, accessed December 10, 2018, https://www.cnet.com/news/gamergate-donald-trump -american-nazis-how-video-game-culture-blew-everything-up.

20. Mattie Brice, "TED Talk: Using Play for Everyday Activism." *Mattie Brice* (blog), January 25, 2017, http://www.mattiebrice.com/ted-talk-using-play-for -everyday-activism.

201. Mattie Brice, "The Lost Woman in Games," *Mattie Brice* (blog), March 11, 2015, http://www.mattiebrice.com/the-lost-woman-in-games.

22. Brice, *Mainichi*.

23. Brice, *Mainichi*.

24. Namaste, *Invisible Lives*, 39.

25. Namaste, *Invisible Lives*, 50.

26. Aizura et al., "Introduction," 308.

27. Aizura et al., "Introduction," 309, emphasis added.

28. Ferguson, *Aberrations in Black*, 39.

29. Gossett, "A Wall Is Just a Wall."

30. Muñoz, *Disidentifications*, 19.

31. Muñoz, *Disidentifications*, 108.

32. Brice, *Mainichi*.

33. Ahmed, *Queer Phenomenology*, 15.

34. Ahmed, *Queer Phenomenology*, 14.

35. Ahmed, *Queer Phenomenology*, 432.

36. Ahmed, *Queer Phenomenology*.

37. Dylan Scott, "COVID-19's Devastating Toll on Black and Latino Americans, in One Chart," *Vox*, April 17, 2020, https://www.vox.com/2020/4/17/21225610/us -coronavirus-death-rates-blacks-latinos-whites.

38. Gossett, "A Wall Is Just a Wall."

39. Gossett, "A Wall Is Just a Wall."

40. Timothy Stewart-Winter and Whitney Strub, "Queer Newark: The Murder of

Sakia Gunn and LGBT Anti-Violence Mobilization," *Outhistory.org*, accessed March 20, 2019, http://outhistory.org/exhibits/show/queer-newark/murder-of-sakia-gunn.

41. Ahmed, *Queer Phenomenology*, 432–33.

42. Mattie Brice, "Assimilation and the Double-Bind of Respectability," *Mattie Brice* (blog), August 21, 2015, http://www.mattiebrice.com/assimilation-and-the -double-bind-of-respectability.

43. Brice, "Assimilation and the Double-Bind of Respectability."

44. Salamon, *Assuming a Body*, 1.

45. Salamon, *Assuming a Body*, 64.

46. Stryker and Whittle, *Transgender Studies Reader 2*, 231.

47. Stryker and Whittle, *Transgender Studies Reader 2*, 230.

48. Stryker and Whittle, *Transgender Studies Reader 2*, 231.

49. Brice, "Assimilation and the Double-Bind of Respectability."

50. Pearce, "Toward a Game Theory of Game," 147.

51. Pearce, "Toward a Game Theory of Game," 147.

52. Pearce, "Toward a Game Theory of Game," 147.

53. Art is still subject to market demands, and artists such as Brice are also still forced to reckon with market concerns within games and art to build careers, but these demands seem to exert a less direct influence on Brice's work than, say, the games marketed as products by large corporations such as Sony. Large corporations such as Sony and Microsoft often do purchase independent games and market them, demonstrating how no one is totally free of capitalist demands in a global neoliberal economic system.

54. Belman and Flanagan, "Designing Games to Foster Empathy," 5.

55. Belman and Flanagan, "Designing Games to Foster Empathy," 7.

56. Belman and Flanagan, "Designing Games to Foster Empathy," 9–10.

57. Belman and Flanagan, "Designing Games to Foster Empathy," 7.

58. Belman and Flanagan, "Designing Games to Foster Empathy," 7–8.

59. Mattie Brice, "Empathy Machine," *Mattie Brice* (blog), June 30, 2016, accessed July 20, 2021, http://www.mattiebrice.com/empathy-machine/.

60. Mattie Brice, "Postpartum: *Mainichi*—How Personal Experience Became a Game," *Mattie Brice* (blog), November 12, 2012, http://www.mattiebrice.com /postpartum-mainichi-how-personal-experience-became-a-game.

61. Brice, "Postpartum."

62. American Association of University Women, "Why So Few? Women in Science, Technology, Engineering and Mathematics," *AAUW: Empowering Women since 1881* (blog), accessed March 19, 2019, https://www.aauw.org/resource /why-so-few-women-in-science-technology-engineering-mathematics.

63. Brice, "Postpartum."

64. Butler, *Gender Trouble*, 191.

65. Chronically ill, trans, femme, nonwhite, and queer are all categories with which I identify.

66. Butler, *Parables of the Sower*; Hopkinson, *Brown Girl in the Ring*; Smith; *Life on Mars*.

67. cárdenas et al., *The Transreal*, 46.

68. McPherson, "Why Are the Digital Humanities So White?," 153–54.

69. Morgensen, "White Settlers and Indigenous Solidarity."

70. Savkin et al., *Decentralized Coverage Control Problems for Mobile Robotic Sensor*, 132.

71. Sohn, Christophe. "Navigating Borders' Multiplicity: The Critical Potential of Assemblage." *Area* 48, no. 2 (2016): 185.

72. Anzaldúa, *Borderlands/La Frontera*, 2012, 34.

73. Quoted in McKittrick, *Sylvia Wynter*, 50.

74. McKittrick, *Sylvia Wynter*, 23.

75. Here I am borrowing a term from Dwight Conquergood that refers to ethnography as performance but using it more loosely to describe what players of personal experience games do, as described in Madison, *Acts of Activism*.

76. Studio XX, "HTMlles 11—2014," October 20, 2014, accessed August 30, 2018, https://htmlles.net/2014/index.php?page=festival&lang=en.

77. cárdenas et al., *The Transreal*.

78. Maria Alejandrina Coates and Julieta Maria, "Editorial," *Voz-à-Voz*, accessed September 1, 2018, http://www.vozavoz.ca/editorial.

79. Skawennati, "Biography," posted December 2015, accessed September 1, 2018, http://www.skawennati.com/bio/bio.html.

80. "Artist Statement," *Voz-à-Voz*, accessed September 1, 2018, http://www.vozavoz.ca/artist-bio/skawennati.

81. Nasrin Himada, "The Colour of Spatial Infinity Is Red: On micha cárdenas's *Redshift and Portalmetal*," *Voz-à-Voz*, accessed September 1, 2018, http://www.vozavoz.ca/aresponse/micha-cardenas.

82. Himada, "The Colour of Spatial Infinity Is Red."

83. micha cárdenas, "*Redshift and Portalmetal* Performance," event announcement, Yyz Artists' Outlet, accessed September 1, 2018, https://www.facebook.com/events/157795964565983.

84. Video footage of Ravyn Wngz's performance is available online at https://www.youtube.com/watch? v=gdOhGns4cG4.

85. Glissant, *Poetics of Relation*, 191.

86. Moten, *Poetics of the Undercommons*, 24.

87. Abril Valdes and Imelda Mejia, "'My Son Is Traumatized': One Separated Family's Reunion," American Civil Liberties Union website, August 24, 2018, accessed August 29, 2018, https://www.aclu.org/blog/immigrants-rights/immigrants-rights-and-detention/my-son-traumatized-one-separated-familys.

88. Glissant, *Poetics of Relation*, 192.

Chapter Five. The Stitch

Portions of chapter 5 were published in Scholar and Feminist Online as "Trans of Color Poetics," http://sfonline.barnard.edu/traversing- technologies/micha-cardenas-trans-of-color-poetics-stitching-bodies-concepts-and-algorithms.

1. Luis Gerardo Rosero's performance can be viewed at http://scalar.usc.edu

/works/poetic-operations/museo-travesti-versin-editada-transvestite-museum
-edited-version-1.

2. Hemispheric Institute of Performance and Politics, "E6.2—El Museo Travesti Performance," accessed April 26, 2019, https://hemi.nyu.edu/hemi/en /campuzano-performance.

3. "E6.2—El Museo Travesti Performance."

4. Jarrín, "Untranslatable Subjects."

5. The interview can be viewed at http://scalar.usc.edu/works/poetic -operations/interview-with-giuseppe-campuzano. See also Marcela Fuentes, *Interview with Giuseppe Campuzano*, video, Hemispheric Institute Digital Video Library, August 6, 2009, accessed April 17, 2019, http://hdl.handle.net/2333.1/vxok6fvt.

I am deeply grateful to Zia Puig, a graduate student in feminist studies at the University of California, Santa Clara, for helping me understand and translate the interview and for the joy we shared as Campuzano's brilliance unfolded for us together.

6. La Fountain-Stokes, "Giuseppe Campuzano and the Museo Travesti del Perú."

7. Beauchamp, *Going Stealth*.

8. Fuentes, *Interview with Giuseppe Campuzano*.

9. "Quipu: Incan Counting Tool," *Encyclopedia Britannica*, online ed., accessed April 17, 2019, https://www.britannica.com/technology/quipu.

10. Fuentes, *Interview with Giuseppe Campuzano*.

11. Fuentes, *Interview with Giuseppe Campuzano*.

12. Stephen Wolfram, "Untangling the Tale of Ada Lovelace," *Writings* (blog), December 10, 2015, accessed September 5, 2018, http://blog.stephenwolfram.com /2015/12/untangling-the-tale-of-ada-lovelace.

13. Deleuze, *Fold*, 26.

14. Deleuze and Guattari, *What Is Philosophy?*, 5, 8.

15. Fuentes, *Interview with Giuseppe Campuzano*.

16. Lorde, *Sister Outsider*, 112.

17. Lorde, *Sister Outsider*, 112.

18. Stiles and Selz, *Theories and Documents of Contemporary Art*, 2.

19. Kester, *One and the Many*, 3–7.

20. Raley, *Tactical Media*, 8.

21. Campuzano, *El Museo Travesti del Perú*, 8.

22. "Giuseppe Campuzano: Linea de Vida—Museo Travesti del Peru," *The Visible* (blog), November 27, 2015, https://www.visibleproject.org/blog/art-as -something-else-20n-gender-giuseppe-campuzano-linea-de-vida-museo-travesti -del-peru/nggallery/thumbnails.

23. Hemispheric Institute of Performance and Politics, "E6.2—El Museo Travesti Interview," accessed April 17, 2019, http://hemi.nyu.edu/hemi/en /campuzano-interview.

24. Mealey, "We Still Need to Talk about Edward Snowden."

25. Mealey, "We Still Need to Talk about Edward Snowden."

26. Mealey, "We Still Need to Talk about Edward Snowden."

27. "About," Adam Harvey website, accessed April 18, 2019, https://ahprojects.com/about.

28. Adam Harvey, "Stealth Wear: Anti-Drone Fashion," Adam Harvey website, December 3, 2013, accessed April 18, 2019, https://ahprojects.com/stealth-wear.

29. Joanne McNeil, "Artist Profile: Adam Harvey," *Rhizome*, June 11, 2012, accessed April 18, 2019, http://rhizome.org/editorial/2012/jun/11/artist-profile-adam-harvey.

30. Adam Harvey, *TEDxVilnius: From 1 to 100 Pixels*, video, TEDx Talks, posted July 6, 2017, accessed April 18, 2019, https://www.youtube.com/watch?v=bfhcc09gS30.

31. Harvey, *TEDxVilnius*.

32. Harvey, "Stealth Wear."

33. Aliev et al., "Mirage Effect"; Institute of Physics, *Mirage Effect Helps Researchers Hide Objects*, video, posted September 29, 2011, accessed April 18, 2019, https://www.youtube.com/watch?time_continue=19&v=3Yo4TTpYg7g.

34. Harvey, *TEDxVilnius*.

35. Adam Harvey, "HyperFace: False-Face Camouflage," Adam Harvey website, March 1, 2017, accessed April 18, 2019, https://ahprojects.com/hyperface.

36. Campuzano, *Museo Travesti del Perú*, viii.6a; "Chonguinada, la danza que nació como burla," *RPP Noticias*, June 7, 2013, accessed April 18, 2019, https://rpp.pe/peru/actualidad/chonguinada-la-danza-que-nacio-como-burla-noticia-602246; Oscar García, "Tunantada: Jauja vivió cinco días de fiesta," *El Comercio*, February 4, 2017, https://elcomercio.pe/peru/tunantada-jauja-vivio-cinco-dias-fiesta-162778.

37. Blas states in this interview that his father is Puerto Rican: Katrina Sluis, "Artist Profile: Zach Blas," *Rhizome*, March 1, 2017, accessed July 31, 2018, http://rhizome.org/editorial/2017/mar/01/artist-profile-zach-blas.

38. Zach Blas, "Facial Weaponization Suite," Zach Blas website, accessed April 26, 2019, http://www.zachblas.info/works/facial-weaponization-suite.

39. Blas, "Facial Weaponization Suite."

40. Zach Blas, *Facial Weaponization Communiqué: Fag Face*, video, 2013, https://vimeo.com/57882032.

41. Blas, "Facial Weaponization Suite."

42. Zach Blas, *Facial Weaponization Communiqué: Fag Face*, video, 2013, https://vimeo.com/57882032.

43. Blas, "Facial Weaponization Suite."

44. Kyle Chayka, "Biometric Surveillance Means Someone Is Always Watching," *Newsweek*, April 17, 2014, http://www.newsweek.com/2014/04/25/biometric-surveillance-means-someone-always-watching-248161.html.

45. Tosten Burks, "An Artist's Pioneering Masks Shield Us from Future Surveillance," *Good*, January 26, 2015, https://www.good.is/features/biometric-policing-zach-blas-masks.

46. Blas, "Informatic Opacity."

47. Blas, "Informatic Opacity."

48. Luiza Prado and Pedro Oliveira, "Questioning the 'Critical' in Speculative

& Critical Design," *Medium*, August 31, 2017, accessed July 21, 2021, https://medium .com/a-parede/questioning-the-critical-in-speculative-critical-design-5a355cac2ca4.

50. Sluis, "Artist Profile."

51. Dunne and Raby, *Speculative Everything*; "Teaching Game Design for a Reimagined World—Marcelo Viana Neto—GDC," conference announcement, Games and Arts, University of California, Santa Cruz, March 18, 2019, accessed April 18, 2019, http://games.arts.ucsc.edu/news/teaching-game-design-reimagined -world-marcelo-viana-neto-gdc.

52. Lawrence Bird, "Global Positioning: An Interview with Ricardo Dominguez," *Furtherfield* (blog), n.d., http://www.furtherfield.org/global -positioning-interview-ricardo-dominguez.

53. Hirsch, "Contestational Design," 11.

54. Electronic Disturbance Theater 2.0/b.a.n.g. lab, *Sustenance*, 4.

55. Stalbaum et al., "The Transborder Immigrant Tool."

56. David Schwartz, "Activists Say Transgender Woman Raped at Arizona Immigrant Center," Reuters, July 31, 2014, http://www.reuters.com/article/2014/07/31 /us-usa-arizona-rape-idUSKBN0G02T920140731.

57. Bird, "Global Positioning."

58. See micha cárdenas, *Net. Walkingtools. Transformer. Shift()*, video, posted April 14, 2011, Center for Race and Gender, University of California, Berkeley, accessed March 21, 2019, https://www.crg.berkeley.edu/conference-videos/net-walkingtools -transformer-shift. See also Peterson, *Troubling the Line*, 391; Dominguez and Carroll, "Operation Faust y Furioso."

59. McPherson, *Feminist in a Software Lab*.

60. Frances Richard, "Multitudes," *Poetry*, 2014, https://www.poetryfoundation .org/poetrymagazine/articles/70111/multitudes.

61. Zach Blas, "Queer Technologies," Zach Blas website, n.d., http://www .zachblas.info/works/queer-technologies.

62. Anzaldúa, *Borderlands/La Frontera*, 2012, 88. For a discussion of critiques of generalizations about indigeneity in Anzaldúa, see Keating, "Speculative Realism."

63. Anzaldúa, *Borderlands/La Frontera*, 2012, 88.

64. Electronic Disturbance Theater 2.0/b.a.n.g. lab, *Sustenance*.

65. Kester, *Conversation Pieces*.

66. See the online companion at https://scalar.usc.edu/works/poetic-operations for an image of the *Autonets* prototype dress.

67. Taylor, *Archive and the Repertoire*.

68. Mignolo, *Local Histories/Global Designs*.

69. Mignolo, *Local Histories/Global Designs*.

70. Mignolo, *Local Histories/Global Designs*.

71. Braidotti, *Metamorphoses*.

72. Nakamura, *Digitizing Race*, loc. 1767–68.

73. Nakamura, *Digitizing Race*, loc. 1763.

74. Braden, "RFC1122: Requirements for Internet Hosts—Communication Layers."

75. "The Internet Engineering Task Force (IETF®)," accessed May 26, 2015, https://www.ietf.org/.

76. Thiong'o, *Decolonizing the Mind*, 27.

77. Available to view at https://scalar.usc.edu/works/poetic-operations/local -autonomy-networks-find-each-other-2012-zero1-san-jose-biennial.

78. As I described in chapter 2, the GJLA is an organization of trans and gender-queer people of color with which I collaborated.

79. Stryker and Whittle, *The Transgender Studies Reader*, 12.

80. I described the algorithm for flocking in chapter 2.

81. Michael I. Niman, "Five Forces Driving the Rise of Fascism in 2019," *Truthout*, January 13, 2019, accessed April 26, 2019, https://truthout.org/articles /five-forces-driving-the-rise-of-fascism-in-2019.

82. Jarrín, "Untranslatable Subjects."

83. Rose, "Giuseppe Campuzano's Afterlife."

84. Rose, "Giuseppe Campuzano's Afterlife."

85. Sandoval and Davis, *Methodology of the Oppressed*, 732; Anzaldúa, *Borderlands/ La Frontera*, 2012, 88.

86. Glissant, *Poetics of Relation*, 190.

87. See the website of the Audre Lorde Project at https://alp.org/do-not -militarize-our-mourning-orlando-and-ongoing-tragedy-against-lgbtstgnc-poc.

88. Lorde, *The Black Unicorn*.

89. Lorde, "Power."

90. Mohanty, *Feminism without Borders*.

91. Anastasia Moloney, "Silence Surrounds Colombia's 92,000 Disappeared: ICRC," Reuters, August 29, 2014, https://www.reuters.com/article/us-foundation -colombia-missing/silence-surrounds-colombias-92000-disappeared-icrc-id USKBN0GT22520140829.

92. Sibylla Brodzinsky, "Colombia Acts on Massacres—Punishing Whistleblower and Promoting Officers," *Guardian*, June 24, 2015, https://www .theguardian.com/world/2015/jun/24/colombian-army-killed-thousands -civilians-human-rights-watch.

93. Brodzinsky, "Colombia Acts on Massacres."

94. Brodzinsky, "Colombia Acts on Massacres."

95. Mignolo, *Local Histories/Global Designs*, 5.

96. Mohanty, *Feminism without Borders*.

97. "Toronto Event: Autonets Convergence—November 13," *Shameless* (blog), November 11, 2013, accessed April 24, 2019, http://shamelessmag.com/blog/entry /toronto-event-autonets-convergence-november-13.

98. "Building Local Autonomy Networks," workshop announcement, Transmediale, accessed April 24, 2019, https://transmediale.de/content /building-local-autonomy-networks.

99. micha cardenas, "Movements of Safety, A Safety Movement, Safety in Movement," in *Plants, Androids and Operators*, ed. Josephine Berry Slater, Anthony Iles, Clemens Apprich, and Oliver Lerone Schultz (London: Mute, 2014), 114–24.

100. "Building Local Autonomy Networks," *Thinking C21* (blog), March 14, 2013, https://www.c21uwm.com/2013/03/14/building-local-autonomy-networks; "Autonets," *micha cárdenas* (blog), accessed April 24, 2019, https://michacardenas.sites.ucsc.edu/autonets.

101. Kaleigh Rogers and Brian A. Anderson, "Ignored by Big Telecom, Detroit's Marginalized Communities Are Building Their Own Internet," *Motherboard* (blog), November 16, 2017, https://motherboard.vice.com/en_us/article/kz3xyz/detroit-mesh-network.

102. Lorde, *Sister Outsider*, 112.

103. Anzaldúa, *Borderlands/La Frontera*, 2012, 100–101.

104. "Spotlight—Coded Bias Documentary," accessed April 1, 2021, https://www.ajl.org/spotlight-documentary-coded-bias.

105. Ridley, "Imagining Otherly."

Conclusion: Visionary Trans of Color Futures

1. Sylvia Rivera, "Queens in Exile, the Forgotten Ones," *Street Transvestite Action Revolutionaries: Survival, Revolt, and Queer Antagonist Struggle* (n.p.: Untorelli Press, 2013), http://untorellipress.noblogs.org/post/2013/03/12/street-transvestite-action-revolutionaries-survival-revolt-and-queer-antagonist-struggle.

2. Cheryl Morgan, "The Future of Gender Is the Present for Trans* Characters in SciFi Novels," *Autostraddle*, April 30, 2013, https://www.autostraddle.com/the-future-of-gender-is-the-present-for-trans-characters-in-scifi-novels-174737; Michael Cieply, "In Search for Gay Characters, Don't Turn to Action or Fantasy Films," *New York Times*, July 22, 2014, http://www.nytimes.com/2014/07/23/business/media/in-search-for-gay-characters-dont-turn-to-action-or-fantasy-films.html.

3. Rodríguez, *Sexual Futures*, 327.

4. Merritt K, "Marginalized Communities Suffer the Most at the Hands of Online Harassment," *Ravishly*, March 31, 2015, accessed May 1, 2019, https://ravishly.com/2015/02/25/merritt-kopas-online-trolling-conversation.

5. Anzaldúa, *Borderlands/La Frontera*, 2012, 44.

6. Michelle Goldberg, "What Is a Woman? The Dispute between Radical Feminism and Transgenderism," *New Yorker*, July 28, 2014, https://www.newyorker.com/magazine/2014/08/04/woman-2.

7. Scott Shane, "These Are the Ads Russia Bought on Facebook in 2016," *New York Times*, November 1, 2017, accessed September 4, 2018, https://www.nytimes.com/2017/11/01/us/politics/russia-2016-election-facebook.html.

8. Lisa Tolin, "President Trump and the 'Shock and Awe' Doctrine," NBC News, February 1, 2017, https://www.nbcnews.com/news/us-news/president-trump-shock-awe-doctrine-n714766.

9. Glenn Thrush and Maggie Haberman, "Trump Gives White Supremacists an Unequivocal Boost," *New York Times*, January 20, 2018, https://www.nytimes.com/2017/08/15/us/politics/trump-charlottesville-white-nationalists.html; Samantha Cooney, "These Are the Women Who Have Accused President Trump of Sex-

ual Misconduct," *Time*, December 13, 2017, accessed September 4, 2018, http://time
.com/5058646/donald-trump-accusers.

10. "Donald Trump Has Lost Popular Vote by Greater Margin than Any US
President," *The Independent*, accessed September 4, 2018, https://www.independent
.co.uk/news/world/americas/us-elections/donald-trump-lost-popular-vote-hillary
-clinton-us-election-president-history-a7470116.html.

11. "Inside Story: How Russians Hacked the Democrats' Emails," Associated
Press, November 4, 2017, https://apnews.com/article/hillary-clinton-phishing
-moscow-russia-only-on-ap-dea73efc01594839957c3c9a6c962b8a.

12. Mattha Busby and Anthony Cuthbertson. "'Killer Robots' Ban Blocked
by US and Russia at UN Meeting," *The Independent*, September 3, 2018, accessed
September 4, 2018, https://www.independent.co.uk/life-style/gadgets-and-tech
/news/killer-robots-un-meeting-autonomous-weapons-systems-campaigners
-dismayed-a8519511.html.

13. Noble, *Algorithms of Oppression*; Joy Buolamwini, "When the Robot
Doesn't See Dark Skin," *New York Times*, June 22, 2018, https://www.nytimes
.com/2018/06/21/opinion/facial-analysis-technology-bias.html; Eubanks,
Automating Inequality.

14. Noble, *Algorithms of Oppression*, 36.

15. Rivera, "Queens in Exile."

16. Costanza-Chock, "Design Justice."

17. Costanza-Chock, "Design Justice."

18. Costanza-Chock, "Design Justice."

19. Evan Hill, Ainara Tiefenthäler, and Christiaan Triebert et al., "Eight Minutes and Forty-six Seconds: How George Floyd Was Killed in Police Custody," *New
York Times*, May 31, 2020, https://www.nytimes.com/2020/05/31/us/george-floyd
-investigation.html.

20. Laura Thompson, "The Police Killing You Probably Didn't Hear about This
Week," *Mother Jones* (blog), accessed June 9, 2020, https://www.motherjones.com
/crime-justice/2020/05/tony-mcdade-tallahassee-florida-police-shooting-death.

21. Northwest Tap Connection and Shakiah Danielson, *#HELLYOUTALMBOUT*,
video, posed September 24, 2016, accessed June 9, 2020, https://www.youtube.com
/watch?v=Fr-FyI-3wZo&feature=youtu.be.

22. Trudy Ring, "Trans Woman Nina Pop Stabbed to Death in Missouri,"
The Advocate, May 6, 2020, https://www.advocate.com/crime/2020/5/06/trans
-woman-nina-pop-stabbed-death-missouri.

23. Rayvn Wngz is the two-spirit Black dance artist I discussed in chapter 4
who performed in *Redshift and Portalmetal*.

24. Muriel Draaisma, "Police Charge Three People after Black Lives Matter
Protesters Splatter Paint on Statues in Toronto," CBC News, July 18, 2020,
https://www.cbc.ca/news/canada/toronto/statues-defaced-paint-toronto-defund
-the-police-1.5654829.

25. bml_to (Black Lives Matter—Toronto), Instagram.com, August 9, 2020,
accessed September 30, 2020, https://www.instagram.com/p/CDrHsqwg9UZ.

26. Doha Madani, "Rally for Black Trans Lives Draws Enormous Crowd in Brooklyn," *NBC News*, June 14, 2020, accessed September 30, 2020, https://www.nbcnews.com/feature/nbc-out/rally-black-trans-lives-draws-packed-crowd-brooklyn-museum-plaza-n1231040.

27. Kaitlan Collins and Noah Gray, "Trump Briefly Taken to Underground Bunker during Friday's White House Protests," CNN, accessed November 1, 2020, https://www.cnn.com/2020/05/31/politics/trump-underground-bunker-white-house-protests/index.html; Azi Paybarah and Nikita Stewart, "Symbol of N.Y.C. Unrest: A Burning Police Car," *New York Times*, June 2, 2020, https://www.nytimes.com/2020/05/31/nyregion/police-cars-nyc-protests.html; "Council Advances Plan to Dismantle M[inneapolis] P[olice] D[epartment]," MPR News, accessed November 1, 2020, https://www.mprnews.org/story/2020/06/26/minneapolis-council-puts-plan-to-dismantle-police-in-motion.

28. Richard A. Oppel Jr., Derrick Bryson Taylor, and Nicholas Bogel-Burroughs, "What We Know about Breonna Taylor's Case and Death," *New York Times*, October 2, 2020, accessed October 6, 2020, https://www.nytimes.com/article/breonna-taylor-police.html.

29. Astead W. Herndon, "How a Pledge to Dismantle the Minneapolis Police Collapsed," *New York Times*, September 26, 2020, https://www.nytimes.com/2020/09/26/us/politics/minneapolis-defund-police.html; Rachel Sadon, Hannah Schuster, and Matt Blitz, "Activists Painted 'Defund the Police' next to the New Black Lives Matter Mural," National Public Radio, June 8, 2020, accessed November 1, 2020, https://www.npr.org/local/305/2020/06/08/872234932/activists-painted-defund-the-police-next-to-the-new-black-lives-matter-mural.

30. Rivera, "Queens in Exile."

BIBLIOGRAPHY

Aha, David W., Dennis Kibler, and Marc K. Albert. "Instance-based Learning Algorithms." *Machine Learning* 6, no. 1 (1991): 37–66.

Ahmed, Sara. *Queer Phenomenology: Orientations, Objects, Others.* Durham, NC: Duke University Press Books, 2006.

Aizura, Aren Z., Trystan Cotten, and Carsten/Carla Balzer/LaGata et al. "Introduction." *TSQ: Transgender Studies Quarterly* 1, no. 3 (August 1, 2014): 308–19. https://doi.org/10.1215/23289252-2685606.

Alexander, M. Jacqui. *Pedagogies of Crossing: Meditations on Feminism, Sexual Politics, Memory, and the Sacred.* Durham, NC: Duke University Press, 2005.

Aliev, Ali E., Yuri N. Gartstein, and Ray H. Baughman. "Mirage Effect from Thermally Modulated Transparent Carbon Nanotube Sheets." *Nanotechnology* 22, no. 43 (October 2011): 435704. https://doi.org/10.1088/095 7-4484/22/43/435704.

Anthropy, Anna. *Rise of the Videogame Zinesters: How Freaks, Normals, Amateurs, Artists, Dreamers, Drop-Outs, Queers, Housewives, and People Like You Are Taking Back an Art Form.* New York: Seven Stories Press, 2012.

Anzaldúa, Gloria E. *Borderlands/La Frontera: The New Mestiza.* San Francisco: Aunt Lute, 1999.

Anzaldúa, Gloria E. *Borderlands/La Frontera: The New Mestiza,* 4th ed. San Francisco: Aunt Lute, 2012.

Anzaldúa, Gloria E., and AnaLouise Keating. *The Bridge We Call Home: Radical Visions of Transformation.* New York: Routledge, 2002.

Aristotle. *Aristotle's Poetics.* Montreal: McGill-Queen's University Press, 1997.

Barad, Karen. *Meeting the Universe Halfway: Quantum Physics and the Entanglement of Matter and Meaning*. Durham, NC: Duke University Press, 2007.

Beauchamp, Toby. *Going Stealth: Transgender Politics and U.S. Surveillance Practices*. Durham, NC: Duke University Press, 2019.

Belman, Jonathan, and Mary Flanagan. "Designing Games to Foster Empathy." *International Journal of Cognitive Technology* 15 (January 1, 2010): 5–15. https://tiltfactor.org/wp-content/uploads2/cog-tech-si-g4g-article-1-belman-and-flanagan-designing-games-to-foster-empathy.pdf.

Benford, Steve, Chris Greenhalgh, Andy Crabtree, et al. "Performance-Led Research in the Wild." *ACM Transactions on Computer-Human Interaction* 20, no. 3 (2013): 1–22.

Blas, Zach. "Informatic Opacity." *Journal of Aesthetics and Protest*, no. 9 (summer 2014). http://www.joaap.org/issue9/zachblas.htm.

Braden, Robert, ed. "RFC1122: Requirements for Internet hosts-communication layers." 1989. Accessed April 1, 2021. https://dl.acm.org/doi/pdf/10.17487/RFC1122?casa_token=ottyFAPsYAoAAAAA:Alznc8lyhqWd1qKh8odQYPjojtWl7hbvUNn8WitfBpS4UoKOoHUOfOPPXTE2kIZOowtTg20q3-87nw.

Braidotti, Rosi. *Metamorphoses : Towards a Materialist Theory of Becoming*. Cambridge: Polity, 2002.

Brice, Mattie. "Assimilation and the Double-Bind of Respectability." *Mattie Brice* (blog), August 21, 2015. http://www.mattiebrice.com/assimilation-and-the-double-bind-of-respectability.

Brice, Mattie. "Empathy Machine." *Mattie Brice* (blog), June 30, 2016. Accessed July 20, 2021. http://www.mattiebrice.com/empathy-machine/.

Brice, Mattie. *Mainichi*, November 6, 2012. http://www.mattiebrice.com/mainichi.

Brice, Mattie. "Postpartum: Mainichi—How Personal Experience Became a Game." *Mattie Brice* (blog), November 12, 2012. http://www.mattiebrice.com/postpartum-mainichi-how-personal-experience-became-a-game.

Brice, Mattie. "Talk: Using Play for Everyday Activism." *Mattie Brice* (blog), January 25, 2017. http://www.mattiebrice.com/ted-talk-using-play-for-everyday-activism.

Brice, Mattie. "The Lost Woman in Games." *Mattie Brice* (blog), March 11, 2015. http://www.mattiebrice.com/the-lost-woman-in-games.Browne, Simone. *Dark Matters: On the Surveillance of Blackness*. Durham, NC: Duke University Press, 2015.

Burks, Tosten. "An Artist's Pioneering Masks Shield Us from Future Surveillance." January 26, 2015. https://www.good.is/features/biometric-policing-zach-blas-masks.

Burton, Johanna, Eric A. Stanley, and Tourmaline, eds. *Trap Door: Trans Cultural Production and the Politics of Visibility*. Cambridge, MA: MIT Press, 2017.

Butler, Judith. *Bodies That Matter*. New York: Routledge, 2011.

Butler, Judith. *Gender Trouble: Feminism and the Subversion of Identity* (Routledge Classics). Kindle ed. New York: Taylor and Francis, 2006.

Butler, Octavia E. *Parable of the Sower: A Powerful Tale of a Dark and Dystopian Future*. London: Headline, 2019.

Campuzano, Giuseppe. *El Museo Travesti del Perú*. Peru: Institute of Development Studies, 2008.

cárdenas, micha. "The Android Goddess Declaration: After Man(ifestos)." In *Bodies of Information: Intersectional Feminism and the Digital Humanities*, edited by Elizabeth Losh and Jacqueline Wernimont, 25–38. Minneapolis: University of Minnesota Press, 2019.

cardenas, micha. "Movements of Safety, A Safety Movement, Safety in Movement." In *Plants, Androids and Operators*, edited by Josephine Berry Slater, Anthony Iles, Clemens Apprich, and Oliver Lerone Schultz, 114–24. London: Mute, 2014.

cárdenas, micha, Zach Blas, and Wolfgang Schirmacher. *The Transreal: Political Aesthetics of Crossing Realities*. New York: Atropos, 2011.

Chun, Wendy Hui Kyong. *Programmed Visions: Software and Memory*. Software Studies. Cambridge, MA: MIT Press, 2011.

Chun, Wendy Hui Kyong. "Race and/as Technology, or How to Do Things to Race." In *Race after the Internet*, edited by Lisa Nakamura and Peter Chow-White, 38–60. New York: Routledge, 2012.

Colectivo Situaciones. *19 & 20: Notes for a New Social Protagonism*. Brooklyn, NY: Autonomedia, 2011.

Cooper, "Intersectionality." In *The Oxford Handbook of Feminist Theory*, ed. Lisa Disch and Mary Hawkesworth, 85. New York: Oxford University Press, 2016. https://doi.org/10.1093/oxfordhb/9780199328581.001.0001.

Costanza-Chock, Sasha. "Design Justice, A.I., and Escape from the Matrix of Domination." *Journal of Design and Science*, July 16, 2018. https://doi.org/10.21428/96c8d426.

Crenshaw, Kimberlé W. "Mapping the Margins: Intersectionality, Identity Politics, and Violence against Women of Color." *Stanford Law Review* 43, no. 6 (July 1, 1991): 1241–99. https://doi.org/10.2307/1229039.

Crossley, John N., and Alan S. Henry. "Thus Spake Al-Khwārizmī: A Translation of the Text of Cambridge University Library Ms. Ii.vi.5." *Historia Mathematica* 17, no. 2 (May 1, 1990): 103–31. https://doi.org/10.1016/0315-0860(90)90048-I.

Davis, Angela Y. *Are Prisons Obsolete?* New York: Seven Stories, 2003.

DeLanda, Manuel. *Intensive Science and Virtual Philosophy*. London: Continuum, 2002.

de Lauretis, Teresa. *Technologies of Gender: Essays on Theory, Film, and Fiction*. Bloomington: Indiana University Press, 1987.

Deleuze, Gilles. *Expressionism in Philosophy: Spinoza*. Translated by Martin Joughin. New York: Zone, 1992.

Deleuze, Gilles. *The Fold: Leibniz and the Baroque*. Illustrated edition. Minneapolis: University of Minnesota Press, 1992.

Deleuze, Gilles, and Félix Guattari. *Anti-Oedipus: Capitalism and Schizophrenia*. Minneapolis: University of Minnesota Press, 1983.

Deleuze, Gilles, and Félix Guattari. *A Thousand Plateaus: Capitalism and Schizophrenia*. Translated by Brian Massumi. 2nd ed. Minneapolis: University of Minnesota Press, 1987.

Deleuze, Gilles, and Félix Guattari. *What Is Philosophy?* European Perspectives. New York: Columbia University Press, 1994.

Dominguez, Ricardo, and Amy Sara Carroll. "Operation Faust y Furioso: A Trans [] Border Play on the Redistribution of the Sensible." *Leonardo Electronic Almanac* 21, no. 1 (2016). Accessed December 21, 2019. https://www.academia .edu/23228474/Operation_Faust_y_Furioso_A_Trans_Border_Play_on_the _Redistribution_of_the_Sensible.

Driskill, Qwo-Li. *Asegi Stories: Cherokee Queer and Two-Spirit Memory*. Tucson: University of Arizona Press, 2016.

Driskill, Qwo-Li, Chris Finley, Brian Joseph Gilley, and Scott Lauria Morgensen, eds. *Queer Indigenous Studies: Critical Interventions in Theory, Politics, and Literature*. Tucson: University of Arizona Press, 2011.

Dunne, Anthony, and Fiona Raby. *Speculative Everything: Design, Fiction, and Social Dreaming*. Illustrated edition. Cambridge, MA: MIT Press, 2013.

Dutta, Aniruddha. "An Epistemology of Collusion: *Hijras, Kothis* and the Historical (Dis)continuity of Gender/Sexual Identities in Eastern India." *Gender and History* 24, no. 3 (October 24, 2012). https://doi.org/10.1111/j .1468-0424.2012.01712.x.

Dutta, Aniruddha, and Raina Roy. "Decolonizing Transgender in India: Some Reflections." *TSQ: Transgender Studies Quarterly* 1, no. 3 (August 1, 2014): 320–37. https://doi.org/10.1215/23289252-2685615.

Electronic Disturbance Theater 2.0/b.a.n.g. lab. *Sustenance: A Play for All Trans [] Borders*. New York: Printed Matter, 2010.

Eubanks, Virginia. *Automating Inequality: How High-Tech Tools Profile, Police, and Punish the Poor*. New York: Picador, 2019.

Ferguson, Roderick A. *Aberrations in Black: Toward a Queer of Color Critique*. Minneapolis: University of Minnesota Press, 2003.

Field, J. V. "The Unhelpful Notion of 'Renaissance Man.'" *Interdisciplinary Science Reviews* 41, nos. 2–3 (July 2, 2016): 188–201. https://doi.org/10.1080/03080188 .2016.1223585.

Fisher, Simon D. Elin. "Pauli Murray's Peter Panic: Perspectives from the Margins of Gender and Race in Jim Crow America." *TSQ: Transgender Studies Quarterly* 3, nos. 1–2 (May 1, 2016): 95–103. https://doi.org/10.1215/23289252-3334259.

Frasca, Gonzalo, "Videogames of the Oppressed." In *First Person: New Media as Story, Performance, and Game.*, ed. Noah Wardrip-Fruin and Pat Harrigan. Cambridge, MA: MIT Press, 2006.

Galarte, Francisco J. "On Trans* Chican@s: Amor, Justicia, y Dignidad." *Aztlan* 39, no. 1 (spring 2014): 229–36.

Galloway, Alexander R. *Gaming: Essays on Algorithmic Culture*. Minneapolis: University of Minnesota Press, 2006.

Gao, Li. "Materials Selections and Growth Conditions for Large-Area, Multilayered, Visible Negative Index Metamaterials Formed by Nanotransfer Printing." *Advanced Optical Materials* 2, no. 3 (2014): 256–61.

Gibson, William. *Neuromancer*. New York: Ace Books, 2000.

Glissant, Édouard. *Caribbean Discourse: Selected Essays*, 3d ed. Charlottesville: University of Virginia Press, 1999.

Glissant, Édouard. *Poetic Intention*. Translated from the French by Nathanaël. Callicoon, NY: Nightboat Books, 2010.

Glissant, Édouard, and Betsy Wing. *Poetics of Relation*. Ann Arbor: University of Michigan Press, 1997.

Gossett, Che. "A Wall Is Just a Wall: Anti-Blackness and the Politics of Black and Prison Abolitionist Solidarity with Palestinian Struggle." *Decolonization* (June 16, 2014). https://decolonization.wordpress.com/2014/06/16/a-wall-is-just-a-wall-anti-blackness-and-the-politics-of-black-and-prison-abolitionist-solidarity-with-palestinian-struggle/.

Graham, Mark. "Inequitable Distributions in Internet Geographies: The Global South Is Gaining Access, but Lags in Local Content." *Innovations: Technology, Governance, Globalization* 9, nos. 3–4 (July 2014): 3–19.

Grefenstette, John J. "Genetic Algorithms for Changing Environments." In *Parallel Problem Solving from Nature 2: Proceedings of the Second Conference on Parallel Problem Solving from Nature, Brussels, Belgium, 28–30 September, 1992*, vol. 2, edited by Reinhard Männer and Bernard Manderick, 137–44. New York: Elsevier Science, 1992.

Guattari, Félix, and Suely Rolnik. *Molecular Revolution in Brazil*. Los Angeles: Semiotext(e), 2008.

Haiken, Elizabeth. *Venus Envy: A History of Cosmetic Surgery*. Revised ed. Baltimore: Johns Hopkins University Press, 2000.

Halperin, David M. "The Normalization of Queer Theory." *Journal of Homosexuality* 45, nos. 2–4 (2003): 339–43. https://doi.org/10.1300/J082v45n02_17.

Haraway, Donna J. *Staying with the Trouble: Making Kin in the Chthulucene*. Durham, NC: Duke University Press Books, 2016.

Harding, James M. "Outperforming Activism: Reflections on the Demise of the Surveillance Camera Players." *International Journal of Performance Arts and Digital Media* 11, no. 2 (July 3, 2015): 131–47. https://doi.org/10.1080/14794713.2015.1084797.

Haritaworn, Jin, Adi Kuntsman, and Silvia Posocco, eds. *Queer Necropolitics*. Abingdon, UK: Routledge, 2014.

Hayward, Eva S. "More Lessons from a Starfish: Prefixial Flesh and Transspeciated Selves." *Women's Studies Quarterly* 36, no. 3 (2008): 64–85. https://muse.jhu.edu/article/255359.

Hayward, Eva, and Jami Weinstein. "Introduction: Tranimalities in the Age of Trans* Life." *TSQ: Transgender Studies Quarterly* 2, no. 2 (January 1, 2015): 195–208. https://doi.org/10.1215/23289252-2867446.

Heaney, Emma. "Women-Identified Women: Trans Women in 1970s Lesbian Feminist Organizing." *TSQ: Transgender Studies Quarterly* 3, nos. 1–2 (May 1, 2016): 137–45. https://doi.org/10.1215/23289252-3334295.

Heyes, Cressida J., and Meredith Rachael Jones. *Cosmetic Surgery: A Feminist Primer*. Burlington, VT: Ashgate, 2009.

Hirsch, Edward A. "Contestational Design: Innovation for Political Activism." PhD thesis, Massachusetts Institute of Technology, Cambridge.

Hong, Grace Kyungwon. *The Ruptures of American Capital: Women of Color Feminism and the Culture of Immigrant Labor*. Kindle ed. Minneapolis: University of Minnesota Press, 2006.

Hopkinson, Nalo. *Brown Girl in the Ring*. New York: Warner Books, 1998.

Huizinga, Johan. *Homo Ludens: A Study of the Play-Element in Culture*. Eastford, CT: Martino Fine Books, 2014.

Imarisha, Walidah, and adrienne maree brown, eds. *Octavia's Brood: Science Fiction Stories from Social Justice Movements*. Oakland, CA: AK Press, 2015.

Jagoda, Patrick. "Gaming the Humanities." *Differences* 25, no. 1 (2014): 189–215. https://doi.org/10.1215/10407391-2420045.

Jarrín, Alvaro. "Untranslatable Subjects: Travesti Access to Public Health Care in Brazil." *TSQ: Transgender Studies Quarterly* 3, nos. 3–4 (November 1, 2016): 357–75. https://doi.org/10.1215/23289252-3545095.

Johnson, Jessica Marie. "Life x Code: DH Against Enclosure." Accessed July 26, 2021. https://www.lifexcode.org/.

Keating, AnaLouise. "Speculative Realism, Visionary Pragmatism, and Poet-Shamanic Aesthetics in Gloria Anzaldúa—and Beyond." *Women's Studies Quarterly* 40, nos. 3 (2013): 51–69. https://muse.jhu.edu/article/493862.

Keeling, Kara. "I = Another." In *Strange Affinities: The Gender and Sexual Politics of Comparative Racialization*, edited by Grace Hong and Roderick Ferguson, 53–75. Durham, NC: Duke University Press, 2011.

Keeling, Kara. "Looking for M—: Queer Temporality, Black Political Possibility, and Poetry from the Future." *GLQ* 15, no. 4 (2009): 565–82.

Keeling, Kara. "Passing for Human: Bamboozled and Digital Humanism." *Women and Performance* 15, no. 1 (2005): 237–50. http://www.tandfonline.com/doi/abs/10.1080/07407700508571495.

Keeling, Kara. "Queer OS." *Cinema Journal* 53, no. 2 (2014): 152–57. doi:10.1353/cj.2014.0004.

Keeling, Kara. *Queer Times, Black Futures*. Sexual Cultures. New York: New York University Press, 2019.

Keeling, Kara. *The Witch's Flight: The Cinematic, the Black Femme, and the Image of Common Sense*. Durham, NC: Duke University Press, 2007.

Kember, Sarah, and Joanna Zylinska. *Life after New Media: Mediation as a Vital Process*. Cambridge, MA: MIT Press, 2012.

Kester, Grant H. *Conversation Pieces: Community and Communication in Modern Art*. Berkeley: University of California Press, 2014.

Kester, Grant H. *The One and the Many: Contemporary Collaborative Art in a Global Context*. Durham, NC: Duke University Press, 2011.

Koyama, Emi. "The Transfeminist Manifesto." In *Catching a Wave: Reclaiming Feminism for the 21st Century*, edited by Rory Dicker and Alison Piepmeier. Northeastern University Press, 2016.

Laurel, Brenda. *Computers as Theatre*. Upper Saddle River, NJ: Addison-Wesley, 1993.

Lorde, Audre. *The Black Unicorn: Poems*. Reissue edition. New York: W. W. Norton, 1995.

Lorde, Audre. "Power." In *The Collected Poems of Audre Lorde*. New York: W. W. Norton, 1997. https://www.poetryfoundation.org/poems/53918/power-56d233adafeb3.

Lorde, Audre. *Sister Outsider: Essays and Speeches*. Berkeley, CA: Crossing, 2007.

Madison, D. Soyini. *Acts of Activism: Human Rights as Radical Performance*. Cambridge: Cambridge University Press, 2010.

Mbembe, Achille. "Necropolitics." Translated by Libby Meintjes. *Public Culture* 15, no. 1 (2003): 11–40.

McKittrick, Katherine, ed. *Sylvia Wynter: On Being Human as Praxis*. Durham, NC: Duke University Press, 2015.

McPherson, Tara. *Feminist in a Software Lab: Difference + Design*. Cambridge, MA: Harvard University Press, 2018.

McPherson, Tara. "Why Are the Digital Humanities So White? Or Thinking the Histories of Race and Computation." In *Debates in the Digital Humanities*. Minneapolis, MN: University of Minnesota Press, 2012. https://dhdebates.gc.cuny.edu/read/untitled-88c11800-9446-469b-a3be-3fdb36bfbd1e/section/20df8acd-9ab9-4f35-8a5d-e91aa5f4a0ea.

Mealey, Lexi. "We Still Need to Talk About Edward Snowden." *Harvard Political Review: Harvard University*. January 18, 2018. Accessed April 18, 2019. https://advance.lexis.com/api/document?collection=news&id=urn:contentItem:5TC1-NB01-DY7P-T1XG-00000-00&context=1516831.

Mignolo, Walter D. *Local Histories/Global Designs: Coloniality, Subaltern Knowledges, and Border Thinking*. Revised ed. Princeton, NJ: Princeton University Press, 2012.

Mohanty, Chandra Talpade. *Feminism without Borders: Decolonizing Theory, Practicing Solidarity*. Durham, NC: Duke University Press, 2003.

Monge, Alvaro E., and Charles Elkan. "The Field Matching Problem: Algorithms and Applications." In *Kdd* 2 (1966): 267–70. https://www.aaai.org/Papers/KDD/1996/KDD96-044.pdf.

Moraga, Cherríe L. *A Xicana Codex of Changing Consciousness: Writings, 2000–2010*. Durham, NC: Duke University Press, 2011.

Moraga, Cherríe, and Gloria Anzaldúa. *This Bridge Called My Back: Writings by Radical Women of Color*. Expanded and rev. 3rd ed. Berkeley, CA: Third Woman Press, 2002.

Morgensen, Scott L. "White Settlers and Indigenous Solidarity: Confronting White Supremacy, Answering Decolonial Alliances." *Decolonization*, May 26, 2014. https://decolonization.wordpress.com/2014/05/26/white-settlers-and-indigenous-solidarity-confronting-white-supremacy-answering-decolonial-alliances.

Moten, Fred, and Stefano Harney. *A Poetics of the Undercommons*. New York: Sputnik and Fizzle, 2016.

Muñoz, José Esteban. *Disidentifications: Queers of Color and the Performance of Politics.* Minneapolis: University of Minnesota Press, 1999.

Nakamura, Lisa. *Cybertypes: Race, Ethnicity, and Identity on the Internet.* New York: Routledge, 2002.

Nakamura, Lisa. *Digitizing Race: Visual Cultures of the Internet.* Minneapolis: University of Minnesota Press, 2007.

Nakamura, Lisa, and Peter Chow-White, eds. *Race after the Internet.* New York: Routledge, 2012.

Namaste, Viviane K. *Invisible Lives: The Erasure of Transsexual and Transgendered People.* Chicago: University of Chicago Press, 2000.

Noble, Safiya Umoja. *Algorithms of Oppression: How Search Engines Reinforce Racism.* New York: New York University Press, 2018.

Ochoa, Marcia. *Queen for a Day: Transformistas, Beauty Queens, and the Performance of Femininity in Venezuela.* Durham, NC: Duke University Press, 2014.

Ono, Yoko, and John Lennon. *Grapefruit.* New York: Simon and Schuster, 2000.

Oshii, Mamoru, dir. *Ghost In the Shell.* Lionsgate, 1996.

Parra, Esdras. *The Collected Poems of Esdras Parra.* Translated by Jamie Berrout. CreateSpace Independent Publishing Platform, 2018.

Pearce, Cecilia. "Toward a Game Theory of Game." In *First Person: New Media as Story, Performance, and Game,* edited by Noah Wardrip-Fruin and Pat Harrigan, 143–53. Cambridge, MA: MIT Press, 2004

Peterson, Trace. *Troubling the Line: Trans and Genderqueer Poetry and Poetics.* Edited by T. C. Tolbert. Callicoon, NY: Nightboat, 2013.

Plant, Sadie. *Zeros + Ones: Digital Women + the New Technoculture.* London: Fourth Estate, 1998.

Prado, Luiza, and Pedro Oliveira. "Questioning the 'Critical' in Speculative & Critical Design." *Medium,* August 31, 2017. Accessed July 21, 2021. https://medium.com/a-parede/questioning-the-critical-in-speculative-critical-design-5a355cac2ca4.

Puar, Jasbir K. "'I Would Rather Be a Cyborg than a Goddess': Becoming-Intersectional in Assemblage Theory." *PhiloSOPHIA* 2, no. 1 (2012): 49–66.

Puar, Jasbir K. *Terrorist Assemblages: Homonationalism in Queer Times.* Durham, NC: Duke University Press, 2007.

Quinn, Zoë. *Crash Override: How Gamergate (Nearly) Destroyed My Life, and How We Can Win the Fight against Online Hate.* New York: Public Affairs, 2017.

Raley, Rita. *Tactical Media.* Minneapolis: University of Minnesota Press, 2009.

Ridley, LaVelle. "Imagining Otherly: Performing Possible Black Trans Futures in *Tangerine.*" *TSQ: Transgender Studies Quarterly* 6, no. 4 (November 1, 2019): 481–90.

Rivera-Servera, Ramón H. *Performing Queer Latinidad: Dance, Sexuality, Politics.* Ann Arbor: University of Michigan Press, 2012.

Rodríguez, Juana María. *Sexual Futures, Queer Gestures, and Other Latina Longings.* New York: New York University Press, 2014.

Rose, Malú Machuca. "Giuseppe Campuzano's Afterlife: Toward a Travesti Methodology for Critique, Care, and Radical Resistance." *TSQ: Transgender Studies Quarterly* 6, no. 2 (May 1, 2019): 239–53.

Salamon, Gayle. *Assuming a Body: Transgender and Rhetorics of Materiality*. New York: Columbia University Press, 2010.

Sandoval, Chela, and Angela Y. Davis. *Methodology of the Oppressed*. Minneapolis: University of Minnesota Press, 2000.

Santana, Dora Silva. "Transitionings and Returnings." *TSQ: Transgender Studies Quarterly* 4, no. 2 (May 1, 2017): 181–90. https://doi.org/10.1215 /23289252-3814973.

Savkin, Andrey, et al. *Decentralized Coverage Control Problems for Mobile Robotic Sensor and Actuator Networks*. Hoboken, NJ: John Wiley, 2015.

Schechner, Richard. *Performance Studies: An Introduction*. London: Routledge, 2013.

Sharpe, Christina. *In the Wake: On Blackness and Being*. Kindle ed. Durham, NC: Duke University Press, 2016.

Smith, Tracy K. *Life on Mars: Poems*. Minneapolis, MN: Graywolf Press, 2011.

Snorton, C. Riley. *Black on Both Sides: A Racial History of Trans Identity*, 3d ed. Minneapolis: University of Minnesota Press, 2017.

Spade, Dean. *Normal Life: Administrative Violence, Critical Trans Politics and the Limits of Law*. Brooklyn, NY: South End, 2011.

Stalbaum, Brett, Amy Sara Carroll, and micha cárdenas. "The Transborder Immigrant Tool: Violence, Solidarity and Hope in Post-NAFTA Circuits of Bodies Electr(on)/ic." *Tactical Media Files*, May 6, 2011. Accessed June 15, 2020. http:// www.tacticalmediafiles.net/articles/3470/The-Transborder-Immigrant-Tool _-Violence_-Solidarity-and-Hope-in-Post_NAFTA-Circuits-of-Bodies-Electr _on__ic.

Stiles, Kristine, and Peter Selz. *Theories and Documents of Contemporary Art: A Sourcebook of Artists' Writings*. Berkeley: University of California Press, 1996.

Stone, Allucquère Rosanne. *The War of Desire and Technology at the Close of the Mechanical Age*. Cambridge, MA: MIT Press, 1995.

Stone, Sandy. "The Empire Strikes Back: A Posttranssexual Manifesto." In *The Transgender Studies Reader*, edited by Susan Stryker and Stephen Whittle, 221–35. New York: Routledge, 2006.

Stryker, Susan. *Transgender History: The Roots of Today's Revolution*, 2nd ed., Kindle. New York: Seal, 2017.

Stryker, Susan, and Aren Z. Aizura, eds. *The Transgender Studies Reader 2*. New York: Routledge, 2013.

Stryker, Susan, Paisley Currah, and Lisa Jean Moore. "Introduction: Trans-, Trans, or Transgender?" *Women's Studies Quarterly* 36, nos. 3–4 (fall–winter 2008): 11–22.

Stryker, Susan, and Stephen Whittle, eds. *The Transgender Studies Reader*. New York: Routledge, 2006.

Taylor, Clyde. *The Mask of Art: Breaking the Aesthetic Contract in Film and Literature*. Bloomington: Indiana University Press, 1998.

Taylor, Diana. *The Archive and the Repertoire: Performing Cultural Memory in the Americas*. Durham, NC: Duke University Press, 2003.

Thiong'o, Ngugi wa. *Decolonising the Mind: The Politics of Language in African Literature*. Oxford: James Currey Ltd/Heinemann, 1986.

Thom, Kai Cheng. *A Place Called No Homeland*. Vancouver, BC: Arsenal Pulp, 2017.

Tuck, Eve, and Wayne Yang. "Decolonization Is Not a Metaphor." *Decolonization: Indigeneity, Education and Society* 1, no. 1 (2012): 1–40. http://decolonization.org/index.php/des/article/view/18630.

Turner, Victor W. "Symbols in African Ritual." *Science* 179, no. 4078 (1973): 1100–1105.

Valentine, David. *Imagining Transgender: An Ethnography of a Category*. Durham, NC: Duke University Press, 2007.

Wald, Gayle. *Crossing the Line: Racial Passing in Twentieth-Century U.S. Literature and Culture*. Durham, NC: Duke University Press, 2000.

Wardrip-Fruin, Noah, and Pat Harrigan, eds. *First Person: New Media as Story, Performance, and Game*. Cambridge, MA: MIT Press, 2004.

Wilding, Faith, and Michelle Wright. *Domain Errors! Cyberfeminist Practices*. Brooklyn, NY: Autonomedia, 2002.

Wynter, Sylvia. "Unsettling the Coloniality of Being/Power/Truth/Freedom: Towards the Human, after Man, Its Overrepresentation—An Argument." *CR: New Centennial Review* 3, no. 3 (2003): 257–337.

INDEX

Dark Side of the Digital Conference, 163

data structures, 81

Davis, Angela, 19

Davis, Vaginal, 103

Dazed magazine, 72

decolonial: 71; acts, 52, 68; cut, 45; geo-body-politics, 151; malware, 117; movement, 3; performance, 140; poetics, 37–38, 41, 169; politic, 28; social change, 17; solidarity, 23; strategy of poetics, 139; theory, 4

Decolonial Aesthetics from the Americas, 123

decolonization, 5, 39, 67–68, 113, 123, 126, 159–60, 164, 169

DeLanda, Manuel: *Intensive Science and Virtual Philosophy*, 39

de Lauretis, Teresa, 59

Deleuze, Gilles, 9, 29, 39–40, 45, 75, 133–34

Depression Quest, 100

Derrida, Jacques, 29

design justice, 136

Design Justice Network, 173–74

design principles, 109

desire, 45

Detecta, 61–62

detection, 139

diasporic, 41

Difference Engine, 133

Different Games conference, 100

differential consciousness, 16. *See also* Sandoval, Chela

digital: algorithms, 81; communications, 25, 51–52; computing devices, 133; games, 22; humanities, 98, 115, 134; identity document tracking, 65; media, 5, 75, 81, 119, 160, 169, 172; media art, 17, 89; photography, 56; poetics, 9; redlining, 21; simulation, 32

disabled, 124, 149, 171

discrimination, 14

disidentification, 103

disorientation, 104, 106–7

do-it-yourself (DIY), 130

Domain Awareness System, 61. *See also* Microsoft

Domain Errors!, 53. *See also* subRosa

domain name system (DNS), 151, 165

Dominguez, Ricardo, 143

Dragon Age, 96

drag queens, 46

Driskill, Qwo-Li, 22, 34

driver's license, 65

Dubois, W. E. B., 81

Dunne, Anthony, 142

Dys4ia, 100–101. *See also* Anthropy, Anna

Electronic Disturbance Theater, 24, 130, 135–37, 143, 145, 169. See also *The Transborder Immigrant Tool* (TBT)

electronic media, 172

embodiment: 87; colonial control of, 4; longer genealogy of, 10

emotional empathy, 110

empathy, 97, 108, 122, 156, 157, 169

empathy games, 111

empathy induction, 110

empathy machine, 98, 111

Este suelo secreto, 31. *See also* Berrout, Jamie

ethnoclass, 81

ethnography, 102

Eubanks, Virginia, 14, 172

events, 20

Eyebeam, 140

Facebook, 14, 137, 171

Face Cages, 140

facial recognition, 14

Facial Weaponization Suite, 24, 140. *See also* Blas, Zach

Fag Face, 140

Fanon, Frantz, 85, 104

fascism, 156

felt sense, 107. *See* Salamon, Gayle

feminism: black, 88; contemporary, 89; cyberfeminism, 53; trans of color, 135, 170; women of color, 4, 8, 25, 35, 128, 134–35, 156–57, 164, 170

feminist, 6, 74, 100, 102, 114, 134, 136, 142, 149, 164, 168–70

Femme Disturbance, 91

femme science, 118

Ferguson, Roderick, 10, 27, 60, 103
first-person accounts, 13
Fisher, Simon D. Elin, 9
Flanagan, Mary, 109
flocking (dance technique), 57
Floyd, George, 175–76
Fluxus, 47
forgery, 2
Foucault, Michel, 45, 92, 116, 149
Fourth Amendment, 137
Frasca, Gonzalo: *Videogames of the Oppressed*, 99
fugitivity, 82
full-body millimeter wave scanner, 66
functions, 20
fungibility, 80, 82
FUSE magazine, 123
futurity, 168

Gabrieliño-Tongva people, 67
Galarte, Francisco, 76
Gallerie de L'Erg, 137
Galloway, Alexander: *Gaming: Essays on Algorithmic Culture*, 99
#GamerGate, 101, 168–69
game(s): AAA video, 98, 118; design, 142; digital, 100–101, 109, 123; interactive narrative, 108; narrative, 98; personal games movement, 100; text-based, 100
Gamino, Marichuy Leal, 145
Gao, Li, 76
gay and lesbian studies, 59
gender, 25, 58, 59, 71, 78, 81, 101, 103, 106, 115–16, 126, 131–32, 134, 164, 168; assigned at birth, 59; binary, 105, 132, 156; binaries, 28, 67, 69; cisgender, 74, 83, 105, 119, 121, 157; confirmation surgery, 54, 156; dysphoria, 104; expression, 105–6; gender justice, 68; gender-non-conforming, 61, 72, 79–81, 84, 87–89, 94, 102, 124, 151, 153–54, 158, 169–70; gender pronouns, 2; identification, 158; identity, 111; performativity, 18, 112; subversion, 140
gender fluid, 82
Gender Justice LA (GJLA), 62, 152–54, 165–66, 170

genderqueer, 69; lives of, 62; performers, 46
genealogy, 28
geo-body-politics, 52
geography, 40, 123
gesture, 60, 162
Gesture in Naples and Gesture in Classical Antiquity, 60
Ghost in the Shell (1995 film), 76
Gibson, William: *Neuromancer*, 76
giles, kumari, 124
Glissant, Édouard, 4, 20, 29, 35, 37–38, 45, 68–69, 84, 127, 142, 152, 157; *Poetic Intention*, 36; *Poetics of Relation*, 35, 68, 78, 106, 126, 156, 164
global poetic system, 145. See also *Electronic Disturbance Theater*
global positioning system (GPS), 24, 144
global South, 134, 159, 161, 164
Google, 137, 173
Gossett, Che, 103–4
government identification card, 63. *See also* driver's license
Gravning, Jager, 82
Greenberg, Clement, 135
Gruppo, Erro, 49
Guattari, Félix, 9, 45, 75, 134
Gunn, Sakia, 79, 105
Gutiérrez, Juan B., 145

hacktivism, 49
Halberstam, Jack, 92
Hall, Mya, 80
Haraway, Donna, 53, 149
Haritaworn, Jin, 16
Harrell, D. Fox, 81
Harvey, Adam, 24, 25, 130, 136–37, 165, 169. *See also* Stealth Wear
HASTAC.org, 121
Hatcher, Ian, 91
Haus der Kulturen der Welt, 91
Hayward, Eva, 13, 55; *Transgender Migrations*, 54
Hebrew, 41
Heemskerk, Joan, 91
hegemonies, 46

Transportation Safety Administration algorithm, 149
Transportation Security Administration (TSA), 66, 173
transreal, 91, 114, 122
transsexual, 11, 54, 94, 156
trans-subjectivity, 54
transvestite, 6, 28
trauma, 127
travesti, 5–6, 25, 28, 33, 131, 136, 155–56
tropicalization, 61
TSQ: Transgender Studies Quarterly, 5, 171
Tuck, Eve, 67
Tunantada, 140
Turner, Victor, 8
Twine, 100
Twitter, 172
two-spirit, 5, 28, 33, 34, 153, 170, 172
two-spirit critique, 34

U-Bahn, 163
Ulay, 49
undocumented, 158
universal health-care system, 156
Universidad Nacional de Colombia, 49, 129–30
University of California's Berkeley Center for Race and Gender, 145
University of Texas, Dallas, 138
University of Washington, 140
Urban Interventions, 49
USA PATRIOT Act, 138
US Department of Defense, 152

Vargas, Chris, 37. See also Museum of Transgender History and Art (MOTHA)
Venezuela, 32
violence: against women, 170; anti-Black, 170; anti-LGBT, 46; community-based responses to, 49; cis-heteronormative, 52; gendered, 35, 143, 169; genocidal, 171; histories of colonial, 169; inequality, 114; misgendered, 96; misgendering, 29; through exclusion, 89; transmisogynist, 128; transphobic, 73, 98, 105, 112, 168. See also colonization
virtual reality, 91
visibility, 2, 4, 69, 72–73, 75–76, 78, 84–86, 130, 140, 142, 169–71
visuality, 4
VNS Matrix, 53
Voz-à-Voz (exhibition), 123

"We Already Know and We Don't Yet Know," 49, 55, 57–58, 61–62, 130, 156–58, 169
wearable electronics, 24, 50, 70, 155
Weinstein, Jami, 13, 55
white supremacists, 101
white supremacy, 139, 172
Wiccan spells, 41
Wilson, Paris, 78
Wing, Betsy: Poetics of Relation, 20. See also Glissant, Édouard
wireless mesh networks, 24
The Witch's Flight, 93
women of color, 10, 61, 74, 162
women's studies, 102
working class, 158
Wygz, Rayvn, 23, 25, 123, 167, 175
Wynter, Sylvia, 80–81, 116

Xtravaganza, Venus, 82–83. See also Paris Is Burning

Yang, K. Wayne, 67
YYZ Artist Run Centre, 123

zine, 101
Zylinska, Joanna, 52, 55, 58, 67–68, 88; Life After Media, 18. See also Kember, Sarah